INDIAN DIASPORA IN WEST ASIA: A READER

Indian Diaspora in West Asia: A Reader

Edited by
PRAKASH C. JAIN

MANOHAR
2007

First published 2007

ISBN 81-7304-727-8

Published by
Ajay Kumar Jain *for*
Manohar Publisher & Distributors
4753/23 Ansari road, Daryaganj
New Delhi 110 002

Typeset by
Ajay Arts
Delhi 110 006

Printed by
Lordson Publishers Pvt. Ltd.
Delhi 110 007

Distributed in South Asia by
FOUNDATION BOOKS
4381/4, Ansari Road
Daryaganj, New Delhi 110 002
and its branches at Mumbai, Hyderabad,
Bangalore, Chennai, Kolkata

Contents

PART II: PRESENT

PART III: SUMMING UP

Tables

Preface

This book is a collection of essays on the subject written by distinguished scholars during the past two decades or so. The essays highlight the past and the present of the Indian diaspora in West Asia. The contemporary Indian diaspora in West Asia, unlike in other parts of the world, has been a discrete phenomenon – temporary, short-term, shifting and 'circulatory'. Two major exceptions are Israel and Yemen where the Indians have been permanently-settled in sizeable numbers for the past several decades, and can be called Diaspora in proper sense of the term. Elsewhere in West Asia, particularly in the Gulf Cooperation Council countries, the Indian Diaspora is in 'incipiency', to use the term suggested by late Professor Myron Weiner.

Although a considerable amount of work has been done on Indian migration to, and return migration from, the Persian Gulf countries, there is a conspicuous absence of any work on the Indian Diaspora in West Asia. A few studies done on the Indian diaspora in Israel and some of the articles, chapters or book excerpts reproduced here in this volume remain an exception. It was for this reason that this anthology was conceived with a view to providing a secondary source material at one place on the subject. The anthology, it is hoped, would stimulate further research on various aspects of this incipient diaspora.

The idea to work on this volume came to me almost five years ago but the work kept on lingering for years for one or the other reason. Nevertheless even this delay had a proverbial silver lining. Had this volume been finalized even a year ago, it would have missed the work of our two important contributors, i.e. Maganmal J. Pancholia and Ram Buxani. My unscheduled or rather a chance meeting with both of them in the Krishna Temple of Dubai on the same day in early January 2005 eventually turned out to be an extremely fruitful event.

I am thankful to all my research students as well as colleagues at the Centre for words of encouragement from time to time about the project. Two of my doctoral students Kallol Bhattacharjee and Ginu Zachariah Oommen require special mention here for assisting me in procuring copyright permissions from the contributors and their publishers. I gratefully acknowledge the financial assistance received from the Gulf Studies Programme of the Centre for word processing the manuscript. I also wish to thank the publisher of this book Ramesh Jain and Ajay Kumar Jain for taking more than professional interest in the work.

Centre for West Asian & African Studies PRAKASH C. JAIN
School of International Studies
Jawaharlal Nehru University, New Delhi

Acknowledgements

The editor and publishers wish to thank the authors and the following publishers who have kindly given permission for the use of copyright material.

Society for Indian Ocean Studies for the articles: Surendra Gopal, 'Indian Diaspora in West, Central Asia and Russia in Medieval Times', *Journal of Indian Ocean Studies*, 1998, vol. 5, no. 2, pp. 116-28; Prakash C. Jain, 'Indian Diaspora in Yemen', *Journal of Indian Ocean Studies*, vol. 11, no. 1, pp. 99-111.

India International Centre for the excerpts from: Abdulla Elmadani, 'Arabian Gulf during the British Era: The Impact of India', in N. N. Vohra (ed.), *History, Culture and Society in India and West Asia*, India International Centre and Shipra Publications, Delhi, 2003, pp. 109-24.

The School of Oriental and African Studies for the article: Calvin H. Allen, Jr., "Indian Merchant community of Masqat in the 19th Century", *Bulletin of the School of Oriental and African Studies*, 1981, vol. XLIV, part 2, pp. 39-53. For the sake of consistency the diacritics used in the original have been removed for this volume.

Frank Cass and Co. Ltd. for the article: Fatma Al-Sayegh, 'Merchants' Role in a Changing Society: The Case of Dubai, 1900-90', *Middle Eastern Studies*, 1998, vol.34, no.1, pp. 87-102.

Friday Magazine (Dubai) for the interview-article: Suchitra Bajpai Chaudhary, 'Maganmal J. Pancholia: A Man for All Seasons', *Friday Magazine*, 2003, pp. 10-15.

Population Council, Inc. for article: Myron Weiner, 'International Migration and Development: Indians in the Persian Gulf', *Population and Development Review*, 1982, vol. 8, no.1, pp. 1-36.

Taylor and Francis Ltd. for the article: Akbar S. Ahmed, ' "Dubai *Chalo*": Problems of Ethnic Encounter between Middle Eastern and

South Asian Muslim Societies', *Asian Affairs*, 1984, vol. 15, no. 3, pp. 262-76.

Motivate Publishing for the excerpts from Ram Buxani, 'The Orphaned NRI', in *Taking the High Road*, Motivate Publishing, Dubai, 2003, Chapter 16, pp. 171-82.

Duke University Press for the article: Margaret Abraham, 'Ethnicity and Marginality: A Study of Indian Jewish Immigrants in Israel', *South Asia Bulletin: Comparative Studies of South Asia, Africa and the Middle East*, 1995, vol. XV, no. 1, pp. 108-23.

Indian Council of World Affairs, New Delhi for the excerpts from High Level Committee, Ministry of External Affairs, Government of India, *High Level Committee Report on the Indian Diaspora*, Indian Council of World Affairs, New Delhi, 2001, Chapter 4, pp. 33-44 and Chapter 9, pp. 111-15.

Introduction

PRAKASH C. JAIN

Trade and cultural contacts between India and West Asia go back to antiquity.[1] These contacts were widespread, extending upto the eastern Mediterranean and also covering large parts of Central Asia. Archaeological and literary evidence suggest that India and West Asia had trade relations since at least the days of the Indus Valley civilization. Three major trade routes have connected India with the West. Perhaps the oldest of these was the Persian Gulf route running from the mouth of Indus to the Euphrates. The second was the overland route from the Indian passes to Balkh, down the Oxus to Caspian Gates, passing through and reaching at Antioch. Finally, there was the sea route down the Persian/Arabian coasts of Aden and upto the Red Sea. Until at least the beginning of the Christian era the Indo-West Asian trade was indirect, that is, part of Indo-Roman or Indo-Greek trade.[2]

Maurya period was a milestone in Indo-Roman/Greek trade relations. Mauryan emperor, Ashoka the Great, not only exchanged ambassadors with Syria, Egypt and Macedonia, but also took up the cause of spreading Buddhism to parts of Central and West Asia. Arab scholar al-Beruni found the traces of Buddhism in Khorasan, Persia, Iraq and Syria. The cultural traditions of Central Asian countries were similarly influenced by the spread of Buddhism during the Kushan period, especially in its later phase. Trade relations were further strengthened by the great Silk Route trade between China and West in which Indians acted as intermediaries. 'During the medieval period the friendly visits of the Khwarezmian scholars al-Beruni and Abdulrazzak Samarkandi form a glorious chapter in the history of contacts between India and Central Asia.'[3] These contacts were multifaceted involving not only trade and political/diplomatic relations but also literature, philosophy, religion, medical knowledge, musical instruments, etc.

The Indo-West Asian relations have persisted throughout the historical period: the rise and spread of Islam since the seventh century AD., Muslim invasions and conquest of India resulting in the establishment of the great Mughal empire and the coming of the European powers in the region following Vasco de Gama's 'discovery of India' in 1498 and the opening of the all-sea route from Europe to India, and the eventual dominance of the British in India as well as the West Asia. Since the coming of Islam to India *Haj* pilgrimage has been another major reason (besides trade) for Indians to travel to the Arab world, specifically to Mecca and Medina. The Shia Muslims have been journeying to Karbala and Mashad for the same reason.[4]

It is against this backdrop that Surendra Gopal's paper included in the present volume seeks to highlight the migration, settlement and evolution of Indian communities in West Asia since the sixteenth century. These small Indian diasporic communities until very recently largely consisted of merchants and personnel related to trade. The communities were predominantly male. The material on the first three centuries regarding the Indian diaspora in the Gulf region is extremely sketchy. Thus the paper takes a wide sweep covering at least two centuries and three major regions, West and Central Asia and Russia.

Vasco da Gama noted the presence of Indians on the shores of East Africa in 1498 and subsequently in the ports of the Red Sea and in the interior of the Arabian Peninsula.[5] Port towns of Mocha and Aden and inland cities of Taif and Sanaa were also inhabited by the Indians. As early as in 1549 Hindu and Jain *Banians* lived on the island of Ormuz.[6] The ruins of a Hindu temple were found at Kalhat, the principal Omani port of the fifteenth century which further suggests the settlement of Indians in Oman.[7]

In Iran besides Ormuz, Indians in small numbers had settled down in Yezd, Shiraz, Isfahan, Tehran, Resht, Gilan, Khorasan and Mashad. Following the establishment of a new port Gombroon or Bandar Abbas in the late seventeenth century Ormuz declined to insignificance and Indians shifted to the new city. In 1760 when Bandar

Abbas was abandoned by the Persians, the Indians shifted to Abu Shehr, Bushahr, and to the Iraqi port of Basra. Towards the end of the eighteenth century Gujarati Baniyas were replaced by a new group of emigrants known as Shikarpuris who hailed from Sindh.[8]

In the seventeenth and eighteenth centuries Indians travelled via Iran to Central Asia, Caucasus region and the Tzarist Russia. They were active as merchants as well as moneylenders in Bukhara, Samarkand, Tashkent, Baku, Semakha, Derbent, Kokand, etc. Gopal also points out the existence of a Hindu temple in Iran and another at Baku 'where a perpetual fire burnt and a priest was always in attendance'.[9] Outside of India, Nepal and Tibet, the temple at Baku was a major centre of Hindu pilgrimage.

In contrast to the seventeenth and eighteenth centuries in which India's impact on the Persian Gulf region was sporadic confined mostly to trade, it was quite comprehensive in the later nineteenth and the first half of the twentieth centuries. This is forcefully brought out in the paper 'India's Impact on the Gulf's Economic and Socio-Cultural Life during the British Era' by Abdulla Elmadani.[10] Indo-Gulf relations during this period were 'varied and multi-faceted'. For about a century or so India was not only a major partner in the Indo-Gulf trade and commerce, its impact on the Gulf countries in terms of initial modernization and cultural renaissance, reform movement and many other aspects of socio-cultural life such as cuisines, musical instruments, interior designing and architecture was also substantial. It was also during this period that a number of Indian merchant communities were more firmly established throughout the Gulf/Red Sea region. Though large parts of the paper are not directly concerned with the Indian diaspora, it nevertheless is important from the point of view of underlining the fact that the Gulf region was virtually an extension of British India and that the Indians in the Gulf enjoyed privileges as British subjects.

'The Indian Merchant Community of Masqat' by Calvin H. Allen, Jr. is perhaps the first and most systematic study of its kind of the subject.[11] It focuses on the late eighteenth and nineteenth centuries. During this period there were three distinct Indian merchant communities in Muscat. The first were the Sindhi or Thatta Bhattias, so-called after the city of Thatta located on the Indus River in Sind – who had been living in Muscat under Portuguese dominance at least since the sixteenth century and continued to prosper through most of the eighteenth century. But strong competition both in India and Muscat and decline of Thatta as a commercial centre drove the Sindi Bhattias from Muscat to Bahrain and other Gulf ports.

The Sindhi Bhattias were replaced by Kutchi Bhattias since the early nineteenth century who came in two phases: before 1830 and following Said b. Sultan's transfer of residence to Zanzibar after 1830. It was in this second phase that the Kutchi Bhattia community grew in size and influence, and continued to thrive until the brief establishment of the conservative Ibadi regime during 1868-71. Due to unsettled conditions in Muscat by 1870 the Kutchi community had declined to 250 from 2,000 only to be restored to 1,500 by 1900. Meanwhile, in the post-Ibadi period a new group of Kutchi Bhattias with international business connections and dealing in a wide variety of merchandise had emerged on the scene. These included such illustrious business families as Virji Pursottam Toprani, Premji Jamnadas Bhimani, Ratansi Pursottam, Dowlatgirji Marupgirji, Virji Ratansi and Damodar Dharamsi. The last four families were considered the 'four pillars' of the Hindu society in nineteenth century Muscat. 'Upon this base a number of other Banians established prosperous businesses that have continued to flourish in Muscat. These include Khimji Ramdas, Dayal Pursottam, Danji Murarji, Vallabdas Umarsi and Gopalji Walji.'[12]

A third group of Indians during the period under review were the Khojas (Khwajas) – also called Luwatiyyas – originating in Hyderabad, Sind. They were settled in Matrah (Sur Luwatiya) living in segregation from the Arabs as well as the Hindu. Like the Kutchi Bhattias Luwatiyyas also reached Oman in two phases. 'The earliest Luttis came in the wake of the establishment of the state in Muscat in 1785. The disruptions of Azzan b. Qays's reign may have had the same impact on the Luti commercial community as it had on the Bhattias. Following the re-establishment of moderate rule in 1871, a new group of Luwatiyyas came to Uman and came to dominate the community.'[13] Luwatiyyas had monopolized the trade of dried fish, besides trading other usual items. Mohammad Fadl born in Bombay in 1858 was one of the well-known Luti merchant in the late nineteenth century Muscat. The Luti community was more or less permanently settled in Oman.

Due to the two treaties of 1820 and 1853, the seven Sheikhdoms were referred to collectively as the Trucial Coast – under truce with Britain. All seven emirates were primarily exporters of foodstuffs, pearls, and items for the peninsular transit trade, which linked the Sheikhdoms to the Southern Iranian coast, to each other and to the Indian Ocean. Thus, many merchants, brokers, and money changers in the Sheikhdoms were Iranian or Indian.[14]

The paper 'Merchants' Role in a Changing Society: The Case of Dubai, 1900-90' by Fatma Al-Sayegh makes an intersting reading on the role of the merchant communities in Dubai. It examines the rise and decline of the merchant power in the city's political economy in the pre-oil era. Since the late nineteenth century the Indians comprised the second largest merchant group after the native tribal Arabs who dominated the pearl fishing and trading – two honourable occupations. The Indian merchants called *Banians* financed the pearling expeditions, besides taking to banking. They monopolised shopkeeing and retail trade. A number of them 'represented British Indian firms in Bombay'.[15] The Indian merchants were rich and enjoyed commensurate political privileges and influence alongwith the other merchant groups. The merchant oligarchy continued until the collapse of the pearl industry and advent of the oil revenues in the early 1930s when rulers began to have direct income and political independence.

In the post-depression period and particularly after the Dubai reform movement of 1938 the Indian merchants continued to enjoy relative prosperity, but less political influence. Thus, in the *Majlis al Tujjar* in the early 1950s and the Dubai Municipal Council elections of 1957 the Indian as well as Persian merchants were excluded. These developments however, did not preclude them from participating in Dubai's evolution as a centre of international trade and exchange, and a cosmopolitan city with excellent educational, community and social services. Thus, as Sayegh put it, 'Merchants were and are still dominant figures in Dubai, playing a vital role in its continued growth and development. Dubai's ancient calling as a "city of merchants" is as strong as it was two hundred years ago'.[16]

Though this article provides only sketchy information about the Indian merchants, it does provide a framework within which their role and contribution can be fruitfully narrated and imagined.

'My life and work in Dubai' by Maganmal J. Pancholia, a prominent Indian businessman, resident in Dubai for several decades now, is not only a portrait of his own contribution to the development of Dubai but also underlines the role of Indians merchants in general.[17] Sindhis in particular have played a vital role in the trade of textiles, foodstuff, provisions and more recently electronic goods. Thus, of about 600 wholesale dealers in textile in Dubai, about 450 are Sindhis. Similarly Gujaratis continue to dominate the gold trade in the UAE. The contribution of the recently migrated entrepreneurs from Kerala is too numerous and diverse to be stated in a few words or sentences. In fact it is a pity that we hardly have any information on Indian entrepreneurship in the Gulf countries.

In the Red Sea region Yemen is one of the countries where Indians have been settled for a long time. Prakash C. Jain's paper attempts to outline the evolution of the Indian diaspora in Yemen in modern times.[18] Although Indo-Yemeni trade and cultural relations go back to antiquity, the evidence of the Indians' presence in Yemen is available since only the early seventeenth century. The Indians were found to reside in almost all the major towns of Yemen, including Mocha, Sana'a, Hodeida and Beit-al-Faqui. The Indians began to settle in the port town of Aden after its occupation by the British in 1839. By the time the British left Aden in 1967 their population had risen to more than 20,000. Besides Aden, there must have been thousands of Indians in other towns of Yemen, but their history is sketchy. Therefore the case of the Indian diaspora in Yemen in this article is largely built on the Adeni component. Today Yemen hosts the largest permanently-settled Indian diaspora in West Asia.

The migration of Indian labour to the Gulf countries appears to be a recent (i.e. post-oil boom of 1973) phenomenon, but in fact it is not so. The Indian manpower presence in the region dates back to the early oil exploration days when some Indians had been employed by the D'Arcy Exploration Company in 1902. Anglo-Persian Oil Company incorporated in 1909 employed 158 Indians in January 1910 and 379 in 1911, and in subsequent years this figure was to reach a peak of 4,890 in 1925. The pattern was repeated in other oil companies in the 1930s and 1940s.[19] In spite of the restrictive nationality clause in the oil concession agreements regarding recruitment and employment of foreign labour in various jobs categories such as senior/junior staff, artisans, domestics, etc, the workers from the Indian sub-continent constituted an important segment of immigrant manpower during the first half of the last century.

The Persian Gulf region, particularly the GCC countries are the major destination in West Asia where Indian labour migration has been taking place for the past few decades. Late Professor Myron Weiner's paper included here was first published in *Population and Development* in 1982 and was the first major systematic attempt to put the Indian Diaspora in the Persian Gulf region in proper perspective.[20] In a subsequent work he called it as 'incipient diaspora'.[21] Weiner takes into account only five of the six GCC countries excluding Saudi Arabia. He discusses in detail the political economy of the Gulf states which dictates them to import foreign labour, the state policies within which such importation takes place and its impact on the receiving countries as well as India. He also briefly mentions the history of Indian immigration into the region and the future prospects of the diaspora and comes to the conclusion that 'politics not economics, will ultimately be decisive'.[22] Such a conclusion is not wide off the mark given the fact that the Gulf countries continue to remain patriarchal and authoritarian in nature.

Prakash C. Jain's second paper included in this volume in some respects compliments and supplements information and arguments provided in the preceding paper.[23] The countries in the Persian Gulf region now host about 4 million Indian 'immigrants'. Such a large scale migration from India to this region is relatively a recent phenomenon. Most migrants (about 60 per cent) originate in Kerala and other south Indian states, and happen to be young, unmarried or recently married, less educated (except professionals) and were unemployed or underemployed at the time of migration. Though migration is 'circular' in nature (migrants preferring to stay only for a few years at a time and looking for an opportunity to migrate again), there is continuity of socio-cultural associations and institutions since at least the Second World War. Not surprisingly, as already pointed out, Weiner described the Indian communities in the Persian Gulf region as 'incipient diaspora'.

The paper 'Aspects of Indian Labour Diaspora in the United Arab Emirates' by K.C. Zachariah, B.A. Prakash and S. Irudaya Rajan provides the first ever survey research based analysis of the Indian workers in the United Arab Emirates. Covering a sample of 361 Indian immigrants (all from the Kerala state of India) in the UAE, the study focuses on their socio-economic background, employment, wages and working conditions. A structured interview schedule was used for collecting relevant data. The survey was conducted in 2001. The study revealed that the largest proportion of workers (36 per cent) was engaged in unskilled, semi-skilled and skilled categories of jobs in construction, production and transport activities. Nearly 20 per cent were in professional and technical work. Clerical, sales and services provided employment to the rest of the sample immigrants. These and many more findings portray a distinctive profile of the Indian labour diaspora in the UAE. Needless to say, many more such studies are required to be conducted in other countries of the Gulf as well.

Noted Arab scholar Hisham Sharabi conceptualizes the contemporary Arab society as 'neo-patriarchal' and argues that the reproduction of neo-patriarchal Arab society derives from its ability to satisfy basic needs of the people: their material interests, security and identity.[24] If Arab secular nationalism could not take roots in the Arab societies, it is mainly due to the entrenched position of neo-patriarchy in social relations, social identity and social consciousness. So pervasive is the hold of neo-patriarchy on the Arab societies that unless there are extended long-term socio-political changes, the social structural transformation away from neo-patriarchy is simply impossible. That, in spite of the 1990-1 Gulf crisis and the current Iraqi situation, the desired socio-economic forces to break the hold of neo-patriarchy could not be unleashed is, however, a hard reality which is further buttressed by three more features of the contemporary Arab societies: the bilateral integration of the Arab economies into the world capitalist system, the rentier nature of the Arab state, and the political culture of accommodation rather than that of mobilisation.[25]

With 70 to 75 per cent budget revenues derived from oil, the Gulf societies are characterised by the rentier nature of their economies and states which not only tends to strengthen patriarchy at social level but also hampers political participation for the masses. According to Hazem Beblawi, rentier economies rely on substantial external rent (wealth) without a strong productive domestic sector. A small fraction of society is involved in the creation of wealth; majority being involved in the distribution or consumption only. As the government happens to be the principal recipient of the external rent in the economy, it also tends to exercise hegemony in political power. The rentier state is essentially an allocative state rather than productive one, and as such, it tends to promote only rentier mentality and ethics, which are essentially ethics of idleness and the easy life. In such a situation, there is no relationship between work and reward, except in the case of expatriates. Citizenship of a rentier state thus becomes both a privilege and a source of income.[26]

Against this conceptual background it is easier to appreciate Akbar Ahmed's paper which is written with the focus on Pakistani migrants in the UAE.[27] The 'Dubai *Chalo*' syndrome in its varied manifestations is indeed the characteristic feature of all South Asian migrants to the Gulf countries. So is the nature of ethnic encounter between the native Arabs and the South Asian immigrants. Perhaps the most important dimension of this ethnic encounter is *watani* (native or citizen) *vs.* non-*watani* (non-native or expatriate). Although in the case of Muslim immigrants the concept of *watani* is antithetical of that of *ummah,* and thereby it goes against the spirit of Islam, Ahmed rightly argued that Islam also 'helps to bridge the ethnic and cultural alienation between the groups and allows a sense of familiarity – through mutually accepted mythologies, rites, customs – to be fostered in spite of difficult conditions'.[28] Non-Muslim immigrants, particularly from the South Asian sub-continent obviously suffer from deeper sense of alienation in the Gulf countries.

If Akbar Ahmed's paper underscores the various nuances of 'ethnic encounter' of South Asians in the host Gulf countries, Ram Buxani's on the 'Orphaned NRIs' complements the former by highlighting their problems at home. In his article he portrays the negative perception of the non-resident Indians held by the Indian people and the Government.[29] Buxani, himself a NRI for over 40 years now, feelingly writes about the plight of NRIs, particularly during the period 1960-90 when the NRI was regarded and caricatured as 'selfish, loud, unpatriotic'. Fortunately things have been changing since then in the wake of liberalisation and globalisation. He forcefully argues for better educational facilities in India for the NRI children, establishment of free ports in India and the political representation of NRIs in the Indian parliament. The article also tells us about his own role in abolishing the estate duty in India. He warns against stereotyping the NRIs in the mass media and underlines the need for 'some basic acceptances on both sides'. On the whole the author provides a comprehensive account of the problems faced by the NRIs in India.

The Indian Jewry which has been living in India for about 2,000 years consisted of three distinct communities: Bene Israel, Cochinis and Baghdadis. Whereas the origins of Bene Israel, and Cochin Jews who lived for centuries in the Konkan region and the Malabar Coast of India respectively are lost in antiquity, the Baghdadis immigrated into India from Iraq, Iran, Syria, Turkey, Yemen, etc., in the eighteenth and nineteenth centuries and were mostly settled in Bombay and Calcutta.[30]

At the time of the creation of Israel in 1948 the total population of the jews in India was less than 30,000. In 1951 their estimated population was as follows: the Bene Israel 20,000, Cochinis 2,500 and Baghdadis 5,000.[31] Since then emigration, mainly to Israel and other countries has reduced their population in India to about 2,000. According to one estimate, 25,214 Indian Jews had emigrated to Israel between 1948 and 1987.[32] These emigrant Indians Jews and their descendents particularly the Bene Israel and Cochinis, are now very well settled in their new homeland. Today, about 70,000 Jews of Indian origin constitute a separate diaspora in Israel.

The settlement and 'absorption' of Indian Jews in Israel has not been an easy task. Thanks to the Israeli constituted 'Absorption of the Immigrant' policy, the Indian Jews who in India constituted mainly a city-based community were forced to settle in *moshavim* or development towns.[33] This 'from ship to village' settlement policy in the case of the Indian and other Oriental Jews initially resulted in their economic marginalisation in the Israeli society.[34] The marginalisation process was further compounded by the educational, cultural and welfare policies and programmes of the government.

The State Education Law of 1953 and the 'Jewish Consciousness Programme' of the late 1950s advocated 'single curriculum' for all Jewish children which was heavily loaded with Ashkenazi history and literature. Extensive courses in European subjects kept the children of Oriental Jews at a disadvantage. In the 1960s the Bene Israel were socially discriminated against on the ground that they were not 'full Jews'. Their marriages were subject to verification. A socio-religious issue soon turned into a major political controversy. In 1963 a bill declaring the Bene Israel as 'full Jews' was defeated by the Mapai and national religious parties. Finally in 1964 the relevant directive against the Bene Israel was removed by the Chief Rabbinate following a resolution passed by the *Knesset* in a specially convened session on the issue. Though the controversy was resolved, it left the community stigmatized.[35]

Since then the Indian Jews in Israel have made significant progress in all walks of life. There is considerable educational and occupational mobility among them. Initially they had to work extremely hard in order to get adjusted in the new economic and socio-cultural environment in Israel. In spite of discrimination and challenges the Indian Jews have been successful in adapting themselves to the Israeli society.[36] Israeli case is comprehensively represented by Margaret Abraham's article.[37] Conditions and causes of migration, settlement, status of Indians Jewry, their problems and prospects are all neatly analysed.

In part III, a summing up of the volume is done by having relevant excerpts from the *Report of the High Level Committee on the Indian Diaspora* which was tabled in the Indian Parliament in 2001.[38] The five member committee was chaired by eminent jurist and former High Commissioner to the United Kingdom L.M. Singhvi. Though the Committee did extensive travelling in major countries hosting the Indian diaspora and met concerned academics as well as prominent Indians, the report was essentially based on a questionnaire-derived input from various Indian ambassadors on behalf of the India's Ministry of External Affairs.[39] The data and information provided in these excerpts ought to be taken in that light. The paper also includes a brief excerpt on Iran from the same report. It would be observed that the paper thus constituted fairly summarises the socio-economic position of the Indian Diaspora in the region.

NOTES

1. See G.F. Hourani, *Arab Seafaring in the Indian Ocean in Ancient and Early Medieval Times*, Beirut, 1963/1995: K.N. Chaudhri, *Trade and Civilization in the Indian Ocean: An Economic History from the Rise of Islam to 1950*, Cambridge University Press, Cambridge, 1985. See also Maqbool S. Ahmad, *Indo-Gulf Relations*, Popular Prakashan, Bombay, 1969. Himanshu Prabha Ray and Jean Francois Salles (eds), *Tradition and Archeology: Early Maritime Contacts in the Indian Ocean*, Manohar, Delhi, 1996. See also Nalinee M. Chapekar, *Ancient India and Iran: A Study of their Cultural Contacts*, Ajanta Publications, Delhi, 1982.
2. See H.G. Rawlinson, *Intercourse between India and Western World*, Cambridge University Press, Cambridge, 1926.
3. Devendra Kaushik, 'India and Central Asia: Past and Present Realities and Future Hopes', *Contemporary Central Asia*, vol. 1, no. 1, 1997, p. 64.
4. Surendra Gopal, 'Indian Diaspora in West and Central Asia and Russia in Medieval Times', *Journal of Indian Ocean Studies*, vol. 5, no. 2, 1998, p. 117.
5. Razul Islam, *Indo-Persian Relations*, Tehran, 1970, p. 172; See also Surendra Gopal, 'Indians in Central Asia in 16th and 17th centuries', Proceedings of Indian History Congress, 52nd Session, New Delhi, 1992, p. 220.
6. See William Foster, *Early Travels in India*, New Delhi, 1985, p. 11; Donald Latch, *Asia in the Making of Europe*, vol. 1, Book 1, Chicago, 1965; see also Surendra Gopal, 'Indian Diaspora . . .', op. cit.
7. S.B. Miles, *Countries and Tribes of the Persian Gulf*, 2nd edn., London, 1966, p. 526.
8. Surendra Gopal, 'Indians in Iran in the 17th and 18th Centuries', *Journal of Historical Studies*, no. 2, 1996, pp. 14-36.
9. Surendra Gopal, 'Indian Diaspora . . .', op. cit., p. 121.
10. Abdullah Elmadani, 'Arabian Gulf during the British Era: The Impact of India', in N.N. Vohra (ed.), *History, Culture and Society in India and West Asia*, Shipra Publications, Delhi, 2003, pp. 102-8.
11. Calvin Allen, Jr., 'The Indian Merchant Community of Muscat', *Bulletin of the School of Oriental and African Studies*, vol. 44, no. 1, 1981, pp. 39-51.
12. Ibid., p. 48.
13. Ibid., p. 50.
14. Yahya Amarjani and Thomas Ricks, *Middle East: Past and Present*, 2nd edn., Prentice Hall, New Delhi, 1986, p. 340.
15. Fatma Al-Sayegh, 'Merchants' Role in a Changing Society: The Case of Dubai, 1900-1990', *Middle Eastern Studies*, vol. 34, no. 1, 1998, pp. 87-102.
16. Ibid., p. 101.
17. Suchitra Bajpai Chaudhary, 'A Man for all Seasons', *Friday Magazine*, (Dubai), 2003, pp. 10-15.

18. Prakash C. Jain, 'Indian Diaspora in Yemen', *Journal of Indian Ocean Studies*, vol. 11, no. 1, 2003, pp. 99-111.
19. I.J. Seccombe and R.I. Lawless, 'Foreign Worker Dependence in the Gulf and the International Oil Companies, 1910-50', *International Migration Review*, vol. 20, no. 3, 1986, pp. 548-74.
20. Myron Weiner, 'International Migration and Development: Indians in the Persian Gulf', *Population and Development Review*, vol. 8, no. 1, 1982, pp. 1-36.
21. Ibid. 'Labor Migrations as Incipient Diasporas', in Gabriel Sheffer (ed.), *Modern Diasporas in International Politics*, Croom Helm, London, 1986, pp. 47-74.
22. Myron Weiner, op. cit., 1982, p. 30.
23. Prakash C. Jain, 'An Incipient Diaspora: Indians in the Persian Gulf Region', in Bhikhu Parekh, Gurharpal Singh and Steven Vertovec (eds), *Culture and Economy in the Indian Diaspora*, Routledge, London, 2003, pp. 102-22.
24. Hisham Sharabi, *Neo-Patriarchy: A Theory of Distorted Change in Arab Society*, Oxford University Press, London, 1988.
25. Prakash C. Jain, *Population and Society in West Asia: Essays in Comparative Demography*, National Publishing House, Jaipur and New Delhi, 2001.
26. Hazem Beblawi, 'Rentier State in the Arab World', in Giacomo Luciani (ed.), *The Arab State*, Routledge, London, 1990.
27. Akbar S. Ahmed, 'Dubai *Chalo*: Problems in Ethnic Encounter between Middle Eastern and South Asian Muslim Societies', *Asian Affairs*, vol. 15, no. 3, 1984, pp. 262-76.
28. Ibid., p. 275.
29. Ram Buxani, *Taking the High Road*, Motivate Publishing, 2003, pp. 171-82.
30. For accounts of Indian Jews, see Thomas A. Timberg (ed.), *Jews in India*, Vikas Publishing House, New Delhi, 1986; T.V. Perasuram, *India's Jewish Heritage*, Sagar Publications, 1982; Benjamin J. Israel, *The Jews of India*, Mosaic Press, New Delhi, 1998; R.A. Schermerhorn, 'Jews: A Disappearing Minority', *Ethnic Plurality in India*, University of Arizona Press, Tucson, 1978, pp. 238-61. See also Shalva Weil, *India's Jewish Heritage: Ritual, Art & Life-Cycle*, Marg Publications, Mumbai, 2002.
31. Op. cit., Israel, pp. 8-10.
32. Margaret Abraham, 'Ethnicity and Marginality: A Study of Indian Jewish Immigrants in Israel', *South Asia Bulletin, Comparative Studies of South Asia, Africa and the Middle East*, vol. XV, no. 1, 1995, pp. 108-23.
33. Ibid., p. 115.
34. See, for example, Gilbert Kushner, *Immigrants from India in Israel: Planned Change in an Administered Community*, University of Arizona Press, Tucson, 1973.
35. See Schifra Stritzower, 'The Bene Israel in Israel', *Middle Eastern Studies*, vol. 2, no. 2, 1966, pp. 122-43.

36. See Sreekala S., 'Israel's Policy of "Absorption of Immigrants": A Case Study of the Indian Jews', unpublished Ph.D. thesis, Jawaharlal Nehru University, New Delhi, 2001; Ginu Zackaria Oommen, 'Integration of the Cochin Jews into the Israeli Society', A Ph.D. thesis in progress, Centre for West Asian and African Studies, School of International Studies, Jawaharlal Nehru University, New Delhi.
37. Abraham, op. cit.
38. Ministry of External Affairs, Government of India, *The Report of the High Level Committee on the Indian Diaspora*, Indian Council of World Affairs, New Delhi, 2001.
39. This author had the privilege of interacting with this committee in June 2001 at the University of British Columbia, Vancouver where he happened to be a Faculty Research Fellow under the auspices of Shastri Indo-Canadian Institute, New Delhi and Calgary.

PART I
PAST

CHAPTER I

Indian Diaspora in West Asia in the Seventeenth and Eighteenth Centuries

SURENDRA GOPAL

The emergence of Islam as a trans-continental ideology and political power in the seventh century AD put an end to Indian missionary activities in Central Asia, but the Indian emigration to Indian Ocean countries continued since the Oceanic trade continued to flourish in which the major participants were the Islamicised Arabs, Chinese and Indians.

The Fatimid Caliphs in the tenth century AD ensured that Indian ports on the western coast were regularly visited by ships sailing from the ports of the Red Sea region. The Arab geographers and historians of the period speak of Indians living abroad. The Indian Muslims went on pilgrimage to Mecca and Medina as was the practice of Muslims. But none has left behind any record of his foreign trip. We have no Indian Marco Polo or Ibn Battuta or Ma Huan to tell us about his visits. Some additional information about Indians residing outside the country is gained from European sources after the outbreak of the Crusades.

Vasco da Gama's opening up of the sea route from Europe to India was followed by the establishment of three empires, the Safavid in Iran, the Ottoman in Turkey and West Asia, and the Mughal in India. The landmass extending from the eastern shores of the Mediterranean to the Bay of Bengal, coupled with the commonality of the religion of the ruling elites, and other factors created conditions which made travel and trade in the region attractive despite Portuguese surveillance over the Indian Ocean sea-lanes. While outsiders continued to pour into India in increasingly greater numbers, the Indians kept up their foreign travels. In the sixteenth century their presence is noted on the eastern coast of Africa, in the Arabian peninsula, the Persian Gulf region, Central Asia and South-East Asia, etc.[1]

Journeys to the Red Sea area were regular features because for the devout Muslims, pilgrimage to the holy cities of Mecca and Medina, at least once in a lifetime was a highly cherished dream. Many of the Muslim rulers on the Indian subcontinent supplied ships, money and escort to ensure that their Muslim subjects participated in the annual pilgrimage. When the Portuguese tried to hinder these ships, the Indian rulers used both diplomacy and force to ensure that the Indian Muslims continued to perform the *Haj* regularly. The vessels sailing from the ports of Gujarat and Sindh carried pilgrims from the north-western India and sometimes even from Central Asia. The Shia Muslims also journeyed to places revered by them, such as Kerbala in Iraq and Mashad in Iran.

Occasionally, an intrepid soul would cross into Iran from India by the land route and then go to Mecca and Medina either by taking a ship from some port on the Persian Gulf or by crossing the desert.[2]

After the arrival of the Portuguese in the Indian Ocean some Indians began taking passage in ships owned by the Europeans since they were considered 'more safe' and better equipped to face the 'pirates'. Some Indians were taken by the Portuguese to Madagascar, Mozambique and the neighbouring areas, either as slaves or as a part of the crew on their ships or as merchants.

Braudel mentions the presence of Indian merchants (*Banyans*) in Istanbul. At the moment our knowledge about the presence of Indian merchants in Turkey is meagre, but it would not have been a problem for Indians to move to Turkey either from their base in the Caucasus or in West Asia or in Basra.

The documents of the European East India Companies and travel accounts of Europeans speak of the presence of Indian traders in the Arabian peninsula in the port towns of Mocha and Aden as well as in the inland cities such as Taif and Sana, etc.

A report of 1621 describes the goods brought by Indian to the port town of Mocha. 'In that year, two ships arrived from Dabhol in India, one with 200, the other with 150 passengers, all travelling merchants coming to sell in the port small quantities of precious goods: 'pepper, gum lac, benzoin, cotton cloth (woven with gold thread or painted by hand), tobacco, indigo, cinnamon, nutmeg, cloves, mace, camphor, porcelain, musk, diamonds, drugs . . . the perfumes and gums of southern Arabia'.

Important commodities carried back by the Indians were coral, coffee, horses and frankincense, etc. Even after investing in these items much gold remained with the Indians, which they had received for the goods they had sold.

The state of Indians in Mocha is described in another report. 'In 1626/27 trade was still normal in Mocha; the Indian merchants sold their wares to merchants from Cairo, but lived in constant fear of an Arab attack, and buried their money every time a forthcoming offensive was rumoured.'[3]

The Indians could be found on the eastern side of the Arabian peninsula as well. Their presence in Muskat, the principal port of Oman was noted by the Europeans. Ashin Das Gupta says,

> There were two kinds of Banias engaged in the Red Sea trade. There were those who came and went every year, doing their own trade and handling the business of others who remained at home in much the same manner as the Muslim merchants were wont to do. Banias from lower Gujarat, particularly from the cities of Surat and Cambay were of this kind. Others had been long settled in Yemen and were found not only in every Yemeni city but in this port towns of Habash and Hadramaut as well. Apparently Banias from Kathiawar, the Kapol Banias of the Peninsula, were predominant among those who settled in Yemen, and immigrants from the ports of Gujarat and Kathiawar continued to come to Yemen throughout the first decades of the eighteenth century. The Bania merchants of the Yemeni cities and the Habash ports controlled much of the commercial life of the area, but in Yemen at any rate, they lived like second class citizens.[4]

The Portuguese developed Muskat as their base when they were driven away from Ormuz in 1622 by the Iranians and the English. They had to quit Muskat when they were driven away by a local power in 1650 The new regime unleashed a reign of terror; the Muskat navy off and on ravaged the Gujarat coast. But Indians continued to come to Muskat. The Muskat ships were built either in Gujarat or in Sindh, since local timber was available there. In 1672 a Sindhi envoy visited Muskat. It is highly likely that when the rulers of Muskat extended their power to the eastern coast of

Africa by capturing ports and islands under Portuguese occupations, some Indians might have accompanied them. After all, in the sixteenth century, the Portuguese had found Indians in the port towns below the Horn of Africa. The Portuguese had been regularly sailing to Mozambique from Goa and some Indians were accompanying them.

II

In Iran, the Indian presence was much more formidable than anywhere else. A number of factors explain this. The Portuguese with their hold over the island of Ormuz kept a close surveillance on ships going to or leaving the Persian ports. But collaboration between the Portuguese and Gujaratis ensured that some Indians did manage to go to the Gulf for purpose of trade.[5] Let it not be forgotten that according to Linschoten, the Gujaratis had a whole street to themselves in the Portuguese capital of Goa towards the end of the sixteenth century.[6]

On the island of Ormuz there were many Indians including Hindus, who practised idolatory as narrated by the sixteenth-century traveller Ralph Fitch.[7] These Indians were described as 'Banias', many of them coming from Gujarat.

The Safavids and the Mughals had close and cordial relations throughout the seventeenth century with occasional setbacks. There was a mutual exchange of embassies, and of scholars and artists. A large number of Indians went to Iran by the land route principally via Qandahar. They generally settled down in cities such a Yezd, Shiraz, Isfahan, Tehran, Resht, Gilan, etc. Sometimes, the Kabul-Herat route was preferred for going to the cities of Khorasan (north-eastern Iran) such as Mashad.[8]

The Indians who resided in interior cities of Iran were generally known a Multanis, after the border city of Multan in the Punjab. As in Ormuz, the community of Indians included a good number of Hindus and Jains, easily identifiable by their practice of idol-worship, sandal-paste mark on their fore-head and cremation of the dead.

The liberation of Ormuz from Portuguese control in 1622 by the joint Anglo-Iranian forces made the sea route to Iran freely accessible. All the European trading companies and the Indians took full advantage of this event and intensified their activities. While many Indians arrived in Iran on their own, several others were invited by the European trading companies to assist them as brokers, bankers, interpreters, etc.

In the post-1622 period there was a spurt in the number of Indians visiting Iran. Since peace prevailed between the Mughals and the Safavids, both the land and sea routes could be used unhindered. Besides, the Europeans permitted Indian passengers and goods to be carried on their ships to the Gulf.

The Indian, both Muslims and non-Muslims, came from Sindh, Gujarat, from the Sultanate of Bijapur on the west coast of India, from the Sultanate of Golkonda on the Cormandal coast and from Bengal, etc. As the century advanced, Indian Parsis also visited Iran, from where their forefathers had fled to India to escape religious persecution.

To cater to the increased passenger and goods traffic, the Shah of Persia established a new port, Gombroon or Bandar Abbas on the mainland opposite the island of Ormuz which thereafter lapsed into insignificance. From now onwards till 1760 when the Persians abandoned Bandar Abbas in favour of Abu Shehr, a group of Indians almost continuously resided there, their number rising and declining, depending upon the business environment. The non-Muslim Indians in Bandar Abbas continued to be designated by the term 'Bania', the majority of them hailing from Gujarat, being vegetarians and teetotallers.

Several European travellers write about Indians there. Fryer,[9] the noted English visitor to Iran, found that these 'Banias' possessed a temple with a priest where they worshipped their idols and celebrated their festivals. The Iranian rulers had granted them religious toleration so that they could publicly conduct their religious rituals and ceremonies. There was a strong presence of Indians in the capital city of Isfahan in the seventeenth century. Estimates of their numbers vary between one thousand and twelve thousand.

III

Having established a strong base in Iranian towns, the Indians moved out to the neighbouring countries. They went to the Caucasus region and from thence, in early 1630s, to the Tsarist kingdom of Russia.[10]

In the Caucasus region, they selected Baku, a port on the western Caspian coast as their principal seat of residence. Shemakha and Derbent were other cities where Indians resided. At Baku, the Hindus had built a temple where a perpetual fire burnt and a priest was always in attendance. Many Hindus in India considered this temple as a place of pilgrimage.

The port town of Astrakhan, situated on the northern banks of the Caspian where the river Volga falls into sea, remained their base in Russia till the beginning of the nineteenth century. They could stay there for more than a century and a half because business was profitable and the Tsars followed a policy of religious toleration. Here the non-Muslim Indians were generally called Multanis since the majority hailed from Multan and its neighbourhood in the Punjab. They practised idol-worship, brought their own priests and were permitted to cremate the dead bodies of their compatriots.[11] Some of the Indians married local women and their offsprings were called 'Agrizhanets'. Many were eventually assimilated into the local society; some accepted Islam and others became Christians.

The Tsars recognised the pivotal position of the Indians in the Russo-Persian trade and when the situation demanded, they extended to the Indian various concessions as well as protection. From Astrakhan the Indians spread to other cities of Russia such as Saratov, Kazan, Nizhni Novgorod, Yaroslavi and reached the capital city of Moscow where they constituted an important group among oriental merchants. An Indian mendicant turned trader also showed up. Among the Indian traders, one named 'Lahori Bania' had earned considerable wealth. Obviously, he hailed from Lahore in the Punjab.[12]

The Indian connection with the Armenians was specially close since they had known Armenians both in India and Iran. These Armenians had extensive trade interest in several countries of Europe and Asia including India.

The Indians residing in Iran and Russia also explored the Central Asian markets, especially the cities of Bukhara and Samarkand. Both these cities carried trade with Iranian as well as Russian trade centres.[13] It may be noted that the overwhelming number of Indians in Central Asia had arrived directly from India by the well-trodden land-route which emanated from Lahore, Multan or Peshawar and converged on Kabul and ran on to the Oxus River. After crossing the river, the Indians reached the Central Asian cities of Samarkand, Bukhara, Tashkent located in the upper Syr Darya basin.

A section of Indians in Central Asia also came via Ladakh, the Pamir plateau and the Yarkand-Kashgar route. From Kashgar they turned west and entered into Central Asian steppe land, the Ferghana Valley and its cities, Andijan and Kokand.

In Central Asia there was another group of Indians who had been carried there as slaves.[14] Some of them had been purchased while others had been taken prisoners during the Mughal campaign in Central Asia. They performed menial jobs at the bidding of their masters.

IV

As we step into the eighteenth century, the political environment within our country and the surrounding regions changes. Of the three great empires of the seventeenth century, the Safavid empire in Persia disappears; and the remaining two, the Ottoman and the Mughal enter into various stages of decay. India is gradually taken over by the British, who in course of time succeed in outmanoeuvring their other European rivals, the Dutch and the French, and succeed in establishing their political and economic dominance over the country. The emergence of the British colonial rule did not put an end to the wanderings of the Indians; but certain changes in the number of emigrants and the countries visited by them can be noted.

The Indians could no longer assert their right to trade in the Red Sea area, since the decrepit Mughal empire was in no position to back their claims or to curb the menace of piracy – Arab, Indian and European, which was increasingly hampering shipping in the Arabian Sea. The Indian dependence on European shipping equipped with fire-power to deter the marauders became considerable. The Europeans were not averse to rendering this service because they needed Indian expertise, help and support for carrying on their business. Also they earned money by levying freight charges.

In the Red Sea region, Mocha continued to be the main concentration point of the Indians who, as in the previous century, dominated its economy. The majority of the Indians, both Hindus and Muslims, came from the ports and cities of Gujarat, such as Surat, Diu, Porbandar, Ahmedabad, etc. The economic ties of Mocha with Surat were very close in spite of disturbances caused by Muskat pirates and/or the occasional blockades of the Europeans. They remained the chief supplier of coffee to the Europeans, who were becoming its principal buyers because of its increased sale on their continent and their inability to finance its purchases in Mocha. For accounting purposes the Gujaratis had devised a Yemeni dollar which was 21 per cent less than the Spanish dollar. As a result, 'Gujarati merchants principally Banias from Kathiawad were settled at all the Yemeni towns. . .' Besides they could be found in the capital town of Sana, in Beit-al-Faqui (the principal market for coffee), in the ports of Hodeida and Lohaya and in inland towns such as Tais and Zabid.

In the Gulf area, the Indians were faced with a different dilemma. Iran, their major object of attention, was rocked by political instability. First, the Afghans occupied Iran, which showed the utter incompetence of the Safavids to defend the integrity of their country against foreign aggression. There was a brief interlude in the dismal political scene in Iran. In 1730s Nadir Shah as the leader of Iranian resistance not only drove out the Afghans but created an empire extending from the shores of the Black Sea in Europe to river Yamuna in India. This temporarily revived economic activities in the country. But he was assasinated in 1747, and political turmoil followed. The Zands and then the Qajars became the ruling dynasties in Iran.

The Indians tried their best to cope with the uncertain political situation in Iran. In 1718 the Shahbandar of Bandar Abbas was Kishendas Khatri.[15] When the safety of life and property became uncertain during Nadir Shah's regime, many of the Indians shifted to Russia. The Tsar, well aware of the economic contribution of Indians to Russia's oriental commerce, extended his protection. Some Indians were granted Russian citizenship. When the Russian established Orenburg in 1735 and wanted to make it a focus of their trade with India, it is said 300 Gujarati families came to reside there.

From their base in Astrakhan in Russia, the Indians kept coming to Iran to conduct their business. The moment some political stability returned to Iran, Indians became active again. When Bandar Abbas was abandoned by the Persian authorities in 1760, the Indians shifted to the neighbouring ports, Bushahr and Abu Shehr or to the interior cities, or even to Basra, the chief port of Iraq. Basra was not a new destination for them. The Indians had been going to Basra in the seventeenth century for purpose of trade. Some Shia Muslims also passed through it while going on pilgrimage to the city of Najaf.

Throughout the eighteenth century, the Indians continued to enter Iran both by the land and sea routes and were to be found in all the major cities, Shiraz, Isfahan, Tabriz, Yezd, Teheran, Gilan, etc. Towards the end of the eighteenth century, a *sarai* exclusively meant for the Indians was still functioning in Shiraz.[16]

As in the Seventeenth century, from Iran they also travelled to Central Asia, the Tsarist empire and the Caucasus region. In fact the Indians were as much active in Baku and other commercial centres of Azerbaijan as they were in Astrakhan.

The Indians had their own cavaransarai in Baku. Besides Baku, the Indians were found in other towns of Azerbaijan as well. They had another temple consecrated to the sacred fire in Surkhan.[17] Indians also visited the commercial cities of Shirvan, Derbend, Shemakha, Aresha, etc., in order to purchase the famed silk. In 1670s, Ya. Ya. Streis found on the outskirts of Shemakha, not less than one hundred Banias, the majority of whom were Hindus. A little later, a French traveller counted 200 resident Indians around Shemakha and described them as 'the richest traders'. They were traders, bankers, money-changers and moneylenders. In 1666, an Indian trader exchanged Persian coins worth 7,860 roubles.

The Indian take-over of the Iranian and Azerbaijan economy had begun in the second half of the seventeenth century. In 1637 the Indians of Shemakha built a caravansarai on the road from Shemakha to Ardebil. Of the twenty caravansarai in Shemakha in 1703, Bruyn noted that the Indian one was made of stone, 23 or 24 feet high and 'was the most beautiful'.

Towards the end of the eighteenth century the importance of Indian traders in Russia was reduced to insignificance; their number in Astrakhan considerably dwindled. They no longer played a role in the Perso-Russia trade.

Despite losing their significance in Russia, the importance of Indians in Iran remained undiminished. The English East India Company, concluded a commercial treaty with the Shah of Iran in 1800. It stipulated, 'English and Indian traders and merchants should be permitted to settle, free from taxes, in any Persian seaport, and should be protected in the exercise of commerce in the Shah's dominions'.

The composition of Indians going to Iran now changed. So far the non-Muslims among Indians were generally known as 'Banias' or 'Multanis' but a new category 'Shikarpuris' now appeared. The new group, consisting mostly of Hindu, hailed from a small town Shikarpur in the Sukkur district of Sindh. Soon the newcomers made their presence felt; they acquired so much prominence that their names became synonym for Indians. The 'Shikarpuris' soon spread from Iran to Central Asian cities and in the next century were to be found even around the Pamir mountains. It appears that the Shikarpuris were primarily moneylenders and bankers but simultaneously carried on commercial transactions.

The name Marwari is also met for the first time.[18] Two Marwaris, Marwari Barayav and Rajaram Marwari went to Iran and then journeyed to Russia. The former earned a fortune and was consulted by Russian authorities when they were trying to establish direct trade with India. He moved to Orenburg when the Russians tried to develop it in the eighteenth century as a centre of trade with India. Eventually, he fell foul of the Russian authorities and was imprisoned. After he was freed, he accepted Christianity. Such was his tortuous fate. Rajaram Marwari was active in Russo-Persian trade, but we do not know what his eventual destiny was.

The Russian language sources mention an Indian mendicant who was going to Siberia in the late seventeenth century.[19] In this category, we can also put the Bengal wanderer Swami Pran Puri or Giri who had earlier visited Tibet in the service of the English East India Company, had also gone to the Chinese capital, Peking, and then proceeded on a journey towards Russia.

In a nut-shell, it could be said that Iran attracted the largest number of Indian immigrants during the period under review. The Indian community in Astrakhan on the Russian soil remained fairly stable during the seventeenth and the eighteenth centuries. But then they disappeared at the turn of the nineteenth century.

Indians in the Caucasus region met the same fate though they lingered on a little longer. The territory was annexed by Russia after the Perso-Russian War of 1826-28. It should be noted that many Hindus went to Baku and Sukhan on a pilgrimage to pay their homage to the 'perpetual flame – the Jwala Ji'. Apparently, the tradition lingered on even in the present century. The famous Indian scholar Rahul Sankrityayan met a mendicant in India who claimed to have paid a visit to 'Jwala Ji' in Baku. The Caucasus was the only foreign country other than Nepal and Tibet where Hindus went on a pilgrimage.

In the Arabian peninsula, Mocha, the port of Yemen, was the most frequented place by the Indians throughout our period. On the soil of Oman, Muskat emerged as the major point of Indian activity.

Indian presence in Central Asia (from the eastern shores of the Caspian Sea to the Pamir plateau) continued despite significant political change in both the regions. Bukhara was the ultimate destination through several Indians lived in Samarkand, Tashkent, Kokand, etc. Towards the end of our period, Shikarpuris, hailing from Sindh emerged as the most important group among the Indian.

Indian remained constant visitors to the trade marts of the Pamir plateau, Yarkand, Kashgar and Khotan. The latter was used as a gateway to Lhasa — the capital of Tibet. Of course, Indians flocked to Lhasa via Nepal and via Bhutan as well. Many Hindus going to Tibet were Sanyasis and combined the discharge of religious obligation with that of commercial entrepreneurship.

The obstacles put forward by the Europeans, first the Portuguese and then the English and Dutch East India Companies and others, could not prevent Indians from visiting the countries of Southest Asia, Burma, Thailand, Malaysia, the Indonesia Archipelago, the Philippines, etc., though in this region their influence and significance over the period considerably declined. The wanderlust of the Indians never withered away.

NOTES

1. Surendra Gopal, 'Indians in Central Asia in 16th and 17th Centuries', Proceedings of Indian History Congress, 52nd Session, New Delhi, 1992. For Indians in Central Asia, see also N.B. Baikova, *Rol Srednei Azii V Russko-Indiskikh Torgovykh Svyazakh*, Tashkent, 1964.

2. N.R. Farooqi, *Mughal-Ottoman Relations*, Delhi, 1989, pp. 144-72; Ashin Das Gupta noted that 'About twenty Gujarati ships sailed every year from Surat to Mocha and Jedda carrying pilgrims for the *Haj* as well as annual trade of much of northern and western India.' Ashin Das Gupta, 'Gujarati Merchants and the Red Sea Trade, 1700-25', in Blair B. Kling and M.N. Pearson (eds), *The Age of Partnership*, Honolulu, 1979, p. 124.
3. Ferdinand Braudel, *Civilisation and Capitalism 15th-18th Century*, vol. II, London, 1982, pp. 153, 127.
4. Ashin Das Gupta, 'Gujarati Merchants and the Red Sea Trade, 1700-1726', pp. 123-58.
5. Even in 1549, Ormuz had a colony of Hindus and Jains, who were described 'as complete vegetarians and worshippers of cows'. Donald Lach, *Asia in the Making of Europe*, vol. I, Book I, Chicgo, 1965.
6. Linschoten, *The Voyage of Johan Huyghen van Linschoten to the East Indies*, vol. I, London, 1885, p. 228. The Gujaratis were so well entrenched that on one occasion the Portuguese delayed the departure of the Cambay fleet on their request. M.N. Pearson, *Coastal Western India*, p. 109.
7. William Foster, *Early Travels in India*, New Delhi, 1985, p. 11.
8. See Surendra Gopal, 'Indians in Iran in the Seventeenth and the Eighteenth Centuries', *Journal of Historical Studies*, no. 2, pp. 14-36.
9. John Fryer, *A New Account of East India and Persia Being Nine Years Travels* (1672-81), vol. II, London, 1912, pp. 167-325, 336-38.
10. Oldberg, Antonova and Lavrentshova (eds), *Russko-Indiiskiya Otnosheniya v XVII v* (hereafter cited as R-I O v XVII v). Moskva, 1958, doc. no. 12.
11. Ibid., doc. nos. 76, 141/X, 141/1, 203, 223. For details see Surendra Gopal, 'A Brief Note on Business Organisation of Indian Merchants in the 17th Century', *Journal of the Economic and Social History of the Orient*, vol. XXXIX, pp. 205-12.
12. R-I O v X VII v., no. 103. He reached Moscow in 1672 and was accompanied by an agent of Shah of Persia. See also doc. no. 44. The Indians continued to visit the Caucasian cities throughout the eighteenth centuries, see Surendra Gopal, 'Trading Activities', *Social History Review*, pp. 141-8.
13. Surendra Gopal, 'Indians in Central Asia in 16th and 17th Centuries', Proceedings, Indian History Congress, 52nd Session, 1992, pp. 219-31.
14. Ibid., pp. 225-7; See also D.A. Kolf, *Naukar, Rajput and Sepoy: The Ethnography of the Military Labour Market in Hindustan, 1450-1850*, Cambridge, 1990, pp. 10-15.

The exports of slaves from Bengal in the sixteenth and seventeenth centuries is mentioned by Tapan Roychoudhury, *Bengal under Akbar and Jahangir*, Calcutta, 1953.

15. *Indian Merchants*, p. 83, fn. 3.
16. Franklin who visited Shiraz in 1787 found a caravanserai exclusively meant for the resident Indians, William Franklin, *Observations Made on a Tour from Bengal to Persia*, Calcutta, 1788, p. 59.
17. Sara Ashurdelli, *Ekonomicheskiya Svyazi Azerbaijana s Indiyei v Sredniye*, Baku, 1990, p. 35. Most of the Indians here belonged to Multan.
18. Antonova and Goldberg (eds.), *Russko-Indiiskiye Otnoshenia v XVIII*, Moskva, 1965, doc. nos. 72, 74, 75.
19. I.A. Lapteva and M.P. Lukichev, 'Documents of the USSR State Archive of Ancient Acts Pertaining to the History of Russian-Indian Relations', Proceedings, *Indian Historical Records Commission*, Srinagar, October 1988, p. 53. His name was Pandu and he was permitted to visit the cities of Toblosk, Yeniseisk and Irkutsk during 1681-83.

CHAPTER 2

India's Impact on the Gulf's Economic and Socio-Cultural Life during the British Era

ABDULLA ELMADANI

The relationship between India and the Gulf region is well rooted in history. It stretches back to ancient times. Based on the artifacts like embellished pottery and seashells recovered from the Harappa Valley in north India and those belonging to the Dilmun civilisation of Bahrain or Magan civilization of Oman, some archaeologists suggest that Indo-Gulf interactions can be traced to the third millennium BC.

On the other hand, Sumerian and Acadian versions indicate that the valley of Mesopotamia had profound commercial ties with the Indus civilisation which flourished from about 2500 to 1500 BC or little earlier. One of the three ancient trade routes between India and Europe went through the strait of Hormuz across the Gulf, Mesopotamia and Aleppo. Because of its central location on this route, in addition to its capability to provide the transit traders and sailors with food and water, the Gulf region became a favourable middle-point for the trans-shipment of Indian merchandise to Mesopotamia and further. This led gradually to a greater involvement on the part of the Gulf inhabitants in trade with India. What support such a conclusion, and additionally proves the stationing of some Indians in the Gulf for the purpose of conducting trade in those ancient days, are the many seals discovered in Bahrain. These seals bear typical Indus Valley designs and characters and some of them are prism-shaped like the ones of the ancient Harappas. It is possible that along with these trade relations some socio-cultural exchanges occurred as, according to archaeological evidence, there was resemblance between a number of methods used in certain activities (such as fishing, boat construction, measuring, and weighing) in both civilisations.

Long before the advent of Islam, India and Indian commodities were known to the tribes of Arabia and were admired by them to the extent that they called their daughters '*Hind*'; the Arabic name for India. Moreover, Arabian poems written in pre-Islamic era (*or Jahiliyah*) contain many words praising or referring to Indian swords, silk, musk, and amber. For example, the word *Muhannad*, which means 'from *Hind*', was repeatedly used in these poems as one of the many Arabic names for sword. The fact that many words of Indo-European stock were used in the Quranic versions and in ancient Arabian poetry, the two most important sources of Arabic philology, is in itself evidence of the long process of social and commercial intercourse that must have taken place between India and West Asia in the centuries immediately preceding Islam.

In the pre-Islamic era a large number of Indians migrated to different parts of the Gulf coast, either to establish business, seek employment by Arab traders, or just to escape instability at home. Among the seven Indian groups that migrated to Arabia and settled down in Bahrain, Oman, and Ubulla (Basra) at this period were the Zuth (known in India as Jats), the Bayasira, and the Siabja. Thus at the time of the advent of Islam, there were many Indian settlers in Arabia who were involved in various activities.

The rise of Islam in the seventh century AD was significant for Indo-Arab commercial interactions, particularly in the aftermath of the Arab conquest of Mesopotamia and Persia and the transference of the capital city of the Arab/Islamic empire from Mecca to Damascus and later to Baghdad. The political unification of Arabia, Egypt, Iraq, Syria, Iran and North Africa, and the emergence of new cities along with the growth of old urban centres, created an enormously powerful zone of economic consumption and widened the demand for Indian commodities. These developments stimulated both caravan and maritime trade in the Gulf region. As a result, commercial ties between Arabia and India tangibly grew in terms of both the composition and volume of goods imported from India.

Until the Muslim conquest of India in AD 711 much of Indo-Gulf interactions had been mainly confined to trade exchange. But with the inclusion of Sind and part of Gujarat into the Arab/Islamic empire, the two regions became politically linked, a development which paved the way for greater contacts and, therefore, strong socio-cultural relations.

Commercial and other forms of exchange between Arabia and India continued until the great setback in the sixteenth century caused by the emergence of Portugal as a dominant sea power in the Gulf and Indian Ocean. With the emergence of the Portuguese, Arabia's merchants were deprived of their influence in the Indian Ocean and of their share of Indian and Oriental goods. Their rulers in Hormuz, Muscat, and Bahrain were suppressed and forced to pay annual tributes to the Portuguese. Their mercantile activity in the Gulf and Indian Ocean became subjected to trade licenses and taxes. In Goa, the Indians of Arab origin known as 'Navayats' were excluded from office and deprived of their control over the import and re-export of Arabian and Persian horses which were needed in the cavalry (the backbone of the Hindu armies in those days). However with both regions, India and the Gulf, politically and administratively linked under the British from the late nineteenth century to near the mid-twentieth century, Indo-Gulf relations entered a new era. Until India's independence in 1947, all decisions regarding the fate of the Gulf region and its political and economic affairs have been taken in India and implemented by India's British authorities. The Gulf dependency on India became, therefore, strong in almost every field as its chiefs and people were not allowed to venture further than India. Talking about the Gulf's Indian connection in the British era, Rosemarie Zahlan said:

> The Indian rupee was the currency in circulation... Indian stamps were overmarked 'Kuwait' and 'Bahrain'. The Arabic dialect of the coastal areas contained many Urdu words, and the political officers stationed there.... were members of the British government of India who had been trained for service in India. They applied British Indian regulations throughout the Gulf states.[1]

The above lines, however, show some features of the connection but not all. Indo-Gulf relations during the first half of the twentieth century were so varied, multifaceted, and of significant impact on the Gulf region that further elaboration is needed. This paper, therefore, is an attempt to illustrate the role played by India and Indians in the Gulf's political, economic, and socio-cultural life during that period.

INDIA AND THE GULF PEARLING INDUSTRY

In the pre-oil days, one of the principal sources of livehood in the Gulf was pearl fishing and trade. A large segment of the population in Kuwait, Qatar, Bahrain, the Trucial Sheikhdoms, and the eastern coast of Saudi Arabia was involved in this activity. In those days, Indian merchants, known in the Gulf by the name '*banyan*' came to the region to conduct deals with their local counterparts. Some of these Indians were stationed permanently in the Gulf for this purpose. The Gulf's merchants also travelled regularly to Bombay to market their pearls, as well as to seek loans for the expansion of their pearl-diving operations. Their vessels on return journeys were loaded with an assortment of staple foodstuffs and materials of Indian origin. Some of these merchants chose to settle there, investing their pearl revenues in real estate and other economic activities. Among them were Albassam and Algosaibi from Saudi Arabia, Alebrahim and Aljina'i from Kuwait, Alzayani and Alurrayed from Bahrain, and Almidf'a and Alsayegh'i from the Trucial Sheikhdoms.

In India, the Gulf pearls were bought, pierced, polished, manufactured into jewellry, and re-exported to Europe or sold to Indian Maharajas, bringing both, Arab and Indian merchants, immense wealth.

It is necessary here to state that the Indian role in the Gulf pearling industry was confined to such activities as purchasing, providing loans, and participating in the construction and ownership of the vessels. There was no actual involvement of the Indians in pearl-diving operations, probably due to Bahrain's refusal to grant them permission to compete with the local divers, fearing the outbreak of hostilities between the Arabs and Indians should it decided otherwise. However, this must not lead to a conclusion that the Indians never tried to get involved in the pearl-diving process.

There were a number of occasions in which Indian merchants got permission from the local chiefs to practice pearl-diving, but were interrupted by the British political Resident.[2]

THE GULF'S COMMERCIAL DEPENDENCY ON INDIA

Throughout the nineteenth century and until the immediate post-oil discovery years, India was not only the main market for Gulf pearls but also the Gulf's major supplier of all sorts of merchandise. There are statistical tables dating back to 1873 that prove India's dominant position in Bahrain's imports. The value of Indian exports to Bahrain in that year (1873) was 1,167,375 rupees or more than a third of total imports.[3] India continued to be the biggest exporting country to Bahrain and probably to other Gulf emirates until the early 1930s. For example, Indian goods constituted 72.47 per cent of the total imports of Bahrain in 1929/30.[4]

Annual trade reports in the era under discussion evidently show that Gulf imports from India increased or decreased, in range and volume, in accordance with the rise or decline of pearl prices. What facilitated the conduct of business between the two regions was the existence of a common means of payment, the Indian rupee. In fact, dependency of the Gulf merchants on the Indian market for the sale of their pearls contributed to the emergence of the Indian rupee as the major currency in circulation in the Gulf. This continued until 1959 when the Indian government, under economic pressures caused by continuous smuggling of gold into its territories against obtaining Indian rupees, issued the 'Gulf rupee' as a special currency for the use in the Gulf states. The Gulf rupee, which was at parity with the Indian currency, remained the official means of payment in these states until they issued their own currencies around the mid-1960s.

ENRICHING THE GULF'S MERCHANT HOUSES

It was through establishing business with India or in India at this time that many of today's prominent merchant families in the Gulf made the first portions of their great wealth. The business histories of these families reveal interesting stories about their early modest beginnings and the role of the Indian connection in their riches.

In Kuwait, for example, the head of Alghanim business empire began his business, which has vastly developed in the last four decades under his sons and grandsons, by plying the Basra-Bombay route, selling Iraqi dates to the Indians and buying from India food, cloth, and timber on return to Kuwait.

The wealth of some of the most prominent Saudi merchant families, like Alireza and Algosaibi, was basically attributed to their decisions in the late nineteenth and early twentieth centuries to establish purchasing offices in Bombay and Calcutta through which they sold pearls and exported an assortment of Indian commodities to Jeddah, Bahrain, and Alahsa. Establishing such offices did not only give them a foothold in the Indian commodities market and advantage over other Arab merchants, whose contact with India was confined to occasional visits, but also gave them opportunities to win contracts to represent Indian companies in the Gulf such as the Bombay and Persia Steam Navigation Company which held monopoly over the pilgrim traffic between India and Arabia.

In Bahrain, Yusuf Kanoo, the founder of Kanoo business empire started as a banker with offices in both, Bahrain and Bombay:

> Those merchants who went to Bombay to arrange the sale of their pearls in October and November could leave their money with Yusuf in India and make their drawings a few months later from his Bahrain office. Those who ran food and timber-importing businesses would pay into their accounts in Bahrain and make their drawing in India, either from Yusuf's own offices or from various Bombay merchants with whom Yusuf held accounts.[5]

Similarly, merchant families in the Trucial Sheikdoms made their early fortunes through import-export relations with India. However, the wealth of a number of them basically came from smuggling big quantities of gold into India, an activity also practised by other Gulf merchants but to a lesser degree. These merchants, particularly from Dubai, exploited the relative geographic proximity of their coasts to the Indian shores, and the need by India's huge population for gold as an essential part of every bride's dowry to conduct this practice and to make immense fortunes. Connected to this another illegal trade was run by them, particularly from the immediate post-oil discovery years until the 1960s; the use of the pearling and gold smuggling boats on return journeys in smuggling Indian young men, eager to obtain jobs and earn money, into the Gulf states.

GULF MERCHANTS' ACTIVITIES IN INDIA

The activity of the Gulf merchants, who settled in India or who were stationed there was not only restricted to marketing pearls or capturing business opportunities. In addition, they were very active in India's social and cultural life, observing political developments in the Indian sub-continent, establishing contact with Indian intellectuals, particularly the leaders of the Muslim community, and trying to educate themselves. Not only that, but some of the wealthiest among them constructed mosques, schools, and clubs in India to serve Muslim Indians as well as the Arab community. The Hijazi merchant Muhammed Zainal Alireza, for example, built a number of schools in Bombay, Bahrain and Dubai including the famous Alfalah school in Bombay (1931) for teaching Arabic language, Islamic studies, and other subjects,[6] while the Kuwaiti Alebrahim contributed to the building of schools in both Kuwait and Bombay.[7]

They also generously assisted and looked after the Arab intellectuals and reformers who happened to be passing through Bombay or those who were deported to India for their anti-British activity.

In brief, their multi-faceted activities brought them into contact with British officials and Indian elites and traders, taught them English and Hindi, and introduced them to new ways of business and life, all of which had a significant impact on the socio-cultural developments in the Gulf and constituted the nucleus of a consciousness movement in Bahrain, Kuwait, and the Trucial Emirates.

INDIA'S IMPACT ON THE GULF REFORM MOVEMENTS

Demands for administrative and legal reform and the improvement of some of the traditions and laws related to the pearling industry and labour conditions began in Bahrain in the early 1920s. These demands continued throughout the 1930s and 1940s and expanded to include the call for a greater role in the running of domestic issues and for the reduction of the British Political Agent's responsibilities, gaining much of their momentum from political developments in India.

Major Dickson, the British Political Agent in Bahrain in the 1920s, stated in a report that one of the sources of instability in the

Island was the effect of efforts by the Muslim Indians to revive the notion of Islamic Caliphate.[8] In letters exchanged between the British Agent in Bahrain, Major Clive Daly, and his masters in the Gulf and in Bombay, India's struggle for democracy was mentioned as one of the influencing factors responsible for the anti-British movement in Bahrain.[9]

When the British struck against Bahrain's reform movement in 1923, two of its prominent leaders, Abdulwahab Alzayani and Ahmed bin Lahij, were arrested and sent into exile to Bombay. In India, they received the support and sympathy of many Indians including the Indian National Congress's leaders. And when Alzayani took his case to judicial authorities of British India, his lawyer and defender was the man who later became the founder of Pakistan, Mohammed Ali Jinnah.

The impact of the Indian national movement on the Gulf reform movements was significant as the Gulf merchants who settled in India were in touch with their people at home supplying them with the news of political developments in India and elsewhere. The letters exchanged between them and their colleagues and friends at home contain interesting discussions and exchanges of views regarding these developments and the proper ways to incorporate the experience of other nations into their own struggle for reform and freedom. What probably made the Gulf merchants and reformers keenly observing India's experience was the fact that their efforts were directed against the same colonial power, and the fact that the Indians supported their case. The Indian National Congress passed, as early as 1928, a resolution expressing its sympathy with all Arabs in their struggle for freedom.[10]

INDIA'S CONTRIBUTION TO THE GULF'S EARLY CULTURAL RENAISSANCE

India acted during the early years of the twentieth century as a channel through which the latest news of political and cultural developments in the main centres of the Arab world flowed into the Gulf. In those days, the Gulf region had no direct contacts with these centres as a result of the British policy of isolating the region from the mainstream of Arab cultural developments. The Gulf merchants and reformers stationed at the time in India responded by capturing news of these developments from magazines published in Egypt, Iraq, and Lebanon, to which they had regular subscriptions, and sending them to the Gulf to be passed around. They were very observant and anxious to make their people at home aware of these developments. They were also very interested in learning from relatively open Indian society, and in transferring new ideas to their own society.

Influenced by India's cultural life and its varied phenomena, these merchants undertook the transfer of some of these phenomena to the Gulf. The emergence in Bahrain of the Iqbal Awal Club in 1913 and the Literary Club in 1923, for example, was basically attributed to the effort and support of these reformist merchants.

Indian had also a role in the very beginnings of the press and publishing activity in the Gulf. For example, the appearance of Bahrain's first newspaper, *Albahrain*, in 1939 would not have been possible without the printing presses brought from Bombay by its publisher and editor, Abdulla Alzayed. Alzayed, a pearl merchant, reformer, and poet, himself owed much of his fortune and experience to India where he had lived in exile for two years.

Prior to the 1930s, all official and unoffical written materials in the Gulf were sent for printing to presses in India. It is no surprise, therefore, to know-that the printing and publishing of some of the very first Gulf books took place in Bombay. Among these books are *Ukud Aljawaher* (1918) and *Tuhfat Alnasik* (1925) which are believed to be the first and the second printed books in Saudi Arabia.[11] The first map defining the locations of pearl fisheries in the Gulf was also printed in Bombay in 1914.

Additionally, India was until the post-Second World War years the only favourable destination of the Gulf people for learning English and obtaining advanced education. Many Gulf families, including the Royal Families of Bahrain and Oman, chose Indian schools, such as Aligarh College, for their sons. As a result many of those who led the socio-cultural renaissance in the Gulf in the early twentieth century owed their knowledge, experience, and prominence to India. Among these were: Khalid Alfaraj, Bahrain's most remembered poet and reformer; Ibrahim Alurrayed, a well-known Bombay-born Bahraini poet and literate; Said Alnooman, who played a remarkable role in the cultural movement in Sharjah as early as 1910, and many other names.

INDIA AND THE EARLY MODERNIZATION PROCESS IN THE GULF

In order to have a firm hold on the region, the British colonial authorities began as early as the first decade of the twentieth century to introduce a series of administrative measures under the guise of reform, with much concentration on Bahrain. These measures included the re-organisation of the customs department, establishment of postal and banking services, and imposition of the civil, commercial, and criminal codes of India. In all these reforms, and those introduced in the post-oil discovery years in the municipality, in the communication, health and agricultural sectors, the British largely depended on the Indians to fill most of the white-collar positions. For example, the very first directors or organisers of customs, post, and passport departments in Bahrain were Indians. So were the heads of the first medical clinic in 1925, and the very first doctors, nurses, midwives, banks and customs' senior clerks, and agricultural advisers. Similarly, the Indians were among the first to organize or run medical, postal, and banking services in Qatar, Kuwait, Dubai, and Sharjah.

On the other hand, the discovery of oil in the Gulf in the 1930s and lack of qualified personnel and labourers among the Gulf natives made the British look again towards India for the import of the needed skills. Even in Saudi Arabia, clerical, technical, and other positions created as a result of the development of the oil industry and related sectors in the 1940s and 1950s were partly filled by employees from India. The number of these newcomers increased gradually in accordance with the developments in the industry itself. For example, statistical records show that their number in Bahrain doubled between 1936 and 1937 making them 14 per cent of the total Bahrainis employed by the oil company.[12] This percentage jumped in 1938 to about 26.5 although the actual number of the Indian employees slightly decreased.[13]

Along with the economic prosperity caused by the production of oil, the well-established Indian merchant communities in the Gulf expanded taking the lead in meeting the growing demands by the Gulf inhabitants for modern consumer merchandise from Europe. This led to the emergence of a number of wealthy Indian commercial houses. In a confidential report on the richest among Bahrain's merchants in the 1930s, six out of thirteen names were Indian.[14]

Simultaneously, the Gulf States witnessed the emergence of new Indian communities consisting of all those who were attracted by the region's economic prosperity and who came legally or illegally to work as shopkeepers, cooks, tailors, barbers, drivers, and domestic servants, or to provide other services traditionally avoided by the natives.

To sum up, the role played by the Indians in the early modernisation of the Gulf region was varied. However, it must be remembered that it was this role which caused much grievance among the Gulf natives and ultimately led to strikes and disturbances in Bahrain in the 1930s and 1940s. The Bahrainis were enraged by the importation of Indians to occupy governmental positions and jobs in the Bahrain Oil Company, by the protection and privileges extended to them by the British, and by the better wages and conditions they enjoyed. Because some of these Indians were involved in running the colonial administration, they were regarded as British agents whose assignments were to reinforce and prolong the British presence in the region. However, despite these tense relations between the Bahrainis and Indians, there are no records showing that they developed at any time into violence as the struggle was of a social and economic nature and did not stem from racial hostility. Probably what contributed to the avoidance of violent clashes was the fact that the Indians, in general, confined themselves to earning money rather that getting involved in the politics and domestic affairs of the Gulf countries.

INDIA'S IMPACT ON THE GULF'S SOCIO-CULTURAL LIFE

As mentioned earlier, India's impact on the Gulf's solco-cultural life has been observed since the old days. However, with both regions being linked under one colonial rule, greater and more varied interaction between the two nations took place and consequently such an impact became noticeably stronger.

The first to be noticed, in this context, is the Indian impact on the spoken dialects in the Gulf's coastal towns. Tens of words of Indian origin entered these dialects and became widely used in everyday conversations. These words related to jobs held by the Indians, products imported from India, modern merchandise and items introduced by the Indians, financial methods associated with the use of the Indian rupee, and tools and methods used in the pearl-diving and maritime trade.

Other aspects of the Indian socio-cultural influence include the entrance of many traditional Indian dishes into the Gulf cuisine, the adoption of Indian artistic designs in the formation of gold and silver and in embroidering clothes, the use of a number of musical instruments similar to those used by the Indian musicians, and the adoption of 'Wizar'[15] as an essential part of menswear in many parts of the Gulf. Also affected by the Indian culture, arts, and traditions were the interior decoration of houses and rooms; material, colours, and designs of women's costume; the types of jewellery worn by females in Oman and the southern Gulf; and the rhythmic pattern of music.

Long and continuous intermixture led also to frequent mentioning of India and Indians in the Gulf's traditional poetry, proverbs, sailors' songs, children's games, anthems, and tales.

THE INDIAN PRESENCE IN THE GULF

With British hegemony over the Gulf States, the position of the Indian merchants in the region was reinforced. The number of these merchants increased, and their activities stretched to include businesses other than those related to the pearling industry.

Among the factors leading to this new situation was the protection which the Indian merchants came to enjoy under British rule in the Gulf due to the fact that they were considered to be British subjects. In all treaties conducted between the British Indian Authorities and the Gulf Principalities there were articles asserting such protection and privileges. Prior to these treaties, Indian merchants faced insecurity which restricted their existence in large numbers in the region. Their businesses and commercial vessels were, on many occasions, victims of domestic instabilities in Oman, Qatar, Bahrain, and the Trucial Sheikhdoms or victims of tribal wars between the ruler of these states. On other occasions, they were victims of the struggle for dominance by such forces as the Wahhabis, the Ottomans, and the Persians.

It must be asserted here that Britain's striving to protect the Indians in the Gulf was not because of its preference for them. It stemmed from the perception that such policy would assist the reinforcement of Britain's position and give it an excuse to interfere in the Gulf's domestic affairs. What further encouraged Britain to adopt this policy was the readiness on the part of some Indians to serve British interests in the Gulf by representing British commercial firms or running some of the colonial departments.

Through a maximum exploitation of the protection and facilities extended to them by the British, and by employing their position as money-lenders to the ruling families in Oman, Bahrain, and the Trucial Principalities, the Indians could establish themselves firmly and dominate a large segment of business in the region.

The oldest and strongest Indian merchant communities in the Gulf were in Muscat and Matrah where a wide range of business was, and still is, dominated by the Luwatias; members of an Indian Muslim sect from near Bombay, many of whom crossed to Oman some 200 years ago. Outside Oman, the largest of these communities were in Bahrain and Dubai, and the smallest were in Kuwait and Qatar. The reason given for the modest Indian influence in the latter was the resistance shown by their rulers to any prominent Indian role in businesses as these rulers themselves were merchants and feared competition. For example, the ruler of Kuwait attempted in the 1930s to exclude all Indians from his state and, as a result, he entered into a dispute with the British Political Agent.[16] However, one must not underestimate here the fact that, unlike the Kuwaitis, the natives of Oman, Bahrain, and the Trucial Sheikhdoms were in those days reluctant to be involved in any business other than pearl trading, giving the Indians plenty of opportunity for commercial dominance.

It is interesting to note that some Indian merchants, probably from Bahrain, extended into the coast of Alahsa in the period prior to the rule of Alsaud. According to Lorimer, a small Indian community involved in the import of general merchandise from India and the export of dates settled in Qatif as early as 1864. And when its members began to withdraw under the pressure of high taxation and harassment caused by the ruling Ottoman Authorities, Bahrain's Indian merchants used their money and influence between 1880-1903 to convince the British to establish an Agency in Alahsa for the purpose of protecting their brothers there.[17]

Finally, there were many Indians who succeeded in establishing strong business communities in Hijaz using the pilgrimage access. Many of today's prosperous merchants in Mecca and Madina are of Indian descent whose ancestors came on the pilgrimage and stayed rather than returning to India.

CONCLUSION

The relationship between India and the Gulf region goes back to pre-history days. There is definite archeological evidence of contacts between the ancient civilisations of the two regions since the third millennium BC. These contacts included demographic movements, commercial intercourse and probably cultural communications.

The Gulf has acted for centuries as a bridge connecting India with the rest of the world on the west. History, culture, and religion have all contributed to strengthening the ties created by the factor of geography.

With the advent of Islam and its expansion beyond the Arabian Peninsula, Indo-Gulf contacts deepened. And with the inclusion of part of India into the Arab/Islamic empire, the relationship branched out into fields other than commerce. The mediaeval period is identified by many scholars as a golden age of Indo-Arab relations as it witnessed enormous fruitful exchanges in different fields.

However, with the British dominance over the Indian Subcontinent and the Gulf, the latter became politically, economically, and administratively linked to India. Its fate and entire affairs were decided in Bombay by the British Indian Authorities. As a result, the Gulf's dependence on India increased significantly to cover almost every sector. This led to greater commercial exchanges, demographic movements, and socio-cultural communications, all of which had remarkable impact on all aspects of life in the Gulf.

These long, intimate, and multi-form historical relations between the two nations must, therefore, constitute the basis on which present and future cooperation is planned. In other words, the legacy of the past in the case of India and the Gulf must be employed today in shaping certain, if not all, foreign policy decisions of each side towards the other as this legacy does not contain such irritant factors as territorial dispute, ethnic hostility, or political competition.

NOTES

1. Rosmarie Said Zahlan, *The Making of the Modern Gulf States*, Unwin Hyman, London, 1989, p. 13.
2. See Mohammed Mitwali, *Howdh Alkhaleej Alarabi* (The Arabian Gulf Basin), Maktabat Alanglo, Cairo, 1981, pt. 2, p. 181.
3. Ali Aba Hussain, 'Historical Relations between Bahrain and India', *Alwatheekah* (Bahrain), no. 17, July 1990, p. 217.
4. Mohammad Al-Rumaihi, *Kadhaya Altaghier Alsiyasi Wa Alijtimai Fi Albahrain* (Issues of Political and Social Change in Bahrain 1920-1970), Alwahdah: Kuwait, 1976, pp. 101-2.
5. Michael Field, *The Merchants, The Big Business Families of Saudi Arabia and the Gulf States*, The Overlook Press: New York, 2nd printing 1985, p. 268.
6. Muhammad Ahmad Al-Shatry, *Muhammad Ali Zainal*, Dar Alshuruq, Jeddah, 1977, p. 61.
7. Saif M. Al-Shamlan, *Tarikh Alghous Ala Àlulu Fi Alkuwait Wa Alkhaleej Alarabi* (History of Pearl-Diving in Kuwait and the Arabian Gulf), Kuwait, 1978, pt. 2, p. 253.
8. See Mohammad Al-Rumaihi, op. cit., p. 275.
9. Ibid., p. 286.
10. Ajay N. Jha, *India's Economic Diplomacy in the Gulf*, ABC Publishing House, New Delhi, 1988, p. 84.
11. *Asharq Al-Awsat* (London), 13 March 1999.
12. See I.O.R. R/15/6/536 Persian Gulf Administration Report, 1936; and I.O.R. R/15/6/537 Persian Gulf Administration Report, 1937.
13. See I.O.R. R/15/718 Report for Year 1938.
14. See I.O.R. R/15/2/1362 Confidential C.T.B. Nos. 17 and 18, Enquiries reports about trading companies in Bahrain, 14 July 1936-16 June 1941.
15. Wizar is a length of printed cotton material wrapped around the lower part of the body.
16. See I.O.R. R/15/5/201 Exclusion of Prosperous Indians from Kuwait, 16 July 1936-16 November 1939.
17. See J.G. Lorimer, *Gazetter of the Persian Gulf*, IIB, Historical, pt. 3, pp. 1449, 1474-76 and 1492-95.

CHAPTER 3

The Indian Merchant Community of Masqat

CALVIN H. ALLEN, JR.

In 1836 the Arabian traveller J.R. Wellsted described the Hindu community of Masqat, Uman, as constituting 'a body of the principal merchants'[1] of that port. By the 1870s the Indian merchants dominated the commercial life of Masqat[2] and had replaced the Al Bu Said rulers of the town as the paramount economic power in Uman. While this community has much wider significance than their pivotal role in the commerce of Masqat and Uman (the Indian merchants in Masqat were a component of the great Indian Ocean trading network, and as Hindus and Shiis in a Sunni, more properly Khariji, country they offer potential insights into the status of minority groups in Muslim states) the focus of this study is the more specific problem of their origins, development and social and economic activities in Masqat to the end of the nineteenth century.

Contacts between India and the coast of Uman probably began very early in the commercial history of the Indian Ocean when maritime trade was conducted between Sumer and the Harappan civilization of the Indus valley. Some archaeologists believe that Magan, the source of copper for this ancient trade, was located somewhere in Uman,[3] and this argument is supported by the numerous ancient copper mining sites that have been discovered in the Hajar Mountains behind Suhar. While it is probably safe to assume that Indian merchants called on the coastal ports of Uman, we do no yet have concrete evidence that would support any further generalizations about the role of Indians in this ancient trade.

It is impossible to determine when the first Indian merchant decided to establish a semi-permanent presence in Masqat or anywhere else on the Batina coast, but evidence points to settlement occuring no later than the fifteenth-century. Andrew Williamson gives no indication of Indian settlement at Suhar, the Umani port that flourished in the tenth century,[4] but S.B. Miles reported the ruins of a Hindu temple at Qalhat,[5] the principal Umani port of the fifteenth century. The argument for fifteenth century settlement is supported further by de Albuquerque's report that Hindu merchants from Gujarat escaped from Khayr Fakkan, a secondary port on the Shimiliya coast of northern Uman, before he sacked that town in 1507.[6]

Once we enter the period of Portuguese domination of the Indian Ocean trade, information on Indian commercial activities in 'Uman and Masqat becomes more available. The Portuguese relied heavily on Indian Hindus in their attempts to secure a monopoly of the Indian Ocean/Arabian Gulf trade.[7] Masqat also played an important role in Portuguese commercial policy as the port became the headquarters of their Arabian Gulf operation early in the seventeenth century when Hurmuz was lost.

Masqat's most important Indian trading partner during this period was the city of Thattha located on the Indus River in Sind. Thattha had been an important trade centre between the Indian Ocean and Central Asia before the Portuguese sack of the city in the sixteenth century.[8] During the period of Portuguese control of its trade, Thattha continued to be an active commercial centre, boasting '40,000 weavers of calico and loongees[9] . . . and artisans of every other class and description to the number of 20,000 more, exclusive of bankers, money changers, shopkeepers and sellers of grain, who were estimated at 60,000 more'.[10] Among the goods exported by Thattha were cloth, including elegantly embroidered cashmere shawls[11] and silk,[12] cotton yarn, opium, ghee, indigo[13] and sugar.[14] Thattha's commerce in these goods with Africa and the Gulf was so great that the British believed that the Portuguese position in Masqat was entirely dependent on the customs duties they collected as a result of their policy of forcing all Africa and Gulf bound shipping to call at Masqat for licensing.[15]

The trade between Masqat and Thattha was conducted by Hindu

merchants in Portuguese ships, and many of these Hindus had warehouses and trading establishments at Masqat.[16] Oral traditions of the Indian merchant community in Masqat allege that these Sindis were the first 'Banians'[17] to settle in Masqat and add that they were Bhattis (Bhattiya).[18]

Sindi Bhattias apparently thrived under the Portuguese rulers of Masqat. The Umani chroniclers Ibn Ruzayq and al-Salimi both report that a Banian 'worshipper of the cow' acted as supply agent for the Portuguese garrison at Masqat, and the Portuguese commander seems to have accepted advice freely from his agent. However, the Banian eventually became dissatisfied with the Portuguese, especially as the commander wished to marry his daughter, and helped the Yaariba rulers of Uman expel the Europeans from Masqat in 1650.[19]

Bhattia support for the Yaariba proved to be very beneficial for the Banians. The community was exempted from paying the poll tax (*jizya*)[20] and permission was granted for the construction of a temple. Although the details need not concern us here, oral tradition attributes the founding of the temple in Masqat to Sindi Bhattias some three hundred years ago. The idol for the temple, a representation of the deity Govindaraj, was transported to Masqat from Basra, where the Hindu community was experiencing difficulties. Once their new temple was built and the idol in place, the Bhattias demonstrated their strong ties with their adopted home by including an Umani dagger in its vestments.[21]

The Hindu community was not affected adversely by the civil war which established the Al Bu Said dynasty in the 1740s, and it continued to propser under Ahmad b. Said (1743-82). In January 1765 the Danish explorer Carsten Niebuhr spent two weeks at Masqat and has left the following description of the Banian community:

> In no other Mahometan city are the Banians so numerous as in Maskat; their number in this city amounts to no fewer than twelve hundred. They are permitted to live agreeably to their own laws, to bring thier wives hither, to set up idols in their chambers, and to burn their dead.[22]

Under the benevolent rule of Ahmad the Banians founded their second temple in Masqat, this one a Haveli or Pustimargi sect temple. Other Hindu sects also set up their own shrines so that Masqat eventually had four Hindu places of worship.[23]

Despite these early successes of the Sindi Bhattias, the community was faced by a number of problems that led to its ultimate demise in Masqat. Three factors interacted concurrently between 1785 and 1820 to drive the Sindis from Masqat. First, the economy of Thattha collapsed. Second, a shift in the commercial practices of the rulers of Masqat hindered Sindi Bhattia enterprises. Finally, Bhattias from Kutch began to challenge Sindi Bhattias commercial activities in Masqat.

Sindi Bhattia trade in Masqat was dependent on selling the exports of Thattha either for cash or in exchange for the African and Arabian Gulf products available in the port, goods which included dates, rhinocerous horn, coffee, ivory and African slaves. Unfortunately, Thattha was on the road to becoming an economic backwater with nothing to export and no market for imports. The city's problems had begun with the expulsion of the Portuguese from the Indian Ocean during the last half of the seventeenth century. The collapse of the Portuguese trading network and its replacement by the British network centred in Surat, and later Bombay, was detrimental to Thattha's business interests as trade was drawn away from the city.[24] While these international influences were disrupting commerce, the intolerant Muslim Talpur dynasty was persecuting all Hindus within Sind.[25] Finally, sometime during the period the Indus River changed course, and Thattha found itself some five miles from its principal transportation route. Thattha's economy collapsed. In 1809 it was said of the once thriving city.

> . . . The only manufacturers now carried on in Tatta are those of a few white cloths and coloured loongees, and in lieu of the bustle of a great trading city, the streets are deserted, the few shops that remain are scarcely worthy of being called such, in view of the disreputable figure they cut, and the whole bazaar exhibits a deplorable picture of poverty and depressed commerce.[26]

The situation was so bad in Thattha that the Sindis abandoned it and began developing Karachi as an alternative.[27]

While the Sindi Bhattias might have established alternative markets and sources of supplies to Thattha and continued to conduct business in Masqat with Indian goods via Karachi, the development of strong competition on both Masqat and western India precluded that possibility. In Masqat Hamad b. Said Al Bu Said set up an independent government in 1785 and launched an aggressive commercial policy aimed at securing a monopoly over Arabian Gulf trade.[28] The most important aspect of this new policy to the Sindi Bhattias was Hamad's establishment of direct trading contacts with Afghanistan via the Indus River.[29] This put the Sindi Bhattias in direct competition with state commercial activities.

Competition was also developing in India in the form of another group of Bhattia merchants, the Kutchis. Kutch, lying to the east of the Indus River mouth, is, in many ways, very similar to Uman in that it is an arid, rugged country that is virtually cut off from the rest of India by the sometimes impassable Rann of Kutch. As a result, contacts with neighbours have always been easier by sea, a condition facilitated by the many fine ports along the Kutchi coast, most notably Mandvi (the mart).[30]

These natural conditions combined with a series of events in the late eighteenth century were to encourage the Kutchi Bhattias to become active in the Gulf trade. Most of the credit for this commercial expansion has gone to the Kutchi ruler Godji II (1760-78) who was extremely active in the development of Mandvi's shipbuilding industry.[31] Godji's actions were probably motivated by the collapse of Kutchi agriculture as a result of the damming of the Indus by the ruler of Sind in 1764.[32] A new dam in Sind in 1802, a famine and plague in 1812 and an earthquake in 1819 all served to cause Kutchis to leave the land. Further inducement came in the form of Fath Muhammad, the chief deputy of the Hindu Maharao, whose continuous wars during the late eighteenth–early nineteenth centuries encouraged social disruption.[33] Despite these dislocations, Kutch was relatively prosperous as the court encouraged the arts and crafts. Mandvi flourished as a result of the trade that provided raw materials to Kutchi craftsmen.[34]

Increasingly, Kutchi Bhattias began appearing in Masqat. The Kutchis had every advantage over the Sindis. They were not in competition with the *sayyids* of Masqat as the Kutchis served largely as shippers rather than middlemen. Kutchi merchants transported the few products of Kutch, predominantly cotton yarn and piece-goods, as well as goods from Bombay and the Gujarati ports, to Masqat where they could be sold to the *sayyid* or his agents. By contrast, the Sindis had their business establishment in Masqat, and while they could have sold to the *sayyid*, Sindi overheads and, consequently, prices were higher. A second Kutchi advantage was that they had a market for a wide range of the products that Masqat had to offer due to their secure trading network in India.[35]

Faced with the problem of insecurity and loss of markets in Sind and competition from the Al Bu Said *sayyids* and the Kutchis in both Masqat and India, the Sindi Bhattias began to abandon Masqat in favour of Bahrayn, where they were active in the pearl trade.[36] By 1900 there were only two Sindis still residing in Masqat, and by World War I there were none, although a few continued to live in the coastal towns.[37]

The Sindhi Bhattias were soon replaced by Kutchis. Kutchi settlement in Masqat and the growth of their own commercial establishment to the point where Kutchi Bhattias dominated the trade and economic affairs of the port grew in two stages, separated by Said b. Sultan's transfer of his residence to Zanzibar after 1830. While Sayyid Said remained in Masqat, he kept in tight personal control over commercial affairs. Under these conditions, the Kutchis did not establish an extended presence in the port, although in the early years a merchant may have remained in Masqat for a few months before picking up a suitable cargo for a return voyage. Some Kutchis did establish temporary commercial outlets in Masqat, but these would be operated for only a few years before the merchant retired to Mandvi.[38] A few Kutchi Bhattias even rose to prominence in the service of the commercially-mined Sayyid Sàid.

Two examples will serve to demonstrate this early stage in the development of the Kutchi Bhattia community in Masqat. Virji Purshottam Toprani today owns a small shop in Matrah, but his family claims seven generations of contacts with Masqat. The Topranis originated in the vicinity of the Rann of Kutch but moved to Mandvi when the Rann encroached on their farmlands. Once settled in Mandvi the family turned to commerce. Late in the eighteenth century, Aranji Toprani sailed to Masqat to conduct business, and he was followed in later years by his son and then grandson. The grandson, Umarsi, established the family's first business house in Masqat.[39]

A second example is Umarsi's contemporary Gopal Mawji Bhimani. Family legend claims that Gopal's great-grandfather was the first Bhimani to trade in Masqat late in the eighteenth century.[40] In time, the family founded a business in Masqat, and Gopal Bhimani began to play an active role in Masqati politics. Gopal was among the Banians who encouraged Said b. Sultan to conquer Zanzibar, and his business manager was active in the suppression of piracy.[41]

The second stage in the development of the Kutchi community in Masqat began with Sayyid Said's transfer of his attentions to Zanzibar after 1830. During this period the community grew in size and influence as a result of two factors. First, during Said's extended absences in East Africa he left most of Masqat's commercial affairs in the hands of resident Bhattias. Both the treasurer and chief customs official were Kutchi Bhattias,[42] and it was probably at this time that the practice of farming the Masqati customs was instituted.[43] A second factor that encouraged the Kutchi Bhattias to extend their interests was that Sayyid Said shifted from being a middleman to production. Once settled in Zanzibar, the *sayyid* was no longer interested in buying and selling the goods of others and making his profit on mark-ups and commissions. Instead, Said was selling slaves and cloves.[44] This turn of events left a commercial vacuum in Masqat, and Kutchis began to pour into the port. By 1840 the Banian population had reached 2,000,[45] and, as already stated by Wellsted, the community had become the principal economic power in Masqat.

Conditions in Masqat following the death of Said b. Sultan in 1856 were in no way detrimental of Kutchi Bhattia commercial interests. Thuwayni b. Said (1856-68) had never shown the business acumen of his father, a situation that is explained, at least in part, by Said's practice during his extended absences from Masqat of putting commercial affairs in the hands of Kutchis while Thuwayni was involved in political matters. Thuwayni simply continued this practice, and his reign was marked by an abandoning to state control of trade in favour of attempts to gain greater political influence and control in Uman.[46] This change in policy was disastrous for the Al Bu Said dynasty which lost the great profits from trade that had made Sayyid Said wealthy at a time when governmental expenses were increasing due to involvemnt in tribal politics and squabbles. The Kutchi Bhattias, by contrast, flourished. There was no state competition of any kind, and the Banians continued to control the treasury and customs house. The profits that had formerly filled the coffers of the ruling family now went to the Kutchi merchants.

The apparently bright economic prospects of the Bhattias were clouded by the rumblings in the interior of ʻUman that had resulted from Thuwayni's interference in tribal affairs. A real crisis for Bhattia interests occurred when the Imam Azzan b. Qays and his allies assumed control of Masqat and established a fundamentalist Ibadi regime (1868-71). The new conservative government not only removed the Bhattias from their important financial posts but also sought to extend Ibadi social regulations, including a ban on the use of tobacco, the playing of musical instruments and dress requirements, to all the inhabitants of Masqat. Despite Azzan's assurances that he supported freedom of religious practices, the Hindus, who employ bells, gongs and drums in their ceremonies, often fell foul of the authorities and there were a number of attacks on Banians.[47] The Indians began an exodus from Masqat, and the community of at least 2,000 dwindled to a mere 250 by 1870.[48]

This rapid population decline has been used as evidence to support the argument that Masqat suffered a serious economic depression during the years following the death of Sayyid Said,[49] a depression from which it never really recovered. While there is little doubt that Masqat was faced with economic problems at this time, they were neither so serious nor permanent as has been believed heretofore. In the first place, many of those who left Masqat during this period were family members rather than the merchants themselves. An indication of this is that by 1900, when some, but by no means all, family members were again coming to Masqat, the Banian population was back up to 1,500.[50] The second group that was most affected by the unsettled state of affairs in Masqat was the older generation of merchants, including the remaining Sindis, who abandoned the port for safe retirement in India. This view is supported by the fact that after the overthrow of the Imamate and the establishment of a more moderate government under Turki b. Said (1871-88), a whole new group of young Kutchi Bhattias emerged as the commercial leaders of Masqat.

An examination of one of the leading Banians of Masqat during the late nineteenth century, Shet[51] Ratansi Purshottam Purecha, will serve as an example of the new business class that came to dominate the trade and finances of the port after 1871. Ratansi first went to Masqat in 1857 as a boy of fourteen or fifteen in order to obtain business experience at his uncle's shop. He worked as a clerk for ten years until 1867 when he established his own firm, probably with capital borrowed from his uncle. The company survived the difficult years of the Imamate, and Ratansi developed a thriving business.[52]

Ratansi Purshottam, like most Bhattia businessmen, dealt in a wide range of goods, including grain, textiles, dates, coffee. Acting as a commission agent, Ratansi would distribute these goods throughout the western Indian Ocean basin on consignment and receive a percentage of the profits, when there were profits.[53] To aid in these commercial operations Masqati Banians often established working agreements with merchants in foreign ports. These were quite often family members, such as was the case with Ratansi, whose brother owned a business in Bombay and who, himself, had an office in Karachi. In the absence of family members these arrangements would be made with other Bhattias, although it was not unusual to deal with a non-Bhattia or even a Muslim if the need arose.[54]

An important contribution of the new merchant group of the late nineteenth century was its 'internationalization' of the trade of Masqat. That is to say that trade was expanded beyond the confines of the Indian Ocean basin. The Indian merchants showed great adaptability in this area. Arab and Indian sailing ships were being replaced rapidly by European steamers,[55] and the Banians were able to import products from Europe and America for their traditional markets and export traditional goods to new markets overseas. Ratansi played an important role in this expanded trade as he was a leading arms merchant, dealing with the London firm Schwarte and Hammer and the Hamburg arms dealer Moritz Magnus, and was active in exporting dates to the United States through the New York firm of William Hills (now a subsidary of Nabisco).[56]

Most of the Banians lived and worked in Masqat within the walled portion of the city and close to the sultan's palace. Ratansi was no exception, although the family did move to Matrah in 1915 when that port supplanted Masqat as the commercial centre of Uman. Early in the 1880s Ratansi began to acquire land along the waterfront of Masqat and eventually came to own all the waterfront property with the exception of the palace, customs house and British Political Agency.[57] This was only one of many parcels of land that Ratansi came to own,[58] and by the end of the nineteenth century he and his Banian colleagues owned most of the best property in Masqat and Matrah.[59]

Land holdings were closely linked with the banking functions of the Banian community as many lands transfers were the result of mortgage foreclosures. Land, houses and date palms were about the only collateral that the local population had to offer in return for a loan that would tide them over to the next date harvest. The level of indebtedness was high and foreclosures a regular occurrence. Even if holding a mortgage, though, the Banian lender was not always guaranteed that a debt would be repaid as it was not unheard of to have an obscure *waqf* property mortgaged on the pretence that it was a private holding. When the debtor defaulted or died and the Banian brought charges, the *waqf* document would be presented and the mortgage had to be cancelled.[60]

The Banians of Masqat retained a fairly high degree of community solidarity, this despite economic competition. The community was represented in political matters by the *nagar seth* or *mukhi*, the most respected man in the community. During the later nineteenth century this office was held by a Bhimani.[61] The Hindus celebrated their religious festivals, such as New Year (Divali), with social gatherings and dinner parties. Usually a dish of the best food would be taken to the sultan. Banians were also invited to the palace on special occasions, although they would not eat the food prepared by the ruler's non-Hindu cooks.[62] For the most part, dietary laws were kept, and the community maintained a herd of cows to ensure a steady supply of dairy products.[63] Kutchi or Gujarati remained the principal language spoken within the community, although most did learn Arabic for business purposes, and accounts were kept in Gujarati. Indian dress styles were maintained.[64] In general, the Masqati Hindu made no attempt to assimilate.

Aside from the Bhimani family and Ratansi Purshottam, there were a large number of important Hindu merchants in Masqat during the late nineteenth century. Among them were Dowlatgirji Manrupgirji, a Gosain Brahman from Kutch who owned a business in Masqat but entrusted it to a manager while he continued to reside in a monastery outside of Mandvi; Virji Ratansi, an important banker, and Damodar Dharamsi, who occasionally farmed the customs. These three, along with Ratansi Purshottam, were considered to be the 'four pillars' of Hindu society.[65] Upon this base a number of other Banians established prosperous business that have continued to flourish in Masqat. These include Khimji Ramdas, Dayal Purshottam, Danji Murarji, Vallabdas Umarsi and Gopalji Walji.

A second group of Indians lived within the domains of the sultan, the Khwajas (Khojas). Very little is known about the Khwaja community of Uman, which goes by the name Luti,[66] and virtually nothing has been written. The Luwatiyya claim origins in Hyderabad, Sind and are, therefore, occasionally, given to the *nisba* Haydarabadi.

The origins of the community are obscure with many different legends persisting about from where the Luwatiyya came. A small pamphlet written by a member of the community and based on classical Arabic sources and a manuscript by 'al-Haydarabadi' asserts that the Luwatiyya are the descendants of one al-Hakam b. Awanat at-Lat. According to this account al-Hakam accompanied the first Arab campaigns against India and eventually became the governor of Sind.[67] A second legend claims that the Luwatiyya were originally Banu Lu'ayy Arabs from Hijaz who went to India with Muhammad al-Qasim and were eventually converted to Shiism.[68] A variant of this account is that the Banu Luayy were Kharijites who fled to Uman but were later expelled from this sanctuary and moved on to India where they converted to Shiism.[69] These legends aside, it is fairly certain that the Luwatiyya, like their Khwaja co-religionists in India, were converts from Hinduism. However, unlike the majority of Khwajas, the Luwatiyya were probably not Lohanas but Bhattias. The name Luti provides an important clue to this theory. Among the clans of the Bhattias is the Panchlutiya (the five martyrs, commemorating an important event in Bhattia history),[70] and many Bhattias in Sind were converted to Islam.[71] The Luwatiyya were almost certainly Bhattias of the Panchlutiya clan who were converted to Islam.

None of the elders of the Luti community know when the first Luti migrated from India to Uman. However, most will claim that there have been Luwatiyya in Uman for four hundred years, a view which they support by citing a date on one of the gates that leads into the Luti quarter of Matrah. While it is possible that Luti merchants came to Uman four centuries ago, there is no real documentary evidence to support this contention; the inscription only tells us that the gate was built in the sixteenth century. The earliest mention of Luwatiyya in Arabic sources occurs in Ibn Ruzayq, who tells us that the Luwatiyya were among the principal occupants of Matrah during the reign of Ahmad b. Said (1743–82).[72] That statement is probably based on the fact that the Luwatiyya were prominent in Matrah in the 1850s when Ibn Ruzayq was writing.

There is stronger evidence for much later Luti settlement in Uman. As mentioned earlier, the Luwatiyya claim to have originated in Hyderabad, Sind. Hyderabad was not founed until 1768.[73] Anyone claiming to be a Hyderabadi, therefore, could not have migrated to Uman before that date. Other events in Sind during the last two decades of the eighteenth century would have encouraged the growth of Khwaja commercial interests. First, the Talpur dynasty, established in 1783, destroyed the Hindu merchant class and paved the way for Muslim merchants.[74] Second, Khwajas could have played an important role in the opening up of direct trade between Masqat and Afghanistan during the reign of Hamad b. Said (1785–92). Finally, the best available documentary evidence for Luti settlement in Uman during the late eighteenth century is an 1889 dispute in which the Luwatiyya claim privileges going back for a century.[75] In any event, by the time of the American diplomatic mission to Masqat in 1835, the Luwatiyya were well established in Matrah.[76]

A second wave of Luti settlement appears to have occurred during the second half of the nineteenth century. This opinion is supported by genealogical studies among contemporary Luwatiyya, who, for the most part, can remember back only as far as their great grandfather,[77] and by the fact that a number of Khwajas were British subjects. This could only have occurred if they had migrated to Uman after 1840 when the British assumed control of Sind.[78]

All of this leads to the conclusion that the pattern of Luti settlement in Uman was very similar to that of the Kutchi Bhattias. The earliest Lutis came in the wake of the establishment of the Al Bu Said state in Masqat in 1785. The disruptions of Azzan b. Qays's reign may have had the same impact on the Luti commercial community as it had on the Bhattias[79]. Following the re-establishment of moderate Al Bu Said rule in 1871, a new group of Luwatiyya came to Uman and came to dominate the community.

The Luwatiyya operated within the same kind of mercantile system that the Banians utilized, and there were Khwajas in most of the Gulf ports, Bombay, Karachi, Zanzibar and Mombasa. Besides dealing the standard products, like textiles, grain and dates, the Khwajas also had a virtual monopoly of the trade in dried fish from Masqat as this was a product in which the Hindu merchants, for religious reasons, would not deal. Khwajas were also involved in various skiled crafts, like carpentry and boat building.[80]

Unlike the Banians, the Luwatiyya chose to make Matrah their home, and the community was concentrated in a ghetto, known as Sur Luwatiyya, adjoining the market. The Sur was off limits to non-Luwatiyya[81] and was strictly residential; the Luti merchant would commute to his shop in the markets at Matrah or Masqat, unlike the Banian who usually lived above his shop.

Despite their permanent settlement in Matrah, the Luwatiyya remained segregated from their Arab neighbours. Although Luti men would occasionally take Umani women for brides, Luti women always married within the community.[82] Khwajki, a mixture of Sindi and Kutchi, was the principal language spoken within the household, but Arabic was fairly widely used. The community had an elected shaykh and council of elders which governed communal affairs, and worship took place in a jamaat khana located within the walls of the Sur.

The Khwaja community of Matrah was affected by the controversy that erupted in India during the 1840s concerning the Agha Khan's rights to the *desaudh* or obligatory religious tithe. This dispute came to a head in 1862 with the initiation of legal proceedings by the Bombay merchants who argued that the tithe belonged to the community and not the Agha Khan.[83] All but twenty families in Matrah supported the case against the Agha Khan and were among those excommunicated when the courts ruled in favour of the religious leader. The Matrah Khwajas then became Ithna-Ashari Shiis, the jamaat khana became a Shii mosque, and the community requested that a qadi be dispatched from Najaf (Iraq) to serve Luwatiyya legal needs.[84] The twenty families who chose to support the Agha Khan were expelled from the Sur and established a new jamaat khana just outside the north western wall of their old home.[85]

By far the most important Luti merchant of the later nineteenth century was Muhammad Fadl. Muhammad Fadl was born in Bombay in 1858[86] and eventualy settled in the Sur Luwatiyya. He began his business career as a clerk in the American firm, W. J. Towell, founded in 1865. Muhammad Fadl worked his way through the firm, becoming a partner in 1894 and full owner in 1906.[87] He also served as American Vice Consul and later Consul and was quite active in securing American trade for Masqat. For most of the late nineteenth century and up until First World War, W.J. Towell was the leading exporter of dates to the United States, and the company also acted as agent for Standard Oil. Unlike most of his Banian contemporaries, Muhammad Fadl did not have close relations with the government of the sultan.

Muhammad Fadl and Ratansi Purshottam had, in common with nearly all the Indian merchants, both Banian and Luti, the protection of the British authorities in Masqat. The general rule in determining who was or was not a British subject was that anyone who had settled in Masqat after the British had assumed direct control over his native territory in India could obtain British protection. If he had lived in a native state that was under British protection, he was a British protected subject.[88] The benefits were the same:[89] exemption from search of private property; exemption from local taxes; right of full discharge from creditors if bankrupt; British assistance in recovering debts; British official representation in any local trial and exemption from direct interference by local authorities.[90] In addition to these broad privileges, British subjects and protected persons could obtain the assistance of British diplomatic authorities in collecting damages for losses due to attack by the local population.

Needless to say, there were often difficulties in determining citizenship, and it was not uncommon for individuals to proclaim British protection in certain instances while claiming Masqati citizenship in others. Most of the controversy was settled in 1867 when the British made provisions for the registration of British subjects and protected persons. Registration was not, however, a prerequisite to obtaining protection.[91]

British protection was a mixed blessing for the Indian merchants. While it served to ensure some measure of security for their businesses, the association with the British also had a negative impact. As Landen has pointed out, much of the Umani resentment against the sultans of Masqat had resulted from their belief that the Al Bu Said were mere puppets in the hands of the British.[92] Many of the problems experienced by Indian merchants during the final decades of the nineteenth century, such as the sacking and burning of their shops during the various raids on Masqat and other actions in Sur and some of the other coastal ports, may have resulted from their close association with the British.[93] The Indian merchants were viewed as agents of British designs of Uman.

Over the course of the nineteenth century, Indian merchants came to dominate the economic life of Masqat, replacing the Al Bu Said rulers as the principal merchants of the city and acquiring fortunes that had once gone to the royal family. The Hindu Banians, who had first come from Sind as junior partners to the Portuguese, flourished under the Yaariba but suffered as a result of the combined strains of political and economic dislocations at home and a more aggressive Masqati commercial policy adopted by Hamad b. Said and followed by his successors. Khwajas from Sind and Bhattias from Kutch began to replace the Sindis, who moved on to other Gulf ports. The Kutchis allied themselves with Sayyid Said, and when he moved his capital to Zanzibar, they assumed control of the financial apparatus of Masqat. The Kutchis faced their first serious crisis during the brief but commercially disastrous reign of Azzan b. Qays. However, the disruptions served to allow many younger, more venturesome merchants to become established in Masqat. Once a more moderate regime was established in 1871 this new merchant group, comprising both Banians and Luwatiyya, once again assumed control of trade and fiscal administration and set about to restore Masqat's commercial prominence by broadening the mercantile base of the port through trade with Europe and America.

NOTES

1. J.R. Wellsted, *Travels in Arabia*, London, 1838, I, pp. 18-21.
2. Robert G. Landen, *Oman since 1856*, Princeton, 1967, p. 138.
3. Geoffrey Bibby, *Looking for Dilmum*, New York, 1969, p. 220.

4. Andrew Williamson, *Sohar and Omani Seafaring in the Indian Ocean*, Masqat, 1973.
5. S.B. Miles, *Countries and Tribes of the Persian Gulf*, 2nd edn., London, 1966, p. 526. On Qalhat see J.C. Wilkinson, 'Kalhat', *Encyclopaedia of Islam*, 2nd edn., pp. 500-1.
6. Afonso de Albuquerque, *The Commentaries of the Great Afonso Dalaboquerque, Second Viceroy of India*, ed. Walter de Gray Birch, London, 1875, I, pp. 99-100. Miles (p. 151), incorrectly claims that these Hindus were Kutchis. This view probably derived from the fact that the Hindus in Masqat during Miles's residence (late nineteenth century) were Kutchi.
7. See M.N. Pearson, 'Indigenous dominance in a colonial economy: the Goa Rendas, 1600-1670', *Mare Luso-indicum*, II, 1972, pp. 61-73, for a study of the role of Hindu traders under the Portuguese.
8. James Burnes, *A Visit to the Courte of Sinde*, Karachi, 1974, p. 27. Burnes had visited Thattha in 1828.
9. Loonghee, s. from Hindi *lungi*, a scarf or length of cloth to wrap around the body, See *Hobson-Jobson*, London, 1903, p. 519. In 'Uman these *lungis*, known locally as *wazar*, are worn by all males.
10. E.H. Aitken, *Gazetteer of the Province of Sind*, Karachi, 1907, p. 116. Aitken was quoting a British official, Henry Pottinger, who was a member of the British mission to Sind in 1809.
11. Burnes, op. cit., p. 92. In Uman and the rest of Arabia these shawls are used as turbans.
12. Al-Salimi relates a story about how the Imam Said b. Ahmad (1199/1784) wore a silk 'diwali' or cummerbund, *Tuhfat al-a'yan bi-sirat ahl 'Uman* (5th edn.), Kuwayt, 1974, II, p. 176.
13. William Foster, *The English Factories in India, 1634-1636*, Oxford, 1911, pp. 127-34. Uman had a local indigo dyeing industry centred on Nizwa and Firq.
14. Ibid., *1637-1641*, Oxford, 1912, p. 135.
15. Ibid., *1646-1650*, Oxford, 1914, p. 153.
16. Ibid., *1634-1636*, p. 127.
17. Banian or Banyan derives from the Gujarati *vaniyo*, a man of the trading caste. The term has been adopted to mean all Hindu merchants regardless of caste. See *Hobson-Jobson*, pp. 63-4. Landen claims that the term is 'evidently a corruption of the word "Bhatetia"' (p. 131). This is incorrect.
18. Personal communication to the author from Ranchordas Lalji Purecha, the grandson of Ratansi Purshottam, and Dungarsi Dharamsi Sampat, 'Bhattiya samsthano itihaṣ; pt. 6: Masqat', *Bhattia Yuvak Magazine*,

Magh [vs] 1989, pp. 111-15. This series, written in Gujarati, is an extremely important source for the history of the Bhattia community throughout India and the Indian Ocean basin. I wish to express my thanks to Mr. Dilip Ukka of Mandvi, Kutch, for his assistance in translating the various articles used in this study. On the Bhattias, see also R.E. Enthoven, *The Tribes and Castes of Bombay*, Bombay, 1920, I, pp. 133-45, and James Campbell (ed.), *Bombay Presidency District Gazetter*, V (Cutch, Palanpur and Mahi), Bombay, 1880, pp. 53-4.

19. Humayd b. Muhammad b. Ruzayq, *al-Fath al-mubin fi sirat al-sadah Al Bu Saidiyyin*, Masqat, 1977, pp. 286-91; G.P. Badger, *History of the Imams and Seyyids of 'Oman, by Salil ibn Razik*, London, 1971, XXVI, pp. 81-7; al-salimi, pp. 65-7. The account given by al-Salimi differs from that of ibn Ruzayq in that the former claims that the principal Hindu was named Sakaliba and his assistant was Narutim. Ibn Ruzayq mentions only Narutim. Carsten Niebuhr, *Travels through Arabia and other countries of the East* Edinburgh, 1792, II, p. 116 contains the earliest (1765) published account of this story, although he offers no details. In Mandvi, Kutch, a similar story was related to me in which a prominent nineteenth-century merchant family, known in Masqat as Bayt Shabika, was alleged to have assisted the Al Bu Said in a similar manner.
20. Al-Salimi, p. 67; Ibn Ruzayq, p. 291.
21. D.D. Sampat, 'Part 7: Masqat', Phalgun 1989, pp. 172-8. Sampat doubts that the idol went from Basra. This whole episode is of interest as it provides some clues to early Bhattia religious practices. The majority of Bhattias were converted during the last decade of the seventeenth century to the Pusimargi sect, a Vaishnavite group with principal deties Krishna as a child and as flute player and Sri Nathji (an incarnation of Krishna) founded by the Mahaprabhu Sri Vallabh-acarya. The movement began in, interestingly enough, Thattha and spread to Kutch and the rest of Gujarat. The fact that this was a Govindraj temple rather than a Putimargi temple, known as Haveli, serves either to date the temple before 1700 or may be an indication of a certain amount of conservatism within the Bhattia community of Masqat. Ranchordas Lalji relates that this temple, which was located near the old palace, was torn down in 1917 to make way for the new palace, and the idol was returned to India.
22. Niebuhr, *Travels*, p. 116.
23. These included the Govindaraj temple, the Haveli, known as Bavaji, which is one of the two temples that still exist in Masqat, a Kalka temple situated on the Masqat side of the pass to Riyam and a large Siva temple, known as Motisvar, located in the Rawiyya section of Masqat.

The Kalka temple, utilized by the small but influential Gosain Brahmin community in Masqat, included a graveyard to accommodate the Gosain practice of burying their dead in a seated position. The temple was demolished in 1970 to make way for a road, and the idol is now stored in the Bavaji temple. Motisvar was built near a large banyan tree and contained two wells. The temple became the centre of Hindu social life in Masqat as well as the water source for the community. It has been rebuilt recently, and contains, beside the linga representing Siva. Nandi, Siva's mount, and a turtle, as well as a small shrine to Hanumant. The Hindu community also had, and continues to utilize, a burning ghat for the cremation of its dead, a cow pen, no longer in use, and a *gupha*, or 'holy cave', located in the mountains near Sidab.

24. On the decline of Thattha see the massive work by William Foster, *The English Factories in India, passim*. Also, for a more succinct description of the plight of the former trading centres in Portuguese India *see The Travels of the Abbé Carre in India and the Near East, 1672 to 1674*, ed. Charles Fawcett, London, 1947, I, pp. 214-15 for his decription of Goa.
25. Aitkin, *Gazetteer*, pp. 116-17.
26. Ibid., p. 116. This is Pottinger's description based on personal observation (see n. 10).
27. *Selections from the Records of the Bombay Government*, new series, no. 17, pp. 1-245. Two articles on Karachi from 1838 and 1840. Sampat, 'Part 3; Karachi', Paush 1989, pp. 26-9.
28. See the author's unpublished Ph.D. thesis, 'Sayyids, Shets and Sultans: Politics and Trade in Masqat under the Al Bu Said', University of Washington (Seattle), 1978, pp. 33-67.
29. 'Report on the commerce of Arabia and Persia by Samuel Manesty and Hartford Jones, 1790', in Ahmad Mustafa abu Hakima, *History of Kuwayt* [in Arabic], Kuwayt, 1970, I, pt. 2, pp. 21-82, 59-60.
30. Mandvi is also known as Musca-Mandvi after the neighbouring village of Musca. This name is very intriguing as Masqat is often referred to as Muska in the Arabic chronicles. I visited Musca in May 1977 in search of information on the origin of the name of the town but met with little success. I would speculate that this village is probably named after Masqat, just as Mandvi's newest suburb, Swalli, is named after the Swahili coast. On the early history of Mandvi see Campbel, *Bombay Presidency District Gazetteer*, pp. 1-227, *passim*.
31. L.F. Rushbrook Williams, *The Black Hills: Kutch in History and Legend*, London, 1958, 41. D.D. Sampat, 'Part 65 : Bhattias of Mandvi', Phalgun 1992, pp. 133-8.
32. Campbell, op. cit., 10, states that the rice fields of western Kutch were reduced to grazing lands as a result of this action.

33. Ibid., pp. 10, 17, 40; D.D. Sampat, 'Part 73: Customs of Bhattias', Asadh 1992, pp. 313-16.
34. Marianne Young, *Cutch: or, Random Sketches of Western India*, London, 1838, pp. 10-14; James Tod, *Travels in Western India*, Delhi, 1971, pp. 448-51.
35. Ibid. Both of the above sources give excellent accounts of Mandvi's role in the slave trade.
36. D.D. Sampat, 'Part 4: Sind', Paush 1989, pp. 29-31. Sindi Bhattias still play an important role in the commerce of Bahrayn and Dubay.
37. At least one Sindi merchant family continued to reside in Suhar as late as 1977. The principal Sindi merchant in Masqat today is Meghji Laxmidas Ved from Shahbunder, but this family, which was established in Matrah in 1907, has no direct ties to the early Sindi merchants (personal communication to author from Meghji Laxmidas Ved).
38. D.D. Sampat, *Kacchnu vepartantra*, Karachi [vs] 1991, pp. 17-18; idem, 'Part 105: Trade with Masqat', Karttik 1994, pp. 863-5.
39. Personal communication from Virji Purshottam Toprani. The genealogy of the family is:

Aranji
|
Ramdas
|
Umarsi
|
Valabdas
|
Damodar (c. 1857-1932)
|
Purshottam (1888-1976)
|
Virji

40. Personal communication from Premji Jamnadas Bhimani of Mandvi. The genealogy of the Bhimani family is:

Rawji
|
Bhimji
|
Mawji
|
Gopa
|
Mulji

|
Jivandas
|
Mawdawji
|
Jamnadas (d. 1942)
|
Premji (b.1990)

41. D.D. Sampat, 'Part 62: towards Kutch and Kathiawad', Bhadarvo 1991, pp. 527-34. The association of the Bhattia merchants with Said's African policy is very significant. The standard interpretation of the establishment of Hindu commercial influence at Zanzibar has attributed it to Said b. Sultan encouraging their migration to that port. Abd al-Muhammad Husayn Sharif, in his Ph.D. thesis 'The Rise of a Commercial Empire: An Aspect of the Economic History of Zanzibar, 1770-1873', University of London, 1971, expresses doubt about this theory. He argues that the Hindu merchants encouraged Said. Sampat's evidence supports that view, although it may be more proper to argue that the development of Zanzibar was a joint endeavour.
42. D.D. Sampat, 'Part 105: Trade with Masqat', Karttik 1994, pp. 964-5.
43. The earliest mention of Banian holding the customs farms is in 1827 in R.H. Thomas, *Selections from the Records of the Bombay Government*, new series, no. 24, 1856, 632. D.D. Sampat, *Kacchnu vepartantra*, p. 19, states that Said b. Sultan farmed the customs to the Bhimanis.
44. See Frederick Cōoper, *Plantation Slavery on the East Coast of Africa*, New Haven and London, 1977, for a discussion of the development of Said's Zanzibar plantations. The impact of Said's moving to Zanzibar on Masqat is discussed in my 'Sayyids, Shets and Sultans', pp. 68-86.
45. Thomas, op. cit., p. 631.
46. See my 'Sayyids, Shets and Sultans', pp. 86-92.
47. A good account of the problems of 'Azzan b. Qays's reign, based on India Office Records, Muscat Political Agency, R/15/6/2, is available in Landen, pp. 309-10.
48. India Office Records, Muscat Political Agency, R/15/6/2, Disbrowe to Gonne, Muscat, 20 April 1869. As is usually the case in dealing with statistics from these sources, some error is assumed. Disbrowe says that there are 250 subjects with dependents. It is possible that the population was as high as 750.
49. Landen, *Oman since 1856*, pp. 134-5.
50. India Office Records, Muscat Political Agency, R/15/6/67, Memorandum, Cox, Muscat, 30 July 1900. This once again raises the problem of

numbers. Landen says that there were 250 merchants at this time (p. 141). Ratansi Purshottam's family came in 1900 and was one of the first to do so according to family tradition.

51. Shet, singular, from the Hindi *seth* meaning head of a corporation, merchant or banker. See *Hobson-Jobson*, p. 813. In Masqat the title is used as an address of respect.

52. Most of the facts concerning the life of Ratansi Purshottam were related to me by Ranchordas Lalji, Ratansi's grandson, who also provided the following genealogy:

Mukund
|
Natha
|
Thakersey
|
Damodar——Mawji
|
Purshottam
|
Ratansi ——Virji
|
Lalji —— Nanci
|
Ranchordas
|
Vimal

On the training of a young Banian see D.D. Sampat, 'Part 6: Masqat', Magh 1989, p. 115.

53. Landen, op. cit., p. 137, is very critical of this system.

54. In the course of numerous interviews with many of Masqat's merchants, both Hindu and Muslim, this fact was stressed.

55. Landen, pp. 96-9.

56. Banian utilization of the steamship to the benefit of Masqat is discussed in my 'Sayyids, Shets and Sultans', pp. 140-77.

57. This property was sold to the British Indian government in 1901 and is now included in the British Embassy compound. See Ruth Hawley, *The British Embassy in Muscat: A Short History*, Muscat, 1974, pp. 9-10. India Office Records, Muscat Political Agency, R/15/6/26 contains a detailed record of how Ratansi originally acquired all of this property.

58. In 1906, the year of his death, Ratansi owned one large residence with office building and twelve warehouses, five of which had upper-storey

residences and one with a courtyard, in Masqat; two houses, one with garden, in Sidab; two houses with lower story offices and two warehouses, one with an attached courtyard, in Matrah and two farms with water-rights in outlying villages, Ratansi Purshottam papers, Account Book for 1905-6.

59. India Office Records, Muscat Political Agency, R/15/6/67, Cox to Landsdowne, Maskat, 21 September 1902.
60. Ibid. Muscat Political Agency, R/15/6/25, Cox to Government of India, Muscat, 27 September 1902.
61. Personal communication from Ranchordas Lalji. The Hindu Association known as the Mahajan, was formally incorporated in the 1930s with the president becoming an elected official. During the twentieth century the Mahajan administered most aspects of Hindu communal life, including the schools, temples and cow herd and property donated to the community by merchants who died without heirs or otherwise.
62. D.D. Sampat, 'Part 7: Masqat', Phalgun 1989, pp. 172-8.
63. The cow-pen, *panjarapol*, was located next to the Siva temple in Rawiyya. These cows, unlike most in Masqat, were not fed fish, which resulted in a fishy taste to the milk. Surplus milk was sold for the benefit of the community. When the Uman National Dairy was opened, the cows were donated to the state with the agreement that when the animals stopped producing they would be sent to India rather than slaughtered.
64. On dress distinctions among various levels of Banian society in Masqat see D.D. Sampat, *Kacchnu Veparatantra,* p. 19.
65. These four merchants were given nicknames corresponding to the four high cards in a deck. Dowlatgirji was the 'ace' (*Ikka*), Ratansi was the 'king' (Batsa), Virji was the 'queen' (Rani) but was also called Bayt Bisah (after the Masqat coin) because of his banking activities, and Damodar was the 'Jack' (Ghulam). See also D.D. Sampat, 'Part 7: Masqat', Phalgum 1989, pp. 172-8 for references to Ratansi as Batasa.
66. Luti, pl, Luwatiyya. The origin of the name is unknown, but both the Arabic and Persian roots are unflattering terms.
67. Muhammad Taqi Hassan al-Umani, *Dalil al-sa'il*, n.d., 6 pages.
68. Personal communication from Hajji 'Ali Sultan of Matrah.
69. Personal communication from Muhammad Matwani of Matrah.
70. Girjir Ratansi Sapat, *Bhattiyaoni pracim sthiti*, Bombay, 1899, p. 69. Enthoven also lists the clans, or 'nookhs', of the Bhattias.
71. D.D. Sampat, 'Part 8 : Thattha', Bhadarvo 1991, pp. 525-7; 'Part 73: Customs of the Bhattias', Asadh 1992, pp. 313-16.
72. Ibn Ruzayq, *al-Fath al-mubin*, 356; Badger, *History of the Imams*, p. 163.
73. Aitken, *Gazetteer*, p. 113.

74. See above, p. 42.
75. J.G. Lorimer , *Gazetteer of the Persian Gulf, Oman and Central Arabia, Calcutta,* 1915, I, pt. 1, p. 535.
76. W.S.W. Ruschenberger, *Narrative of a Voyage Round the World during the Years 1835, 36, 37,* I, London, 1970, p. 125.
77. Dr. Nihami Levtzion, on the basis of oral traditions collected in West Africa, has found that migrant groups usually recall genealogy only as far as the first settler in the area. Personal communication. The following genealogies are offered as examples:

(1) 'Ali Sultan:
Muhammad Fadl (d. 1916)
|
Sultan
|
(2) Amin Malallah:
Ali Wansiyah
|
Murad
|
Habib (d. 1938)
|
Malallah
|
(3) Muhammad Musa:
Amin Ghulam
|
Ja'far (d. 1894)
|
Musa (d. 1967)
|
Muhammad

78. India Office Records, Muscat Political Agency, R/15/6/8, *passim.*
79. See n. 53. The Luwatiyya suffered equally under 'Azzan.
80. Landen, *Oman since 1856*, p. 140.
81. The Sur Luwatiyya retains its exclusivity. My one attempt to walk through the quarter was unsuccessful as I did not get past the main gate before I was met by a concierge and told to leave. Ruschenberger was told in 1835 that outsiders were not admitted to the Sur because Luti women went unveiled (p. 125).
82. See J.C. Masselos, 'The Khojas of Bombay', in Imtiaz Ahmad (ed.), *Caste and Social Stratification among Muslims in India,* Columbia, Mo., 1978, p. 101, for a discussion of Khwaja marriage practices.
83. J.N. Hollister, *The Shia of India*, London, 1953, pp. 364-70.
84. Lorimer, *Gazetteer*, I, pt. 2, Appendix H, 'Religions and Sects of the

Persian Gulf Region', 2377-80 and II B, Calcutta, 1908, pp. 1034-5. Personal communication from 'Ali Sultan.

85. The few Agha Khanis (as they were called) who remained in Matrah left in 1965 on the orders of the Agha Khan, who feared for their safety following the revolution in Zanzibar. Their jima'at khana, located in front of the girls' school in Matrah and next to the Jibru roundabout, was bought by the W. J. Towell Company and torn down to make way for an office building.
86. United States National Archives, Muscat Consular Archives, Mirofilm Publication T638, Macquire to Wharton, Muscat, 19 February 1893.
87. The early history of the W.J. Towell Company is unclear. Towell apparently sold the company during the 1870s as in 1880 an Irishman named William Maguire, who became the second American Consul in Masqat, described himself as the 'sole partner' in the company, which, despite Towell's absence, retained his name. Kamal 'Abd al-Rida Sultan of W.J. Towell believes that his great-grandfather, Muhammad Fadl, became a partner in the company in 1884 when he purchased shares valued at RO 11,000. That seems unlikely according to American consular records which show that a Scot, Archibald Mackirdy, became Maguire's partner in 1887 and then inherited the company, and the American consulship, in 1893. Muhammad Fadl probably became a partner in 1894 and inherited the company on Mackirdy's death in 1906. See United States National Archives, Muscat Consular Records, Microfilm Publications T638 and T639, *passim*.
88. India Office Records, Muscat Political Agency, R/15/6/8, *passim*.
89. Ibid. Political Secretary to Resident, Persian Gulf, Simla, 19 October 1875.
90. Landen, *Oman Since 1856*, p. 202.
91. India Office Records, Muscat Political Agency, R/15/6/8, Political Secretary to Resident, Persian Gulf, Simla, 19 October 1975.
92. Landen, op. cit., p. 392.
93. On the various difficulties between the British and the sultans see sections in Lorimer entitled 'Protection of British Subjects in Oman', I, pt. 1A, pp. 513-16, 535-8, 553-5.

CHAPTER 4

Merchants' Role in a Changing Society: The Case of Dubai, 1900-1990

FATMA AL-SAYEGH

Since the turn of the twentieth century, Dubai, the largest city in the United Arab Emirates (known before independence as the Trucial Coast), has derived its fame and prosperity from trade. With little or no other means of livelihood, commerce became the main source of income for the Sheikhdom. Dubai's port became the main entrepôt in the Gulf, and the busiest trading port in the region.

In many respects Dubai typifies the way in which Gulf cities have developed over the past two hundred years. Many have grown rapidly from small merchant communities to thriving commercial centres. In fact Dubai owes much of its prosperity and development to its merchants who played a key role in restructuring the economy and in the government decisionmaking process. As the main contributors to the economy, they played a fundamental role in implementing economic and political reforms, and were the driving force behind Dubai's development in the pre-oil era. When oil was struck in the mid-1930s and revenue began to pour into the state's treasury, many predicted a decline in the influence of merchants whose revenues had shrunk, and who had consequently lost some of their power. A closer examination of Dubai's development shows however that any decline in the merchants' influence was only temporary. Even today they continue to play a fundamental role not only in economic affairs, but also in reformulating the political structure of Dubai. Furthermore, merchants have taken on additional roles as service suppliers, urban planners, culture mediators, and internationlists who represent the Gulf throughout the world. Using

Dubai as a case-study this article examines the rise of the merchant class in the Gulf, its influence in decision-making in the pre-oil era, and its role in shaping the future of the Arab Gulf.

For many decades Dubai was a stopover for boats heading to and from Persia, India, China and East Africa. It was also the starting point of the great caravans to the West. Archaeological findings in the area confirm the historical importance of Dubai as a regional trading centre. In fact since the early twentieth century Dubai has been known as the 'city of merchants'.[1] It has a fine natural harbour; its strategic location on the mouth of the Gulf coupled with the initiative of its merchant community, contributed greatly to its rise as a thriving commercial centre. These assets have resulted in Dubai becoming what it is today, the principal entrepôt of the Arabian Gulf.

Dubai's merchant community has always been cosmopolitan. Indians and Persians have traded freely on equal terms with Arab residents for centuries. So it remains to this day. The cosmopolitan nature of Dubai society allowed no major distinction between the ethnic groups which lived and traded in the city and environs. However, the pure tribal Arabs were regarded as the bourgeoisie, or the *A'yan* of the society. Members of this upper-middle class limited their economic activities primarily to pearl fishing and trading, both of which were considered honourable occupations. Hundreds of Indian British subjects, or Banians, settled in Dubai after 1865. They represented British Indian firms in Bombay and formed a segment of the merchant class. Indians took to banking, since Muslims, bound by religious law, could not practise usury. It was, therefore, the Banians for the most part who financed the yearly pearling expeditions. In addition, the Indian merchants supplied the diving fleets with textiles and imported goods, taking pearls in payment for supplies. They also monopolized shopkeeping and retail trading activities; many became extremely rich. As a result, Indians comprise the second biggest economic class in Dubai.

Persians who had moved to Dubai from the other side of the Gulf and made Dubai their new home, monopolized retail trade and foodstuffs. Their common religion and similar social customs meant the Persians and Arabs mingled freely and often intermarried, thus producing a third important class grouping. As we have seen, the foreign mercantile community controlled the financing sector, which, though it worked well in times of general prosperity, was later to prove disastrous.

With its sophisticated mercantile tradition and a strong commitment to urban planning, even in these early days, Dubai grew in an orderly if rapid manner. Its commercial sector, based on a strong trading tradition, made it prosperous long before the Emirate became an oil producer. It was the good fortune of this mercantile city-state to be governed by liberal and farsighted ruler at the turn of the twentieth century when new commercial opportunities were arising. Shaikh Maktum bin Hasher, who ruled from 1894 to 1906, was a paternalistic merchant prince who governed with little, if any, formal administrative structure. His rule included part of the period during which the pearling industry experienced fast growth.

The 1900-29 era is characterized by two main developments: the growth of the pearl trade, and the emergence of Dubai in 1903 as the main port of the Trucial Coast. Both these factors greatly affected the merchants' role and intensified their influence, making them a primary driving force behind social change.

Like its Gulf counterparts, Dubai was largely dependent on the traditional pearling industry as the backbone of its economy. Pearls have been treasured and traded as beautiful adornments for the wealthy for centuries, and up until the 1930s, the Gulf was one of the most prolific pearl producing areas in the world. The pearling industry reached its peak just before the First World War when demand for pearls in India, Europe and America made this industry very profitable. When we review the available trade statistics of the Trucial Coast for that period, it is immediately apparent how dependent the inhabitants of Dubai were on pearl diving. It was their only means of generating income to purchase the basic necessities of life: rice, sugar, coffee, textiles and wood, items which they did not produce themselves. At the turn of the twentieth century Dubai had the highest number of men employed on pearling boats in the trucial Coast (6,936 according to Lorimer).[2] Dubai's merchants owned around 335 pearling ships, nearly one-third of the total (1,060) owned by the Trucial States' merchant community; this made Dubai's the second largest diving fleet in the area.[3]

This importance was recognized by Paul Harrison, a missionary whose accounts of his travels to the Emirates during that period are considered a good source of information on the area's history. Harrison described the Trucial Coast as 'the second largest diving community in the region whose capital and largest city is Dubai'.[4] As the richest of the pearl fisheries in the Gulf lie between Qatar and Dubai, the latter's port became a centre for provisions and pearl marketing – an economic factor which added to the socio-economic importance of Dubai during this period.

The second significant factor was the decline of Lingah and the subsequent emergence of Dubai as a port of call in the Gulf. Throughout the eighteenth and nineteenth centuries the supply of Indian goods to the Trucial Coast depended mainly on the port of Lingah, on the Persian side of the Gulf, where British steam liners called regularly. The bulk of Indian trade coming to the Coast through the port of Lingah between 1873 and 1902 was redistributed by Dubai's merchants. As a result, Indian merchants settled at Lingah and other Persian towns, and these ports flourished.

However, when the commercial strength of the Persian coastal towns began to decline drastically, owing to the Persian policy of encroaching on the Arab tribes and to the imposition of high taxes – which reached 400 per cent on some goods – the trading post of Lingah slid from prosperity to relative obscurity in a very short period of time. Many Arab, and even Persian merchants began to leave Lingah to settle in Dubai bringing with them their trade and businesses, their shipping experience and craft skills. They also brought Indian associates who were the links between the Gulf pearl merchants and their pearl markets around the world. This drain of expertise from Lingah to Dubai was to be the foundation for the latter's strong commercial growth after 1903.[5]

These two factors – the growth of the pearl industry and the emergence of Dubai's port – laid down the foundation for the merchants' vital role in the development of the economy as well as society over the next several decades. Other factors, however, also contributed to Dubai's prosperity during this period.

Bearing in mind Dubai's position as a merchant community, Shaikh Maktum took progressive measures to encourage local businesses and attract foreign trade by abolishing taxes. This policy drew merchants from across the Gulf. More than 21 steam vessels, mostly belonging to the Bombay and Persian Steam Navigation

Company, entered the port of Dubai in 1904. By 1905 the number of steamers calling at Dubai had risen to 34, with a tonnage totalling, 70,000 tons. British-India Steam Navigation also included Dubai in its timetable early in the same year. This resulted in further growth. H. Burchhardt, a German-Swiss traveller who visited Dubai in February 1904 during a trip to the Gulf, reported that the ruler of Dubai had abolished the 5 per cent customs duty and declared Dubai a free port. Burchhardt was not, therefore, surprised to find German and British merchandise abundant in the markets of the port. He also reported that the influx of immigrants from Lingah, attracted by this pro-business policy, was causing higher commercial and residential rents from which the ruler and the merchants profited greatly.[6]

The unique structure of Dubai's economic and political system was also a factor influencing the role the merchants played in the Emirate's development. While the merchants derived their wealth from many sources including pearling, trade and shipping, the ruler depended entirely on taxes imposed on the pearling fleets and on revenues provided by the customs houses to provide income for himself and the state treasury. While the pearling taxes were collected seasonally by someone appointed and employed by the ruler, the collection of customs duties was not done by a government official. Instead the ruler gave the contract to a merchant who agreed to remit a certain yearly sum to the ruler.[7] This system strengthened the influence of the merchants and gave them power within the ruling order.

Since the ruler's income was not as high as that of the pearl merchants, and sometimes fluctuated with the market, the ruler often turned to the merchants for financial assistance, a fact which increased his dependency on them. This caused a unique situation where in fact the merchants were often in a position to dictate their wishes. The ruler was fully aware of this fact, and in return for merchants' financial contributions he appointed them to his Majlis, or advisory board.

The Majlis was a legislative council considered to be the highest central authority in Dubai. It comprised between 15 and 40 members usually drawn from families with a long tradition of public service. It included merchants and tribal chiefs, each appointed in recognition of his contribution to the welfare state.[8] The Majlis' function was to provide the ruler with advice and political assistance.

Although the Majlis had no binding power, through it the ruler would be warned by his senior advisers if his decisions were proving unacceptable. Without the Majlis' support it was difficult for the ruler to pass any law. Being the town notables, or *A'yan*, and the main contributors to the state's treasury, merchants always held a special position in the Majlis. They held the keys of legitimacy, and gave the rule of the Shaikh a kind of Islamic sanction he greatly needed. Moreover, they were powerful and influential urban politicians who could, within certain limits, raise, support or foster discontent among the middle class, craftsmen, fishermen and slaves. Merchants were also the spokesmen for popular grievances and demands. They had direct access to the ruler and made it virtually impossible for him to rule effectively without them. By exerting pressure on the rules whenever they found it necessary, the merchants wielded a great deal of influence over the economic and political decision-making process of the time.[9]

One of the immediately noticeable results of the rise of merchants status was the influential position which they came to occupy in public and political life. Since no municipal institutions existed, the merchants, by exercising control through the Majlis, became the *de facto* government led by the ruler. It was they who financed internal wars between emirates, and forced the ruler to make alliances with inland tribes and neighbouring shaikhdoms. Merchants such as Mani bin Rashid, Ahmed bin Dalmuk, Salim bin Misabbah, bin Bayat, bin Badur and Muhammad Zainal exercised great political and economic power.[10]

During this period, and afterwards as well, the merchants role went beyond their involvement in the Emirate's economies and policies. Improving economic conditions in the early twentieth century helped them initiate educational development aimed at improving social awareness and introducing modern civilization to Dubai. A number of enlightened philanthropists such as M. Ali Zainal and Mani bin Rashid appeared – the latter would eventually publish the first map of the Gulf pearl fisheries. In 1903 a new modern school, 'Al-Ahmadiyyah', was founded in Dubai by a wealthy pearl merchant named Muhammad Ahmad bin Dalmuk. Students contributed a small fee for their education; but unlike those at the Taimiyyah school, the Al-Ahmadiyyah students sat at desks during lessons. The teachers came largely from Lingah and Al-Hasa, Saudi Arabia and later from Zubair, Iraq.[11]

The period after the First World War witnessed further advances in social and educational awareness. Three more schools financed by wealthy pearl merchants were opened in Dubai. Zainal opened the Al-Falahiyyah school which played an important part in the development of modern education in Dubai. The Al-Sa'adah school was set up by two merchants, Muhammad Al-Badur and Yusuf Sirkal, and Ubaid al-Nabudah founded a third school called the Modern School. At the same time Dubai witnessed a growing movement in cultural activities. Large numbers of poets and writers, among them Ahmad Sultan bin Sulayyim, began to establish themselves in the city. The advantages of being a city-state with a sophisticated, energetic business community, combined with Dubai's favoured position as a trade centre, made it a driving force in the area. Sadly, progress in many areas including education was severely affected by the decline of the pearl industry in 1929. In fact many schools and businesses were forced to close down.

Another important factor in the development of Dubai was the advent of modern communications at the turn of the twentieth century, bringing the Gulf closer to Bombay, the symbol of Western civilization under British rule Bombay had been transformed from a small village into a modern mercantile port which attracted merchants from all parts of the world. Many Gulf as well as Arab merchants gathered in Bombay to sell their merchandise and exchange news. Through their frequent contacts with Arab merchants in Bombay, and through Arabic newspapers and literary journals, Dubai's merchants developed an awareness of world developments which greatly influenced their political thinking. On the other hand, the opening of the Suez Canal connected the Gulf with Egypt. As the Gulf had no Arabic printing press, books and nationalist magazines were sent from Cairo to Gulf subscribers through the port of Dubai. Many Dubai merchants became regular readers of these publications, a fact which created a cultural awakening among the local merchant class and was reflected in Dubai society.[12]

Dubai merchants did not limit their activities to local issues, they also became involved in international causes, playing a significant role, for example, in developing local support for pan-Islamic and Arab nationalist movements. Since the political thinking of the people of the Coast was dominated by a religious rather than a national identity, it had been greatly influenced by the Ottoman propaganda describing the Ottomans as leaders of Islam and defenders of the faith. The Persian merchants of Lingah who had immigrated to Dubai were for the most part Sunni and also fervent supporters of the Ottomans. Their arrival strengthened similar feelings already in evidence in towns along the Trucial Coast. In 1913 the merchants of Dubai collected around Rs. 43,000 to help the Turkish government finance its military efforts in the Balkans.[13] In addition, Dubai's merchants came in contact with Arab reformers such as the Tunisian nationalist leader, Al-Tha 'alibi, who in 1923 met Mani bin Rashid in Bombay and was invited by him to visit Dubai during the former's tour of the Gulf. The visit was to be an occasion for nationalist and literary celebrations held by members of the ruling family and the wealthy merchants.

Socially, the economic boom greatly affected the traditional society of Dubai. A more settled lifestyle was adopted and an appreciation for modern amenities grew. Increased wealth opened the doors to wider prospects and a more sophisticated way of life. Although some merchants ploughed money back into the pearling industry, buying more ships for example, others spent it in providing themselves a slightly more extravagant life-style.

Their newly acquired status was reflected, not only in their own lifestyle, but also in the architecture of the city. While common people had homes made of palm-sticks, prominent merchants fashioned theirs from earth or clay. When merchants emigrated from Persia and India, they also brought with them their own lifestyle and architecture. Many who made their fortunes in Dubai used their wealth to build coral stone palaces with windtowers in the charming districts of Bastakiya and Shaindagah, thus adding a distinctly cosmopolitan flavour to the city-state. Clearly, until the emergence of Dubai's modern administration, changes were mostly instigated by the merchant oligarchy. With the decline of the traditional economy, the status, and therefore the influence of the merchant oligarchy started to wane somewhat, thus paying the way for the emergence of a new socio-economic order.

The 1929-39 era witnessed two major economic changes. The first was the collapse of the traditional pearling industry as a result of the Great Depression, and the second was the emergence of new economic sources such as air travel and oil concessions – two factors which ultimately changed the socio-economic fabric of Dubai, increased the ruler's power at the expense of the merchants', and resulted in the 1938 Dubai reform movement.

The 1929 collapse of the pearling industry greatly affected the role of merchants and led to far reaching consequences in the emirates' society. It changed the economic fabric of the Trucial Coast in general and Dubai in particular. As prices of pearl slumped, many merchants became bankrupt. Merchants who, during the boom, had contributed to the state's treasury lost money as well as influence.

Meanwhile, as the recipient of new revenues the ruler came to enjoy not only an independent but rather a better financial status than his advisers, most of whom were merchants. Merchants who had wielded substantial power throughout their lives suddenly found themselves not only bankrupt but deprived of their social and political privileges. Unhappy with this set of circumstances, the merchants acted fiercely in an attempt to restore their former status. The ensuing conflict resulted in a movement aimed mainly at reforming the economy and restoring to Dubai its commercial character.

Although the Great Depression started officially in October 1929, it began earlier in the Gulf when, in July 1929, 60 pearling boats belonging to Dubai merchants were unable to proceed to the pearling banks for lack of funds. Reports of the day also mention that Muhammad bin Bayat, one of the wealthiest merchants in Dubai, was declared bankrupt, and another, Ahmad bin Dalmuk, was greatly in debt to an Indian merchant.[14] This difficult year was followed by another.

In 1930 many Indian Banians sent complaints to the British Political Resident in the Gulf asking him to use his influence to obtain the repayment of their debts from leading Arab pearl merchants. Protection of the Banians' property and claims was one of the main duties of the Political Resident and the cause of continuous British interference in the affairs of the Sheikhdom. As there was no Order-in-Council to judge the claims of the Indian merchants, the British authorities in the Gulf held the ruler personally responsible for ensuring the repayment of the debts, a fact which increased the already tense relationship between the ruler and the merchant community.[15]

The decline continued throughout the 1930s. In 1933 a drop of 20 per cent in the price of pearls was recorded.[16] This dealt a mortal blow to the merchant community, and meant a further decline in its status. Meanwhile the ruler's economic status was gradually rising. Since 1929 new economic opportunities which generated revenues for the ruler had been exploited. Britain chose Dubai to accommodate an air base in 1934. A few years later, when oil exploration started, royalties began to pour into the ruling shaikh's treasury. Since air and oil royalties were paid directly to the ruler, he considered them personal. The new revenue was his key to independence from the merchants, a situation which was without precedent in the history of Dubai.

Following its annexation from Abu Dhabi in 1833,[17] Dubai survived and prospered by pursuing positive relations with the British and by allowing its sophisticated and well-connected merchant community free rein. As a mercantile community, Dubai functioned politically on a balanced relationship between the ruler who represented the central authority and the merchants who provided him with revenues and made up the bulk of his Majlis. For decades this relationship worked well and contributed to making Dubai the most active trade centre in the Arab Gulf. However, the economic changes of the late 1920s upset this balance.

Suddenly the merchants found themselves deprived of their previous privileges and political status, and the ruler no longer depended on them financially. Faced with this sudden change and economic hardship, the merchants asked the ruler for some reforms in the economic system. They also turned to the only means which seemed available to them: the arms trade, smuggling of provisions and gold, and the slave trade, all of which were considered illegal by the British authorities in the Gulf, and banned by means of treaties and agreements.[18] Britain began waging war against Dubai's merchants both inside and outside the city state. The merchants' discontent increased, culminating in the Dubai reform movement of 1938. Most of the reformers were previous wealthy merchants, a number of them were from the Shaikh's own family. Fired by political development elsewhere in the Arab Gulf and inspired by a successful reform movement in Kuwait, the merchants of Dubai rebelled. In October 1938, they forced Shaikh Said (1912-58) to accept a real consultative council aimed mainly at reforming the economy and restoring to Dubai its multinational merchant character.

With 15 members chosen by the notables of Dubai, and serving under the presidency of the ruler, the new Majlis attempted both practical reforms as well as enlightened political and social innovations, all of which served the needs of the merchant community. The customs service was regulated, the harbour improved and expanded, and a municipal council created. Pearl-divers turned porters, as a result of the decline of the pearling industry, became the subject of discussion. The merchants realized that they could not move their goods without them. Therefore, during the Majlis' short existence, porters' status, payment and working conditions were often the subject of heated discussion. However, the most drastic step taken by the Majlis was to control Dubai's income. The Majlis decided that it would control the income and expenditure of Dubai, and all decisions were to be ratified by the majority.[19] The Majlis also took a decision that the ruler had to have a fixed allowance of one-eighth of Dubai's revenue, and all royalties from air and oil concessions were to go to the state's treasury and not to the Shaikh's, a step which in reality meant a return to the old situation.

As the economic depression hit the merchants hard, the Majlis set as its goal the improvement of the economy. As noted earlier Dubai was dominated largely by three different merchant communities. During the period of economic growth they lived side by side and rarely begrudged one community the privileges which it enjoyed over the others.[20] With the decline of the pearling industry, this situation changed. While the British authorities took several measures to protect the interest of the Indian merchants, and the Persian community knew how to avoid Persian customs restrictions, the Arab merchant community was affected more negatively than others. The Shaikh did little to relieve the suffering of his people, and refused to reform the economy. Unemployment was high, and Britain was threatening to enforce a general manumission of slaves, a measure which if enforced would mean a total collapse of the pearling industry.

The Shaikh's refusal to comply with the merchants' wishes and to cooperate in implementing reforms was understandable. He was apprehensive of their growing power and popularity, fearing that their suggested reforms might further strengthen their resolution. This agitated the merchant community which in turn directed its anger not only against the ruler but also at the British and their Indian subjects.

The ruler's apathy towards the new Majlis was anticipated. The idea of an executive council with real power was unlikely to be accepted by the ruler who felt the Majlis should be an assembly of notables with an advisory function only. Moreover, he saw the reform movement as a direct challenge to his personal authority, and his new status. Therefore, in March 1939, after five months of the Majlis' existence, the ruler forced its dissolution. In its place, he appointed a new committee of merchants known as *Majlis al Tujjar* to continue the reforms started by the old Majlis and to settle commercial disputes.

Majlis al Tujjar was a compromise between the old unpopular autocratic rule of the Shaikh and the popular though short-lived Majlis. Although the new Majlis consisted mainly of merchants, it was presided over by the ruler. Its function was to continue improving the economy, and to reform the economic system. In an effort to reduce the tension between the ruling power and the merchant community, the ruler appointed five members of the old Majlis to the new one. This step was taken in recognition of the merchant community's efforts and to prevent further discontent.[21]

Despite its brief term, the efforts of the Majlis were not all lost. A feeling of pride and a sense of community as well as optimism for the future well-being of the state was generated.[22] The example of the brief experiment and the dynamic mercantile environment that produced it were later to generate lasting reforms and progress; it also served as the foundation of Dubai's current prosperity and as a model of successful urban development for the other emirates.[23]

The 1939-90 stage was characterized by a great deal of socio-political readjustment as well as economic reforms, all of which were of benefit to the merchant community. Although it started with the dwindling influence of merchants and a concurrent rise in the ruler's authority, it ended with a more balanced sharing of community responsibility. It also marked the end of a traditional era wherein the rulers depended financially on the economic elite. Now, the merchant community had to learn to coexist with the new order while pursuing a broader role within its framework.

As mentioned earlier, although the aims of the reformers were to establish a uniform and centralized administration linked directly to the interests of the merchants and working according to their rational principles, the reforms could not be carried out completely. Matters were complicated by the existence of an absolute ruler who determined not to upset the new order or let his power slip away from him, and by outside interference. The British, who for years protected the political system, and benefitted from the new economic revenues, were willing to sanction the new reforms as long as they did not threaten their air and oil interests. The merchant community had two choices: either to continue opposing the existing economic and political pattern or to work within its framework; they chose the latter. As a result, the 1940s were a period of economic growth and readjustment from which the merchants benefited greatly.

Just as the economic ball started rolling with considerable movement, the Second World War broke out. The war brought much of the trade to a standstill and dashed all hopes of enterprising merchants. Worse yet, it meant near-starvation for many inhabitants of the Arabian Gulf. In an effort to alleviate some of the suffering, the British Government supplied the Gulf countries under its control with food rations including sugar, rice and tea which were distributed through local governments and agents. Unused rations were sometimes sold to merchants who in turn sold them on the black markets of the neighbouring countries where these commodities were even scarer. Qatar, for instance, was importing most of its commodities from Dubai, a fact which produced a black market in both countries.[24] Clearly, Dubai's rise was, in this case at least, at the expense of that of other Gulf States. The Shaikh of Bahrain complained many times to the Political Resident in the Gulf that smuggling from Dubai to

Qatar and then to Bahrain, especially sugar and rice, was affecting this country's economy. It was also an indication that other Gulf states were getting a larger quota despite the fact that Bahrain's population was larger. As a solution, the Political Resident suggested, in 1944, reducing the Trucial States' quota by 500 tons.[25]

The merchants of Dubai also profited from political instability in other parts of the Gulf. The unrest prevailing in the Sultanate of Muscat between 1895 and 1920, which blocked the roads between the port of Muscat, Matrah and the interior, enabled the merchants of Dubai to supply inner Oman with provisions.[26]

The considerable progress made in Dubai during the Second World War has already been noted. The advantages of being a compact city-state with a sophisticated, energetic business community, combined with Dubai's favoured positoin as residence of the British Political Agent, briefly gave Dubai the leading role in pointing the Trucial States toward a new era. Therefore, for the rest of the 1940s and 1950s, Dubai gained importance as a platform for international trade and exchange.

From the 1950s onwards the merchant community focused on further diversifying the economy. As they recovered from the economic depression, merchants began actively engaging in new commercial enterprises. The idea of improving the port's facilities were revived, and merchants seemed more than willing to contribute towards the cost. New facilities meant more business. Between 1958 and 1959 the creek was dredged. The improved waterway offered sheltered anchorage for local craft and coastal steamers up to 500 tons. But imports came mostly on large steamers which still had to be offloaded about two miles from port. Therefore, a second improvement of the port was undertaken during the early 1960s, providing merchants with more convenient facilities.

Playing to Dubai's first strength, Shaikh Rashid (1958-90), himself a merchant, institutionalized his relationship with the merchants through his Majlis or court and concentrated his efforts on trade, even after oil had been discovered in the emirates. His initiatives to promote modernization of the port during the 1950s provided a fillip to Dubai's trade-based prosperity. This made possible advances in a number of areas – Dubai provided the only modern medical care in the lower Gulf in the 1950s, built on the educational innovations of the 1938-39 reform movement, established a police force, and set up a modern municipality to provide structure and order to its rapid economic growth.[27] The necessity to improve the town, and to plan future infrastructure development with the idea of keeping Dubai's character as a merchant community, led to many merchants becoming financially involved in development projects. The hub of all these activities remained however the development of the creek and its wharves, loading facilities and warehouses. This was promoted by the Dubai Port Committee which counted amongst its members not only bank managers and representatives of consultancy companies, but prominent merchants.[28]

During the 1950s Dubai was subjected to social and political forces that shaped its history for years to come. As a result of events elsewhere in the Arab world a number of Dubai merchants formed in 1953 a loose organization, the National Front, that opposed the growing influence of Persian and Indian merchants. It included Dubai's luminaries in commerce such as Al Futaim and al-Ghurair. They were responsible for agitating against the British presence and wavered in their opposition to Shaikh Rashid, the then heir apparent. Shaikh Rashid, in what would seem to be an attempt to cajole the merchants, held weekly meetings with the Majlis in which were included members of the National Front. A member of the latter, Murshid al Usaimi, declared that there would be no opposition party in Dubai if Rashid agreed to have a council of merchants to advise on and contribute towards a proper *Baladiya* (Municipal Council). The *Majlis al Tujair* when formed was packed by National Front supporters and excluded Persian and Indian merchants. Furthermore, the Arab merchants intrigued in order to control the Municipal Council which was founded on 5 March 1957.[29] Two years later a British official reporting on the organization of government and the role of merchants in Dubai wrote that on the whole merchants showed very little interest in governmental affairs. Nonetheless, a start in local representative government had been made.

As the need for public services developed between the mid-1950s and the early 1970s, the foundation was laid for a system whereby most community services were undertaken by the private sector. This allowed merchants to participate actively in the economy, while they acquired new roles as service suppliers, a feature which made the economic structure of Dubai very different from that of other Gulf countries. Many services were provided by private companies and not by the government. The Dubai Electricity Company, for example, was owned by a number of local merchants. Similarly, most shareholders in the Dubai Telephone Company were merchants.[30] Merchants also financed other ventures including housing projects.

During the 1970s, the merchants' role developed as a result of Dubai's new economic importance. Oil had been discovered, and oil wealth was used to develop the infrastructure and to provide prosperity to every citizen. The economic growth including large projects brought more merchants' involvement in community services. In the field of construction, for instance, large housing and communication projects were awarded to local merchants. On the other hand, the need to make Dubai an international business centre required new economic and administrative reforms towards which the merchants contributed either as consultants or as financiers. By this time merchants had diversified the scope of their business which ranged from oil to marketing. Then, as now, growth and prosperity were encouraged by the city's tax system. Customs duties in Dubai have never exceeded 2 per cent, and today in Jabal Ali Free Zone (an area west of Dubai) they are non-existent. This feature has always attracted more business and provided a ready stage for development.[31]

The growth of Dubai as reflected in these ambitious development projects was partly in response to the conditions created by an astute merchant community with a network of foreign contacts. The other part of the growth was, however, the result of a deliberate policy to attract additional business to Dubai. Neither the activities of the oil companies nor the income from oil itself actually generated the greater part of the economic growth in Dubai.[32] Since trade is concomitant with communications, all significant development projects up to the end of 1973 were concerned with communications in one form or another. After 1973, it was decided to embark on a programme of industrialization; Dubai's future was not to be based on trade and services alone but also on manufacturing industries. A modern industrial centre was erected at Jabal Ali, giving Dubai new importance.

From the early 1980s until the mid-1990s Dubai's commerce with the Gulf Cooperation Council (GCC) and other Gulf countries such as Iraq and Iran grew and diversified. As far as Iran is concerned, Dubai enjoyed a brisk and lively trade with it during most of the 1980-8 Iraqi-Iranian war. Dubai's merchants revived their previous roles as major entrepôts of trade and created a new one as suppliers of services.[33] Their dhows were plying back and forth to the Iranian coasts laden with a wide variety of consumer goods, foodstuffs and equipment of all kinds. Although most of their cargoes were banned in Iran in order to preserve foreign currency, the merchants of Dubai managed to get them through undetected. The profits were considerable, both to individual traders and to the economy of Dubai. Another lucrative business which witnessed growth during the war was servicing of international shipping which found Dubai a safer place than Kuwait or Iranian ports. Dubai's dry dock, one of the largest in the world, was busy maintaining and overhauling tankers as well as repairing those damaged in the fighting. Dubai was therefore loath to relinquish its neutrality in the war.

Since the Second Gulf War of 1991, the Dubai merchant community, benefiting from political stability and thriving market economy, has played a significant role in turning Dubai into the busiest port in the region. The city itself has evolved as the most active business centre in the region, attracting business from all over the Middle and Far East as well as from Europe.[34] Thus far the 1990s have witnessed development in new sectors. As Dubai will end its dependency on oil by the year 2010, the government tries to diversify its sources of income and give the private sector a greater role in the economy.[35] The private sector has discovered another area with significant growth: up market tourism. It has begun developing tourist attractions, transport, resorts and other facilities, which has in turn generated almost 7 billion dirhams a year in additional revenues for the emirate.[36]

The new broader role played by merchants during the latter part of the twentieth century enabled them to strengthen their position in society; many were powerful and contributed to Dubai's development as educators, philanthropists and cultural advocators. Some ploughed new wealth into the economy thus providing more jobs, i.e. Al-Ghurair, al-Fataim; others used it to establish community services: research centres, public libraries, scientific and academic institutions, all have been financed with merchants money. The Jumah Al-Majid Center for Culture and Heritage and the Dubai

Medical College are two examples of community projects financed and patronized by wealthy Dubai merchants.[37] The example of Dubai often aroused the interest of the other shaikhdoms. Therefore, the emirate also has a vital role to play as a model for the rest of the Arab Gulf countries.

The evolution of the Dubai business sector in the twentieth century went hand in hand with the development of Dubai itself. This development began with the merchant community gaining powerful positions through the control of valuable economic resources which in turn provided political influence; it evolved through the emergence of a new economic structure where power was systematically divided between merchant community and the ruling family. As the relationship between the two involved a certain amount of give and take, both groups agreed to share the responsibility of guiding society's development. This agreement adjusted the balance. It restored merchants to their previous prestigious position, thus, enabling the ruler to benefit from the financial and social backing of the merchant community. Merchants are often rewarded for their community services with honorary positions or appointments to municipal councils and advisory boards. They became part of the political structure in the past because the structure of the economic and political system made it impossible to rule without them. They remain integral to the structure because the conservative capitalist nature of Gulf societies cannot exclude them. Merchants were and are still dominant figures in Dubai, playing a vital role in its continued growth and development. Dubai's ancient calling as a 'city of merchants' is as strong as it was two hundred years ago.

NOTES

1. See Ian Fairservice (ed.), *Dubai, Gateway to the Gulf*, UAE, 1987, pp. 12-13. The Roman traveller and chronicler Pliny travelled to the Gulf during the first century of the Christian calendar and described a river at the lower end of the Gulf, which he named Cynos and which is widely believed now to be the creek which runs through the heart of Dubai.
2. J.G. Lorimer, *Gazeteer of the Persian Gulf, Oman and Central Arabia*, India, 1915, vol. 1, *Historical Part*, pt. 1, p. 743.
3. Ibid.
4. Paul W. Harrison, *The Arab at Home*, New York, 1924, p. 87.

5. Mohammed Al-Fahim, *From Rags to Riches: A Story of Abu Dhabi*, London, 1995, p. 32.
6. See M. Morsy Abdullah, *The United Arab Emirates: A Modern History*, London, 1978, p. 104.
7. See Frauke Heard-Bey, *From Trucial States to United Arab Emirates*, London, 1982, p. 249.
8. The term 'welfare state' is used by both Arab and Western scholars to refer to Arab Gulf states where no income taxes are imposed on citizens (or non-citizens) and where the states are responsible to finance all public services such as health services, etc.
9. Albert Hourani, *The Emergence of the Modern Middle East*, Oxford, 1981, p. 44.
10. M. Morsy Abdullah, *The United Arab Emirates*, p. 104.
11. Ibid., p. 108.
12. Ibid.
13. Ibid., p. 111.
14. Ibid.
15. See Rosemarie Said Zahlan, *The Origins of the United Arab Emirates*, London, 1978, pp. 151-2.
16. The introduction of the Japanese cultured pearl to the market dealt the natural pearl market a blow from which it never recovered; see Saif M. Al-Shamlan, *History of Pearl Diving in Kuwait and the Gulf (ta'rikh al kaws 'ala al l'lu fi al Kuwait wal Khalij)*, Kuwait, 1984.
17. Before 1833 Dubai was part of Abu Dhabi Emirate. In 1833 the Al-Maktoom family (part of the Bani Yas, the ruling family of Abu Dhabi) was able to annexe Dubai from Abu Dhabi and declare it an independent emirate under their rule.
18. For more information on treaties and agreements see C.U. Aitchison, *A Collection of Treaties, Engagements and Sanads Relating to India and Neighbouring Countries*, 5th edn., Delhi, 1933.
19. I.O.L.&R,L/P&S//12,3827, 'Agreement between the Shaikh of Dubai and members of Al Bu Falash'.
20. Heard-Bey, p. 255.
21. Ibid., the Political Resident, Bushire, to Secretary of state for India, London, 28 April 1939, P.Z. 2670.
22. Heard-bey, *From Trucial States*, p. 257.
23. Malcolm Peck, *The United Arab Emirates*, Washington, DC, 1986, pp. 39-40.
24. See Al-Mansour, *Al-tatawur al-siyasi li Qatar*, Kuwait, 1976, p. 73.
25. Ibid.
26. Abdullah, *The United Arab Emirates*, p. 104.

27. Peck, *The United Arab Emirates*, p. 46.
28. Heard-Bey, *From Trucial States*, p. 259.
29. PRO, F0371/120553, from British Resident to Selwyn Lloyd, 9 Oct. 1956, no. 113-1015//1/30/56; also see Albadur Abu-Baker, 'Political Economy of State Formation: The United Arab Emirates in Comparative Perspective' (unpublished Ph.D. thesis, University of Michigan, 1995).
30. See Richard Trench (ed.), *Arab Gulf Cities: Doha, Abu Dhabi, Dubai, Sharjah* (Archives editions, 1994), pp. 393-4.
31. Heard-Bey, op. cit., p. 260.
32. See *Al-Khaleej* daily newspaper, 12 Nov. 1996, No. 6388; also see *Arab Gulf Cities: Doha, Abu Dhabi, Dubai, Sharjah* (n. 30), pp. 332-3.
33. Rosemarie Said Zahlan, *Modern Gulf States*, London, 1989, p. 154.
34. See *Al-Khaleej*, report by Dubai Chamber of Commerce, 11 July 1996, no. 6263.
35. *Al-Khaleej*, 13 Nov. 1996, no. 6388.
36. See *Trade and Industry*, Dubai, Nov. 1996, vol. 21, no. 251, p. 6; also *Al-Khaleej*, 18 Jan. 1997, no. 6454.
37. Interview, Mr. Jumah Al-Majid, Dubai, 14 April 1996.

CHAPTER 5

My Life and Work in Dubai

MAGANMAL J. PANCHOLIA

I've had a fulfilling and challenging life with experiences that have chiselled me to what I am today. I arrived in Dubai in 1942, a fresh matriculate from Karachi and on the threshold of a college career at the DJ Sind College. Those were the days of the Indian freedom struggle and Mahatma Gandhi had given the famous 'Quit India' call. Our colleges were closed. I was betrothed then and, for want of anything better to do, came to Dubai to help my father with the family business. At the time we were handling the Sharjah Customs which we had been doing for over 20 years.

We belong to the Thattai Bhatia community from India, which is the oldest expatriate community to have moved to the then Trucial States. It is a well-knit and closed community with about 10,000 members worldwide.

Our ancestors were pearl traders. In the early days, traders from the Gulf would come to Thatta, a small hamlet near Karachi, to barter pearls and dates for spices and clothes. Along the way, they invited our community elders to set up business in Dubai to facilitate better trading. Our forefathers who came here for pearl trading, gradually diversified into other commodities after the pearl market was badly hit owing to the recession of 1930s. In effect, our family had been here for a good 200 years when I arrived on the scene.

Those days, Dubai was like a small hamlet. There was no electricity, no tap water, no roads, and none of the modern means of transport. Hurricane lamps were in vogue, people travelled on donkeys and drinking water was sold on donkeys – four cans, for one Indian rupee. Many of us who couldn't trust the hygiene of those rusted old cans, preferred to draw water from the small wells that were dug about a furlong away from the souk near Bank Street. These wells were normally seven feet deep and would have sweet water for about eight days, after which the water would turn sour. Then another would be dug. . . we kept digging one well after another. One could pay a labourer Rs 3 to dig a well. Despite filtering the water with white muslin cloth, we could still find a small residue of sand at the bottom of the pot.

But all these things did not matter much. Despite the lack of basic comforts, life was very simple and there was so much love and affection in our interpersonal relationships as well as in our ties with the local people. We were all like a big family. The Bedus are very gentle people and our relationship was based largely on trust. Major cash and jewellery transactions were made without the exchange of a single receipt. Trust was the very foundation of our bonds for so many years. We had and still continue to maintain very strong ties with the leading local business families.

All Indians, basically traders, resided in Souk Baniyan (Bania, in Hindi, means traders) close to the Creek in Bur Dubai. The shops were on the ground floor and residential premises, mostly bachelor's quarters, on the first floor. By the time I was 18, I married the woman I was betrothed to, but she had to reside in Thatta with other women and children. None of us had our families here as we lacked some basic comforts. Also, there were no schools. I lived in one of these houses, first as a bachelor and then with my family, for nearly 20 years.

I remember, the souk had a large entrance door. We would function largely in and around the souk and always kept together. Nobody ventured out after sunset. A few feet away was the prison, which is now the Dubai Museum. In the evening, the souk door would be shut, and a lone watchman, hurricane lamp in one hand and a long stick in the other, would go around the place. The very sight of him made us feel safe and secure.

Our routine was fairly simple. Everyone would get up in the morning and do their daily ablution with a little water. Very few eatables were available in the market. It was basically the local *seemuch* (fish), dates, rice, wheat, sugar and spices from India. There were a few locally-grown vegetables, such as gourds and brinjals, but they were available only during the cooler months. Breakfast was nourishing but frugal – milk (all of us had at least one cow) and hurriedly-rolled out wheat chapattis. This was a staple meal for all traders in the morning.

Nobody really missed any comforts. Those were times of optimism and change, and our family business too changed from pearl, to textile to foodstuff trading, until my elder brother who was my idol, had the idea of starting a currency exchange business. In those days, besides the rupee, the other currency in vogue was the Iranian riyals and tumans. Dubai trade was largely dependent on Iran and directly affected by changes taking place there. One tuman was roughly one Indian rupee and I remember it falling until Rs 60 would fetch us 100 tumans.

People might like to think of us as enterprising individuals, but very often, as they say, necessity is the mother of invention. We were staying away from our families and life was tough. We had to make ends meet. The rent for our homes was Rs 50 per annum while that of our shops was around Rs 100. If we paid Rs 8, we could get a proper Indian lunch and dinner for a month. With so many expenses, it was difficult to save and send some money to our families back home. We had to make ends meet and have something in surplus. So we thought of various ways of improving our income.

My brother once again thought of taking the bold step of diversifying into the gold business. The recession had compelled people to sell off their jewellery. People would come from Iran to sell their jewellery. It was sold at Rs 8 per ten grams (one *tola*). We would buy the jewellery, melt it into ingots and officially send it by steamer to be sold in India. The job was extremely tiring and tough, and we got about four annas per ten grams for our efforts.

But every enterprise that my brother undertook would succeed and I learnt a lot from him. By the mid-1950s, we were busy with our exchange, gold and textile business. In 1958, I started a private electricity company. At that time, there was another national gentleman in Deira who had also started something on similar lines. I set up generators and connected the entire souk, supplying electricity and charging a monthly fee for it. It was a novelty and there was a great demand for it. Later the Ruler, His Highness the late Sheikh Rashid bin Saeed Al Maktoum, started a shareholding company, Dubai Electricity. I was elected director of the company from 1961-

80 as I had made some major investments in the company along with some other Indians.

By the sixties, I was conducting business transactions with the Far East. That was when I also added the Orient Watch agency to our business. I went on my first (and last) world tour in 1968 where I travelled from the Far East to America to Europe. It was tough for a person like me – a teetotaller, vegetarian and a non-smoker – to last for nearly four months in countries where it was difficult to get a decent vegetarian meal. But I am a resourceful person and I managed to find a solution.

It started in Honolulu where I entered a Chinese restaurant and tried explaining to the waiter that I was a strict vegetarian. It took some time, but he finally understood and brought me boiled rice and vegetable chopsuey, a dish, which I realised was available in all parts of the world! So, for the next four months, that became my staple diet – from Osaka to Beirut to Hawaii.

THE TRANSFORMATION

Dubai had begun changing. People had begun getting their families here. My wife was among the first women to arrive here in 1962. Transport was still a problem, but people had begun travelling in taxis. There were no private cars except those owned by the Ruling Family. When we traders would decide to go on a picnic, we would request the Rulers who would provide us cars free of cost with chauffeurs to take us for a picnic around Jumeirah. Jumeirah was a large desert stretch near the sea and there were many *nakhals* (small farmhouses with a well and cluster of date trees). We were provided one of these *nakhals* for our recreation.

It is difficult to say when and how Dubai changed. The progress was so rapid and the changes so dramatic that we did not realise when it all happened. Roads, electricity, buildings . . . the entire infrastructure came up in a period of sustained activity that started from around 1961 but gained momentum after the formation of the UAE in 1971.

The welfare of the expatriate community was an issue close to my heart, and when businesses were fairly established, and I was elected president of the Indian Association, my focus naturally shifted to that. There was no school for our children and laying the foundation of the Indian High School happened as a result of a challenge. An Indian lady teacher named Hemkalaben, who was offering tuitions to children of goldsmiths in the souk, one day walked up to me and said: 'What are you doing for us? You had better take charge of education.'

Her words moved me. I have always considered education as the main instrument of change in any society anywhere in the world. That day I decided to do something about it. I first rented a building from Al Shirawis for Rs 8,000 per year on a five-year lease. Hemkalaben started the school with only nine students. At first, the medium of instruction was Gujarati, but it was later changed to English.

Slowly, as more and more students began enrolling, the school started expanding. To rationalise the steep rent which I was paying, I housed the Indian Association office in the same building. A second teacher was brought in for Rs 200 per month. Then a third teacher, Mariamma Varkey, joined us and a fourth one in quick succession. It is difficult for me to visualise how such a modest institution, which was started on such a small scale, has grown up to become a leading school in the UAE.

TRUST IS THE CORNERSTONE

Trust has been one of the major issues of my life. There were so many people who trusted me, and I feel glad that I did not disappoint anyone of them.

The land where the institution stands was donated to me by our beloved Ruler, the late Sheikh Rashid. There is an interesting tale to it. He donated that land to me four times and every time I gave it up because I was not able to collect funds from benefactors! Finally I went to him for the fifth time and told him: 'If you believe me, this time, I take a pledge to construct the school myself.'

Sheikh Rashid immediately called the then Head of Municipality, Kamal Hamza, and asked him to give the land to me. Immediately, I collected about half-a-dozen people and told them that those who were willing to pay Rs 10,000 would be made trustees of the school. The foundation stone was laid in 1968. When the building was constructed on the plot measuring 500 × 700 sq ft., there was nothing else on that entire stretch.

When the school started functioning there was no constitution as such. A few of my colleagues and I formed a committee to take decisions on major issues. I remained the head of the group for several years until we formed the constitution and, during those years, I was in control of the finances and the funds. The good thing is that so many people believed in me, trusted me and I am glad that I never once let them down.

I am a firm believer in the grace of God. When He wants you to do something, He gives you the determination and the resources. What you need is knowledge, devotion and an ability to work hard. Do this, and success will be inevitable.

Now, at this stage of my life, I still prefer to associate myself with many social and cultural projects here and in India, and try and donate funds for orphanages, women's homes, construction of academic institutions and marriage halls. I share a close bond with my four children – two sons and two daughters – 11 grandchildren and two great grandchildren.

It is difficult to slow down in life because there are so many commitments to fulfill but I try and stick to a simple uncomplicated routine, especially after a heart attack and a bypass surgery which I had. After my morning walks and routine of collecting flowers, I have a light breakfast of fresh salads and a piece of chapatti. I am a frugal eater and, by reading books on nutrition, have learnt that it is better to include larger portions of fruits, vegetables and a lesser quantity of dairy products. I take a bit of everything in moderation.

I also believe in naturopathy. I read a lot on it and keep my own collection of ayurvedic remedies. Although I try and keep myself out of business affairs, I am in office till lunch time and then devote the rest of the day to spirituality, reading, meeting old acquaintances and indulging in a lot of mental sorting. I am a keen reader and have also started a free library. I am constantly trying to do things that will help those in need.

I have worn many hats in my life. Today, I am the head of my community, the head of this business and the head of my large family. I see all the people with love. I always tell people that there may be differences of opinion but everything should be solved amicably or through arbitration.

When I sit back and look at Dubai, I feel that in my own small way, I contributed to the progress of this land that is my home. But there is no pride, just a deep satisfaction of having done my duty well.

CHAPTER 6

Indian Diaspora in Yemen

PRAKASH C. JAIN

Cultural contact and commercial exchange have existed between India and Yemen since ancient times. Geographical proximity and knowledge of monsoon were helpful in establishing cultural and economic relationship between the two countries in ancient times when people from Yemeni kingdoms of Hadramont, Qataban, Ousan and Sheba and subsequent unified Hemiarite Kingdom traded Yemeni myrrh and incense with the Indian silk, textiles and spices. The emergence and spread of Islam in the Arabian Peninsula and beyond had further consolidated these relations. There is reason to believe that two-way migration and settlement took place between the two countries during ancient and medieval times: the Yemenis migrated to Hyderabad and the Indians settled in Yemeni port towns of Aden, Mokha, Shihr, Mokalla, Hodeida and even Socotra.[1] It was also not unusual for some Indians returning from pilgrimage to Mecca to have settled in Yemen.[2] Obviously, such migrations and settlement must have been very small.

When the Portuguese entered the Indian Ocean trade in the sixteenth century, the Indian merchants, particularly the Gujaratis were found in all the major ports between Aden and Malacca.[3] In the seventeenth century Indo-Yemen trade involved locally-produced Yemeni coffee and Gujarati textiles, spices and other necessities.[4] Surat was the main trading partner of Yemen during this period.

In Yemen the port town of Mocha was an important trade centre in the seventeenth century. Thus in 1621 'two ships from Dabhol visited Mocha, one with 200 and the other with 150 passengers, all travelling merchants coming to sell in the port small quantities of precious goods'.[5] Another report for the year 1626/27 suggests that the Indian merchants 'lived in constant fear of an Arab attack, and buried their money every time a forthcoming offensive was rumoured'.[6] In the first quarter of the eighteenth century, 'about twenty Gujarati ships sailed every year from Surat to Mocha and Jedda carrying pilgrims for the hajj as well as annual trade of much of northern and western India'.[7] Apparently for the sojourning as well as resident Indian traders Mocha continued to be an important trading centre until about the middle of the nineteenth century when Aden came into prominence. In 1810, according to the British traveller Valentia, there were about 250 resident Hindu merchants in Mocha who following the annexation of Aden moved there.[8] In the eighteenth century Gujarati merchants were settled in all the Yemeni towns. Besides Mocha, they were found 'in the capital town of Sana, in Beit-al-Faqui (the principal market for coffee), in the ports of Hodeida and Lohaya, and in island towns such as Tais and Zabid'.[9]

A distinction can be made between the sojourning and the settled Indian traders in Yemen. Thus talking about the early eighteenth century, Ashin Das Gupta wrote:

> There were two kinds of Banias engaged in the Red Sea trade. There were those who came and went every year, doing their own trade and handling the business of others who remained at home in much the same manner as the Muslim merchants were wont to do. Banias from lower Gujarat, particularly from the cities of Surat and Cambay were of this kind. Others had been long settled in Yemen and were found not only in every Yemeni city but in the port towns of Habash and Hadramaut as well. Apparently Banias from Kathiawar, the Kapol Banias of the Peninsula, were predominant among those who settled in Yemen, and immigrants from the ports of Gujarat and Kathiawar continued to come to Yemen throughout the first decades of the eighteenth century. The Bania merchants of the Yemeni cities and the Habash ports controlled much of the commercial life of the area but, in Yemen at any rate, they lived like second class citizens.[10]

In the seventeenth and eighteenth centuries Great Britain established a number of commercial agencies and military posts along the coasts of Red Sea, Arabian Sea and the Persian Gulf. In 1798 when Napoleon Bonaparte occupied Egypt and threatened to attack India, Britain occupied Perim Island in 1799, and signed commercial and military treaties with the rulers of Lahej and Aden in 1802. Aden was eventually occupied in 1839 by a combined force of 300 European and 400 Indian troops.[11] The British existence in Aden and its eastern and western Protectorates in the Yemeni hinterland was tied to the British Administration in Bombay until 1937 when Aden became a Crown colony. Talking about the importance of Aden to the British interests the Governor of Bombay said:

> Aden is of great value to us. It is very suitable as a coal depot throughout the year. It could be a meeting place for all ships using the Red Sea route, and as a military base from which we can protect our activities. Aden is like Gibraltar, once in our hands will be difficult to take neither from land nor from sea. There are two great nations conspiring against us and seek to eliminate our influence in the East. The first is Russia which tries to advance through Iran, and the other is France which is coming via Egypt. To confront these threats Britain must have defense post outside its borders.[12]

After six weeks of the British occupation of Aden there were only 35 Indians out of a total Adeni population of 1,294 which also included 624 Arabs, 568 Somalis and 63 Jews. All the Indians were Banyans and male.[13] After three years the Indian population grew by more than ten times. By then the population of Aden had not only increased to about 16,000 but had also diversified as shown in Table 6.1. With the importation of Indian labourers for the construction work related to defence in the late 1840s, 'Aden became more an Indian than an Arab town. In 1849 and again in 1856 the Indians formed somewhat over 40 per cent of the total population and were by far the largest national grouping at Aden, followed by Arabs, Somalis and Jews.'[14]

The major components of the Indian population around this time were 'the old Indian trading community engaged in commerce of the Red Sea, the garrison and the new Indian community which served it'.[15] The new Indian community comprised the merchants especially the Bombay Parsis and the subordinate administrative staff of the settlement and the police force.[16] According to Gavin, the Parsi community at Aden was from the outset closely connected with the garrison. There were no Parsi names on the list of Aden residents in 1839. They came to Aden after the occupation in the wake of the army takeover and probably were mostly engaged in providing

TABLE 6.1: ADEN'S POPULATION IN 1842

Ethnic Groups	*Population Distribution*	
	Male	*Female*
Arabs	8,960	3,270
Somalis	1,430	620
Jews	590	480
Afghans	180	100
Egyptians	146	50
Portuguese	136	
Sidis*	180	
Banyans	196	
Borahs (Bohras)**	111	
Indian Shopkeepers	100	
Parsis	38	
Total	12,067	4,520

Notes: * In Aden, the word 'Sidi' (from Arabic 'Sayyid', 'Lord' or 'master') was jocularly applied to non-Somali Africans, most of whom were former slaves.

** Shi'i Ismaili Muslim mainly from Gujarat.

Source: Z.H. Kour, *The History of Aden, 1839-1872*, Frank Cass, London, 1981, p. 26.

services for the troops. In 1846 they began to move into the gum, hides and coffee trade and they seemed to be the only members of the commercial community with large enough capital at that date to buy the cargoes of American ships.[17]

Some of these Parsi merchants who supplied livestock, fowls, eggs, vegetables, milk, beer, liquor, firewood and other provisions to the steamers and other vessels and the garrison had become quite prosperous and influential in due course of time. Among these, two businessmen Edulji Manockji and Cowasji Dinshaw had been prominent enough in 1854 to be among the principal signatories of an address to British Political Agent Captain S.B. Haines at the time of his departure.[18] Cowasji Dinshaw was the founder of the still prominent firm of Cowasji Dinshaw Bros. at Aden. A third Parsi named Manockji Dinshaw was the Head Accountant and Treasurer of Aden in 1856. A wealthy Parsi merchant Hormusji Dinshaw 'represented commercial Aden on State occasions as the Sultan of Lahej represented the people, or rather the political broker, of the hinterland'.[19]

It is interesting to note that the Aden police force from its very inception in 1840 had been essentially an Indian organization in terms of recruitment as well as style of functioning. It remained so until about the late 1920s when the policy of Arabisation was gradually adopted in spite of the opposition from the Bombay Legislative Council.[20] In 1839 there were only 11 policemen in Aden (9 Arabs and 2 Indians). 'In May 1840 a police force of 20 men (12 Muslims and 8 Hindus) was sent from Bombay on home leave every three or four years. By 1855 the number had increased to 160 which was subsequently reduced and the practice of recruiting police from India was discontinued.'[21]

Indian population in Aden continued to increase to 8,229 in 1856 according to one estimate, and 8,563 according to another (see relevant figures in Tables 6.2 and 6.3 respectively). However, as the population estimates for the years 1867 and 1872 suggest this pace of population growth could not be sustained in the 1860s and 1870s. It was only in 1881 that the population of the Indians in Aden could approximately reach the 1856 level. We do not have any estimates for the next 50 years. The 1931 estimates further suggest that the size of the Indian population in Aden remained more or less the same during all these years. It is difficult to offer any explanation for this demographic stagnation.

Another remarkable feature about the Indian population in Aden in the middle of the nineteenth century was the sharp decline of the Hindu population from 5,611 in 1856 to only 854 in 1872 (Table 6.2). This happened in spite of the fact that the opening up of the Suez Canal in 1869 had given Aden a great commercial boost. The major items of trade around this time were coffee, raw cotton, piece goods, grain and ivory. Much of this trade involved the Bombay Presidency.[22]

But at the same time we also know that 'in 1870 Aden was a financial burden on India costing about £ 150,000 a year. Most of this money was spent on the maintenance of a garrison of one British Battalion, an Indian Regiment, three Batteries and 100 Sabres of the Aden Troops which had been raised in 1865.'[23] Could this be an explanation for the decline of the Hindu population in Aden? Perhaps more plausible explanation can be found in the fact that the volume of trade was relatively lower for a few years around this time.[24]

TABLE 6.2: INDIAN AND OTHER POPULATION GROUPS OF ADEN, 1856 AND 1872

Ethnic Groups	*1856*	*1872*
Arabs	4,812	8,241
Africans	3,627	5,346
Jews	1,224	1,435
Europeans (Christians) (mostly British)	1,129	208
Indians		
-Hindus	5,611	854
-Muslims	2,557	2,614
-Parsis	61	121
Miscellaneous	1,717	470
Total	20,738*	19,289**

Notes: * Includes military (troops and camp followers) whose numbers fluctuated between 3,400 and 3,600.

** Excluding the military personnel numbering 3,433.

Source: Adapted from Z.H. Kour, *The History of Aden, 1839-1872*, Frank Cass, London, 1981, pp. 50-1.

In the early 1870s Indians formed the majority of blacksmiths, carpenters, mechanics, and sweepers. They were also shopkeepers, bricklayers, bumboatmen, and merchants. Some were jewellers. 'The Banyans, who were the wealthiest among the Hindus, had in their hands the wholesale trade of Aden as well as the banking and exchange business. At the other end of the scale, most of the menial servants were Hindus. In contrast with the Banyans, the Parsis were mainly retail merchants.'[25] Most of the Indian Muslims were employed with the police force, and many engaged themselves as masons. 'The poor worked as tailors or domestic servants. In 1872, many of the Borahs worked in tin, and the need for gallon measures was enough to keep them busy, since water was given or sold by the gallon.'[26] Some educated Indians and Parsis were also employed as accountants and clerks with commercial firms and in Government offices.

In 1932 Aden became a Chief Commissioner's province under the Central Government of India. With the intensification of independence movement in India the Adeni leaders feared that they might one day be annexed to an independent India. Therefore they persuaded the British Government in 1937 to make the settlement a Colony administered from London by the Colonial Office.[27] For about a century when Aden was administered by the Bombay Presidency, Aden had experienced tremendous Indian commercial and cultural influence. Building architecture and town planning were particularly affected. Thus describing the Indian influence on the life of Aden one British Officer Harold Jacob in his book *The Kings of Arabia* wrote: 'Aden is painted Indian, the post office have their notices and instructions written both in Arabic and Hindi and Gujarati. Many of the school teachers are Indians. The resonance of Bombay hypnotizes Aden.'[28]

In 1947 Aden's formal link with India ended, and appeal cases were transferred from Bombay to Nairobi. Nevertheless, rupee continued to be the currency until 1951.[29] There were about 16,000 Indians in 1955 out of Aden's total population of 138,000 (Table 6.3).

TABLE 6.3: POPULATION OF INDIAN AND OTHER COMMUNITIES IN ADEN, 1839-1955

Year	*Arabs*	*Somalis*	*Jews*	*Indians*	*Europeans*	*Other*	*Total*
1839	617	63	574	35			1289
1840							4600
1841	7,262		777	207			8,246
1842	12,170	2,050	1,079	481	747		16,527
1849	4,845	2,877	1,150	7,605	778	1,868	19,024*
1856	4,812	2,896	1,224	8,563	791	2,452	20,738*
1867	9,350	3,387	1,275	2,308	49	1,177	17,546
1872	8,241	5,346	1,435	3,589	208	470	19,289*
1881	13,285	9,150	2,121	7,265	2,101	789	34,711*
1891	n.a.	n.a.	n.a.	n.a.	n.a.	n.a.	40,926*
1901	n.a.	n.a.	n.a.	n.a.	n.a.	n.a.	39,986*
1911	n.a.	n.a.	n.a.	n.a.	n.a.	n.a.	42,675*
1921	n.a.	n.a.	n.a.	n.a.	n.a.	n.a.	57,571*
1931	29,820	3,935	4,120	7,387	1,145	331	46,638*
1946	58,455	4,325	7,273	9,452	366	645	80,516*
1955	103,879	10,611	831	15,817	4,484	2,608	138,441

Notes: *Including military.

Source: Adapted from R.J. Gavin, *Aden Under British Rule, 1839-1967*, C. Hurst & Co., London, 1975, p. 445.

In the mid 1960s their population rose to about 20,000.[30] In 1955 a wealthy Indian V.K. Joshi was elected to the Legislative Council. He was reelected in 1959, and was a Minister in the Adeni Government in the early 1960s.[31]

The rise of Arab nationalism in the late 1940s and 1950s, problems of political succession, widening schism between the traditionalists and modernists in the Yemeni society, the unsuccessful *coups d'etat* of 1948 and 1955, dismemberment of the short-lived confederation with the United Arab Republic (1958-61) and the 1962 Yemeni revolution and the British withdrawal from Aden in 1967 – all these events had their unsettling impact on the Indian immigrant and other population groups in both the Yemens which forced them to go elsewhere.[32] According to one estimate, 'about eighty thousand people left Aden after 1967, perhaps half foreigners (mainly Asians and Africans) and the other half Yemeni.'[33] 'Yemeni merchants driven from Aden established their businesses in the North in Saana, Taiz and Hodeida.'[34]

The independence of Aden and its hinterland from the British on 30 November 1967 and subsequently a Marxist revolution led to the establishment of Peoples Democratic Republic of Yemen (PDRY). 'The PDRY built the stronger state order, one based on constitution which had elements of Islamic and British as well as Marxist legal principles. Special privileges of Sultans, Sayyids, foreigners, and property owners were replaced by universal rights to housing, education, health care, and social security.'[35]

The socialist policies of the PDRY Government led to the takeover of Indian businesses and properties.

> The expropriated businesses were given derisory compensation and a fortnight later many of their senior staff were dismissed. Later the Parsee firms, whose names were known to all who had passed through Aden and who had done more than anyone else to build its reputation as a shopping center, were taken over for "not contributing effectively in the service of the national economy" and for allegedly smuggling out currency.[36]

These developments 'resulted in the hasty departure from Aden of many PIOs, either for India or some other country. But a large number belonging to Bohra, Khoja and Kachchi communities decided to remain behind and gradually became Yemeni citizens.'[37]

North Yemen had already undergone a bourgeois revolution in 1962. The country was named the Yemen Arab Republic (YAR). By the early 1970s, 'the border between North and South Yemen, originally drawn between the Turkish and British empires, became a cold war border, and the PDRY and the YAR respectively seemed to represent microcosms of the differences between peripheral capitalism and third world socialism.'[38] Nevertheless, in spite of the seemingly irreconcilable differences between the two Yemens they were united in 1990.

No accurate estimates are available regarding the Indian population in Yemen. About 17,000 Indian expatriates in Yemen were reported by the Ministry of External Affairs in 1979.[39] It is not clear whether this figure refers to the People of Indian Origin (PIO) or Non-Resident Indians (NRI) or both. The picture is further confounded by the reported figures of 100,000 Indians in PDRY (99,000 PIOs and 500 NRIs) in the early 1980s and 3,500 Indians (300 PIOs and 3,200 NRIs) in YAR.[40] These figures cast doubts on the 1979 figures reported above and vice versa. But then these figures appear to be in tune with the estimates for the year 2001 in which 109,000 Indians (100,000 PIOs and 9,000 NRIs) were reported to be present in the united Yemen by the High Level Committee on the Indian Diaspora of the Government of India.[41] According to the report of this Committee, the overwhelming majority of Indians are Yemeni citizens and are settled in major towns like Aden, Sanaa, Mukalla, Haraz, Seyum and Hodeida.[42] The NRIs consists of professionals, skilled workers, nurses and paramedical staff, semi-skilled workers and housemaids. Apart from the availability of simple data regarding migration, settlement and ethnic background of Indians in Yemen, there is no systematic study of other diasporic features of the Indians in Yemen. The Government of India's High Level Committee on the Indian diaspora did collect some information about their economic, political and socio-cultural profile but it is extremely sketchy and brief. Thus besides mentioning the presence of an Indian school in Sana'a and the installation of Mahatma Gandhi's statue in its hall, in a significant passage it does lament the on-going demise of the Indian heritage in Aden:

As many as ten Hindu and Parsi temples have survived in Aden since the time when it was still a British colony. But most of them are now objects of neglect because the small size of their remaining congregations. As these properties are strategically located, they have become attractive targets for illegal encroachment and demolition. The Indian Ambassador in Sana'a is continuing his *demarches* with the Yemeni government to secure protection for these endangered sites. In cooperation with several Western Ambassadors, he had succeeded last year in persuading the country's President to restore similarly endangered Church properties.[43]

The Indian Embassy in Yemen had also requested the Government of India for 'the opening of a branch of any nationalized Indian bank in Aden or Sana'a and increased shipping services between Indian and Yemeni ports'.[44]

To sum up, with about 100,000 people of Indian origin, Yemen hosts the largest permanently settled Indian diasporic community in West Asia – even larger than that in Israel. In spite of this however the Indian diaspora in Yemen remains the least researched one in the Persian Gulf/Red Sea region. Hence this chapter which is perhaps the first ever, up-to-date and systematic though sketchy attempt to outline the evolution of the Indian Diaspora in Yemen in recent times.

NOTES

1. For a brief overview of Indo-Yemeni relations since ancient times see Saleh Ali Basurrah, 'Yemen and India: Development of Historical Relationships', in N.N. Vohra (ed.) *History, Culture and Society in India and West Asia*, Shipra Publications, Delhi, 2002, pp. 32-6.
2. That Aden was an important stopover enroute to Mecca and Medina for pilgrims is borne out by two major incidents reported below:
   'In January 1836 a ship belonging to the family of the Nawab of the Carnatic, carrying a number of pilgrims bound for Mecca which ran aground near Aden was looted by the Arabs. The crew and passengers were grossly maltreated,' Eric Marco, *Yemen and the Western World since 1571*, C. Hurst & Co., London, 1968, p. 28.

   'In September 1854 fire broke out in the quarter chiefly inhabited by Indian Hajj pilgrims claiming nine lives and destroying about 400 huts, several stone houses, and the entire lines of the *Sebundis*,' Z.H. Kour, *The History of Aden, 1839-72*, Frank Cass, London, 1981, p. 40.
3. Claude Markovits, *The Global World of Indian Merchants, 1750-1947*, Cambridge University Press, Cambridge, 2000, p. 11.

4. R.J. Gavin, *Aden Under British Rule 1839-1967*, C. Hurst & Co., London, 1975, p. 17.
5. Surendra Gopal, 'Indian Diaspora in West and Central Asia and Russia in Medieval Times', *Journal of Indian Ocean Studies*, 1998, vol. 5, no. 2, p. 117.
6. Ferdinand Braudel, *Civilization and Capitalism, 15th-18th Century*, vol. II, London, 1982, p. 127.
7. Ashin Das Gupta, 'Gujarati Merchants and the Red Sea Trade, 1700-1725', in Blair B. Kling and M.N. Pearson (eds.), *The Age of Partnership*, Honolulu, 1979, p. 124.
8. Claude Markovits, op. cit., p. 11, n. 5.
9. Surendra Gopal, op. cit., p. 123.
10. Ashin Das Gupta, op. cit., quoted in Surendra Gopal, op. cit., p. 118.
11. Eric Marco, op. cit., p. 29. Aden was a small town with less than 1,000 people when the British occupied it in 1839. But this was not always the case. In the fourteenth and fifteenth centuries, for example, Aden was a prosperous town with a population of about 50,000. Some idea of its glory can be had from the fact that 'embassies came to the rulers of Aden from all parts of the world, from Egypt, from India, from Ceylon and from China' (R.J. Gavin, op. cit., p. 11). Aden declined in the sixteenth century only to be revived in the middle of the nineteenth century following the British occupation.
12. Letter to the Council of Directors of the East India Company, 27 February 1839, quoted in Saleh Ali Basurrah, op. cit., p. 34.
13. Z.H. Kour, op. cit., p. 21.
14. R.J. Gavin, op. cit., p. 59.
15. Ibid., p. 61.
16. Ibid., pp. 60-1.
17. Ibid., p. 371, n. 117. See also D.A Farnie, *East and West of Suez*, Oxford University Press, 1969, pp. 37-8.
18. Ibid., p. 107.
19. Ibid., p. 188.
20. Ibid., p. 290.
21. Z.H. Kour, op. cit., p. 95.
22. Ibid., p. 26. We do not know much about the social life of Indians around this time. It is therefore enlightening to know that before the Aden Act of 1864 'religious and caste disputes among the Hindu immigrants were referred to a *panchayat* (council) composed of their leading men'. Ibid., p. 88.
23. Robin Bidwell, *The Two Yemens*, Longman and Westview Press, Harlow and Boulder, 1983, p. 42.

24. See R.J. Gavin, op. cit., p. 446.
25. Z.H. Kour, op. cit., p. 52.
26. Ibid., p. 53.
27. Peter Mansfield, *The Middle East*, Oxford University Press, London, 5th edn., 1980, pp. 151-2.
28. Quoted in Saleh Ali Basurrah, op. cit., p. 34.
29. Robin Bidwell, op. cit., p. 76.
30. See Sheila Carapico, *Civil Society in Yemen*, Cambridge University Press, Cambridge, 1998, p. 87. It is interesting to note here that late Mr. Dhirajlal Hirachand Ambani (1932-2002), the former Chairman of the Reliance Group of companies was one of the earliest non-resident Indians in Yemen. He stayed there for about a decade between 1949 and 1958 as a petrol pump attendant working with the Shell Oil agents Besse & Co. in Aden. He subsequently rose to become India's top most entrepreneur. Today Reliance is India's largest business group with total revenues of Rs. 65,000 crore (US $13.3 billion). Its activities span petro-chemicals, textiles, oil and gas, telecom, insurance, financial services, etc. See *India Today*, 8 July 2002, pp. 32-41.
31. V.S. Sheth, *South Arabia: 1959-1967*, Somaiya Publications Pvt. Ltd., Mumbai, 1998, p. 109.
32. Mohammed Ahmad Zabarah, *Yemen: Tradition vs. Modernity*, Praeger Publishers, New York, 1982,
33. Sheila Carapico, op. cit., p. 30.
34. Ibid., p. 34.
35. Ibid., p. 31.
36. Robin Bidwell, op. cit., p. 247.
37. *Report of the High Level Committee on the Indian Diaspora*, Ministry of External Affairs, Government of India, New Delhi, 2001, p. 43.
38. Sheila Carapico, op. cit., p. 36.
39. Myron Weiner, 'International Migration and Development: Indians in the Persian Gulf', *Population and Development Review*, 1982, vol. 8, no.1, p. 32, n. 9.
40. See I.J. Bahadursingh (ed.), *Indians in South Asia*, Sterling Publishers, New Delhi, 1984, Appendix I, p. 219.
41. *Report of the High Level Committee*, op. cit., pp. 33 and 43.
42. Ibid., p. 43. A Relatively smaller size of the NRIs component among the Indians in Yemen vis-à-vis other Gulf countries suggests that Yemen is not only the poorest country (with little oil and gas) in the Persian Gulf region but also a major labour exporting country. Following the Kuwaiti crisis in 1990-1 and Yemen's role in it (it sided with Iraq), between 800,000 to one million Yemeni workers were expelled from

Saudi Arabia and other Gulf countries. Ironically, these were replaced by Indian workers whose population in Saudi Arabia alone increased from about 900,000 in 1991 to about 1.5 million in 2002. For details about Indians in the GCC countries, see Prakash C. Jain, *Population and Society in West Asia*, National Publishing House, Jaipur and New Delhi, 2001, Chapter 4.

43. *Report of the High Level Committee*, op. cit., p. 43.
44. Ibid., p. 43.

PART II

PRESENT

CHAPTER 7

International Migration and Development: Indians in the Persian Gulf

MYRON WEINER

In the five small oil-producing states that line the Persian Gulf – Kuwait, Qatar, Bahrain, the United Arab Emirates, and Oman – two-thirds of the labor force is imported. Nowhere in the world have societies experienced such massive labor shortages satisfied not through open migration, but through the use of temporary imported workers. The United States, Australia, and Canada, among others, expanded economically and demographically through permanent migrations. Postwar Europe recruited temporary 'guest workers' from the Mediterranean countries and the United States has also employed temporary migrants (both legal and illegal) from Latin America, but the size of this labor force in relation to the local population in each instance is small compared with the proportion of migrants in the Gulf states.

Moreover, migrants to Europe and the United States from low-income countries have been primarily low-skilled workers, recruited to positions that the local labor force did not want and at wages it would not accept. In contrast, a large proportion of migrants to the Gulf are skilled workers who have entered the modern sectors of the economy in such large numbers that they easily outnumber the local skilled labor force.

Much of our understanding of the characteristics and problems of developing countries and of the role of migration in economic growth clearly does not apply to the small oil-rich countries of the

Gulf. As capital-rich, labor-short countries, they are not concerned with creating labor-intensive industries to increase employment, or with reducing luxury consumption and increasing the rate of savings to stimulate investment; nor are they faced with the problem of obtaining financial resources for delivering medical services, education, drinking water, housing, and sanitation. There is no debate in these countries on the issues of growth versus income distribution, consumption versus savings, industrial versus agricultural development, export-oriented growth versus import substitution. Our understanding of the role of international migration in economic growth, our appreciation of how private and social gains and losses are distributed by international migration, and our assessment of the long-term domestic and international consequences of migration seem inadequate for analyzing what is happening in the Gulf.

The governing elites of the Gulf states have been concerned with two questions: how to use their abundant wealth to develop their countries; and how to do so with the least disruption of the existing political structure. The Gulf states share common strategies: they have each decided to share the wealth (but not political power) with their own populations through the expansion of social services and government employment, to diversify their economy by industrial investment, and to erect modern infrastructure – airports, roads, communications networks. To pursue these objectives, they import workers to construct and operate new facilities and industries and to provide services. They have decided not to permit migrants to become citizens.

As countries with great wealth, low populations, and labor shortages, the Gulf governments might have decided to encourage permanent migration. And if they sought to avoid the social complications associated with increased ethnic heterogeneity, they could have selectively opened their doors to permanent migrants from neighboring Arab countries. But as monarchies the Gulf states fear the political erosion that might accompany massive permanent migration from countries that have overthrown their monarchies; as small states, they fear being politically overrun by their larger neighbors if they allow foreigners to become citizens; and as tribal chieftains – not withstanding pan-Arab and pan-Islamic rhetoric –

their first concern is with maximizing the economic well-being of members of their own tribes.[1]

What have been the consequences of this strategy of development, and what are likely to be the long-term social, economic, and political effects? This article attempts to provide some answers to these questions by exploring the role of the largest single group of migrants to the Gulf states, migrants from South Asia, who constitute nearly half of the 628,000 foreign workers in the Gulf. Among the South Asians, we focus on the Indians who, although less numerous than the Pakistanis, are the most skilled part of the South Asian labor force.

Tables 7.1-7.3 summarize the distribution of nationals and migrants in the total populations and in the labor force of the Gulf states.

In 1975 the Indian population in the five Gulf states numbered 223,000, of whom 134,000 were in the labor force.[2] By 1979, there were an estimated 333,000 Indians living in the Gulf.[3] Pakistanis numbered 335,000 in 1975, of whom 166,000 were in the labor force. In the United Arab Emirates and in Qatar, South Asian workers outnumber native Arab workers by about three to one. What for Pakistan and India represents a small trickle of emigrants constitutes a torrent for the Gulf.[4]

Both the Gulf governments and South Asian governments view this migration as temporary. The Gulf governments insist that in time the local labor force will take over jobs now performed by migrants. The Indian government takes a similar view and considers remittances earned from migrants a short-term contribution to foreign exchange. State governments within India make no particular effort to 'capture' remittances for investment or to take emigration or return migration into account in manpower planning. The Indian migrants themselves assume that their sojourn is temporary, and while they put considerable resources into creating community life within the Gulf, they send most of their money home, return to India regularly, and in most ways act as if their stay is temporary. There is, to anticipate a theme of this article, an illusion of impermanence on the part of all the participants – the host governments, governments of the sending countries, and the migrants themselves.

TABLE 7.1: NATIONAL AND MIGRANT POPULATIONS IN THE GULF, 1975

State	*Citizens*		*Migrants*		*Total population*
	No.	*Per cent*	*No,*	*Per cent*	
Kuwait	472,000	47.4	523,000	52.6	995,000
Bahrain (1976)	224,700	76.1	70,500	23.9	295,000
United Arab Emirates	200,000	30.5	456,000	69.5	656,000
Qatar	60,000	38.0	98,000	62.0	158,000
Oman	550,000	79.1	145,000	20.9	695,000
Total	1,506,700	53.9	1,292,500	46.1	2,799,200

Source: J.S. Briks and C.A. Sinclair, *Arab Manpower: The Crisis of Development* (New York: St. Martin's Press, 1980). Oman migrant and population data computed by author from data provided in Birks and Sinclair.

This paper will present five arguments:

First, that such fundamental structural changes have taken place in the economies and labor markets of the region that non-nationals are an enduring part of the labor force. The removal of all or some of the migrants or a halt to the migration flow would entail considerable social and economic costs for the Gulf states; it would disrupt their capacity to deliver social services and to maintain many economic activities.

Second, the fundamental decisions concerning migration – how many migrants should be allowed to come, from what countries, for what jobs, at what wages, and with what rights and benefits – are all matters of policy, not decisions made in the market place. In the long run the fate of the migrants rests primarily upon what happens politically and only secondarily on the question of long-term manpower needs.

Third, although some observers have expressed concern that migrants would 'overwhelm' the Gulf countries and, by implication, threaten existing regimes, in fact the migrants, at least those from South Asia, dare not oppose the regimes for they are dependent upon the present political order for their security. It is a changed regimes or the movement of these regimes in a more populist direction that could most threaten the South Asian expatriates.

Fourth, the development program pursued by the Gulf states are

TABLE 7.2: NATIONALS AND MIGRANTS IN THE LABOR FORCE IN THE GULF, 1975

State	*Citizens*		*Migrants*		*Total labor*
	No.	*Per cent*	*No.*	*Per cent*	
Kuwait	86,970	29.2	211,440	70.8	298,410
Bahrain (1976)	46,800	60.8	30,200	39.2	77,000
United Arab Emirates	45,000	15.2	251,500	84.8	296,500
Qatar	12,500	18.9	53,800	81.1	66,300
Oman	99,000[a]	54.9	81,200	45.1	180,200
Total	290,270	31.6	628,140	68.4	918,410

Note: The World Bank reports the number of migrant workers for 1975 as 61,000 for Qatar and 104,000 for Oman.
[a]An additional 38,000 workers are abroad.
Source: See Table 7.1

producing a social order divided between a consumer-oriented native population and a productivity-oriented migrant population, with the result that economic growth is occurring without the local population acquiring the values associated with modern productive life.

Fifth, although migrants have become an inextricable part of the economy, they are pressed to live in their own social enclaves, cannot obtain citizenship, own property or join trade unions, have restricted access to social benefits, and are excluded from participation in the political system. The result is a sharply divided political and social order in which less than half of the population are citizens with full rights, while the remainder, constituting two thirds of the labor force, are migrants living in a subordinate position and subject at any time to expulsion.

These arguments will be developed as we first review the impact of emigration upon India, then consider who the migrants are and what role they play in the economies of the Gulf, describe the factors that shape the present and future demand for migrant labor, briefly look at the interaction of migrants and the local population in several Gulf states, and finally examine the migration policies of the Gulf states and the factors likely to influence them in the future.

THE IMPACT OF EMIGRATION ON INDIA

India earned US $2.7 billion dollars in remittances from migrants abroad in 1978 and $3.2 billion in 1979.[5] No official figures are available on the magnitude of the remittances from the Gulf states and other Middle East countries, but unofficially the figure has been placed as high as $1.6 billion.[6] Such a high number would imply either very high average remittances from the estimated half million Indian migrants in the Middle East or a larger number of workers than officially reported; however, the number is not implausible, and comparable figures have been found in a study of remittances of the Pakistani migrants in the Middle East.[7]

The planning board of the Indian state of Kerala estimates that about $500 million in remittances from the Gulf flows into that state alone each year, while the director of the state bureau of economies and statistics estimates that 300,000 Keralites lived abroad in 1979, with the largest share employed in the Gulf.[8] In all, remittances from migrants abroad to India[9] were large enough in the 1970s to cover the deficit in India's trade balance and enabled India to increase its reserves in spite of the rise in oil prices.

TABLE 7.3: SOUTH ASIANS IN THE GULF (1975-79)

State	*Population*		*Labor force (1975)*		*Population*
	Indian	*Pakistani*	*Indian*	*Pakistani*	*Indian (1979)*
Kuwait	32,105	23,016	21,475	11,038	65,000
Bahrain (1976)	17,250	17,750	8,943 (13,200 in 1977)	6,680 (9,200 in 1977)	26,000
United Arab Emirates	107,500	201,750	61,500	100,000	152,000
Qatar	27,800	28000	16,000	16,000	30,000
Oman	38,500	65,000	26,000	32,500	60,000
Total	223,155	335,156	133,918	166,218	333,000

Source: 1975 data from Birks and Sinclair, cited in Table 7.1; 1979 data from the Indian Ministry of External Affairs.

Emigration provides a significant safety valve for India's unemployed, most notably from the states of Kerala, Karnataka, Goa, Maharashtra, and Gujarat on India's west coast, and from the

Punjab.[10] Emigration to the Gulf is particularly high among the educated. The persistently high level of unemployment among the educated, the migration notwithstanding, suggests a brain. In Kerala, for example, 1.2 million job seekers were registered with employment exchanges in December 1979, and half of these were educated – 512,000 high school graduates, 67,000 pre-degree certificate holders, 54,000 college graduates, and 8,500 postgraduates.[11] Although there are shortages of skilled labor in the construction industry in Kerala, and there is an element of selective migration (one study reveals that two-thirds of those who migrate were employed at the time they left), emigration from India has not produced the kind of loss of human resources experienced by some of the Mediterranean countries.

Two public sector Indian firms play an important role in the Middle East, Engineering Projects India, Ltd (EPI) and the National Buildings Construction Corporation. The Government of India permits Indian companies to pay a lower wage to Indian workers so they can successfully compete for contracts in the Gulf against British, American, Cypriot, Korean, and Japanese firms. Indian companies in the Gulf import some of their engineering equipment and construction supplies from India, while the Indian work force in the Gulf imports consumer goods from India, including Indian food, saris and Indian films.

Remittances are an important source of income for the families of migrants, enabling them to pay off debts, purchase land, build new homes, send their children to school, and pay for weddings.[12] Because real estate is a favored investment in Kerala, land values there have risen sharply and the construction industry has boomed. There has been a spurt in the number of cars, refrigerators, and radio, and an increase in the number of taxis. Enrollment in educational institutions has increased as potential migrants study Arabic and the children of migrants are sent to English medium schools. In Kerala, it is generally said, remittances are used to invest in an improvement in the social status of families;[13] in Gujarat, business families reportedly use remittances as working capital; and in the Punjab, many families use remittances to finance permanent migration to the United Kingdom.

And for the migrants themselves, work in the Gulf is financially attractive. Wages are high, and the opportunities to save are great in spite of the high cost of living. Housing, much of it barrack style for construction workers, but some of higher quality as well, is sometimes provided by employers either rent-free or at low rates. Medical care is generally provided by employers. Food is often available in the canteens, and for those prosperous enough to eat out there are low-cost Indian restaurants. There are few costly diversions; no bars, no gambling, no fleshpots. For those with cars, gasoline is cheap. Consumer durables are widely available at price well below those in India.

The incentives to save are also great – to support families in India; to accumulate savings to purchase a home and property in India; to provide against the likelihood of unemployment on the return home. Even cursory interviews with workers reveal an extraordinarily high rate of savings; to send back to India remittances of one-third to one-half of one's income is typical.

Many middle class migrants now expect to remain in the Gulf for many years, possibly for their entire working lives. As a result a certain 'deepening' has begun. Many have brought their wives and children.[14] The migrant community has begun to create a communal life. The process has only recently started, and it is done with a minimum of conspicuousness. Indian sports clubs in Kuwait, Bahrain, Dubai, Abu Dhabi, and Oman – places in which the middle class can meet, eat, engage in sports, and conduct their social life – now have long waiting lists for membership. The club are expanding rapidly, and several have put in new buildings, constructed tennis courts, and added a swimming pool. Indian schools are being built.[15] The demand is high, since middle class parents prefer to keep their smaller children with them rather than send them India for their education.

The government of Kuwait gave the Catholic Church land to build a large church, which serves the religious needs of the large Indian Catholic population. Other Gulf governments have also permitted Christian institutions to function. But the large Hindu population has been more cautious in approaching the government authorities for permission to build Hindu temples. There is a 100-year-old Balakrishna temple located near the souk in Bahrain, and the Sultan of Oman, with his long term connections with the

Indian merchant and banking community, has allowed the Hindu community to build a temple near the palace compound in Muscat, but elsewhere Hindus must observe their festivals in less conspicuous locations, or in private. The Indian community recognizes that the conspicuous display of religion – in the form of temple, religious or marriage processions – can be provocative in Islamic states.

The Indian community now imports Indian films;[16] there is a growing number of Indian restaurants; imported Indian spices, fruit, and other foods are available in the shops. One can readily buy Malayalee books and newspapers, and one of the Kerala newspapers is planning a Gulf edition. Many of the migrants' wives have found employment. Indian families are excluded from Arab social life, but for many this is advantageous: there are no pressures on their children to assimilate, as would be the case in the United States or the United Kingdom.

In the main, then, the Indian government, public and private sector contractors, Indian exporters, Indian banks, the state governments, Indian airlines, and the migrants and their families all look favorably upon this migration. This is not to say that migration does not generate costs: dislocation of households, inflation of land prices in areas from which migrants come, some loss of skilled labor, and problems for the migrants in the Gulf that have created political problems for the Government of India. But on balance, the migration is widely viewed in India as a net gain.

On two occasions, efforts by the Indian government to restrict migration because of mistreatment of migrants were aborted by political pressures within India. In one incident a Cypriot construction firm in Oman was confronted with a strike by Indian workers who complained that their wages, housing, and medical care were below the standards of their contract. When the company, working with the Government of Oman, expelled the protesters, the Government of India responded by prohibiting all new migrant workers from entering Oman. But within months, under pressure from Indians who wanted to migrate to Oman, and following a mild expression of regret from the Oman government, the migration was resumed. On the other occasion, the Government of India banned the migration of single uneducated women to Kuwait, when there were reports that ayahs and domestics were being mistreated. But after protests from Goanese and Malayalee families, Indian officials quietly permitted the resumption of the migration.

Moves by governments in the Gulf to restrict migration have been followed by expressions of concern from the Indian government. In 1980 when the governments of the United Arab Emirates and of Kuwait announced that workers whose permits had expired would be forcibly expatriated, the Government of India quickly dispatched an official delegate to persuade the two governments to slow down deportations so as not to strain the Kerala economy.[17]

Given the benefits that accrue to the migrants and their families, to the sending communities, and to various state and central ministries and agencies in India, it is politically difficult for the Government of India to refuse to allow its citizens to emigrate to the Gulf for employment.[18] The Gulf governments can decide how many migrants to admit, what qualifications they must have, how long they can stay, what wages should be paid, what rights and benefits should be provided, and whether they should be imported from India, Pakistan other parts of Asia, or from Arab countries. The asymmetrical dimension of policymaking is well understood by all. For all practical purposes the power to regulate is primarily in the hands of the labor-importing, not the labor-exporting counties.

WHO ARE THE INDIA MIGRANTS?

The largest single group of Indian workers in the Gulf is in construction. Indian labor is employed in the building of housing projects, drydock facilities, roads, airports, office buildings, and industries. They work for Indian, British, American, Cypriot, and Arab companies. Indians are recruited for the entire spectrum of construction work: unskilled workers, skilled craftsmen, civil engineers, managers. The number of Indian construction workers was at its peak in the late 1970s, but declined thereafter, partly because of the increasing success of Korean companies in winning contracts, but largely because of a slowdown in construction. Construction work is largely short-term – one to two years – but it is common for construction companies to move their labor force from one project to another.

Construction workers live near the construction sites in barracks provided by the employers, with their own messes and medical facilities. Except for the senior engineering and administrative personnel, workers on construction projects come without their families.

A second large group of Indians is employed by private sector firms in industry and in services. Indians are employed as factory workers, department store clerks, hotel staff, engineers for oil companies, bank officials, and in clerical jobs for businesses. These private sector jobs are among the most prized, not only because the wages are good but also because they provide opportunities for staying in the Gulf for an extended period.

Indians are also employed by Gulf governments and by government - run institutions. Hospitals import doctors from India, Pakistan and Bangladesh.[19] Nurses are recruited from among the Christians of Kerala and Sri Lanka. Civil engineers are imported from India to help design highways, communications facilities, and electric power plants. In Oman the personal properties of the Sultan are managed by a staff of Indians. Some Indians employed by Gulf governments are on official deputation from the Government of India, Department of Public Works, though most come in their personal capacity.

Employment in government has less job security than employment in the private sector since Gulf government are on the look out for qualified local Arabs who can take over positions held by foreigners, but the jobs pay handsomely, and in some occupations, notably engineering and medicine there is little likelihood that Indians and other expatriates will be displaced in the near future.

For centuries Indian traders have played a significant role in trade between India and the Gulf and between the Gulf and East Africa. Much of the trade in Dubai and Oman, particularly the pearl and gold trade, was in the hands of Indian merchants. When Oman was a dependency of India under the Government of Bombay, the traditional trade of rice, coffee, tea and cotton goods from India for dates, dried fish, and pomegranates from Oman was handled by Indian merchants. Kutch merchant families from Gujarat also ran the trade between Oman and Zanzibar.

In recent years Indian merchants have moved into the new trade linking the Gulf to Europe and the United States. Indian merchants own many of the franchises and import permits. They operate numerous small shops in the souks and some of the larger modern department stores in the port cities of Kuwait, Manama, Dubai, Abu Dhabi, Muscat, and Mutrah.

The countries of the region (with the exception of Oman and until recently, Dubai) require that businesses and shop must be owned by local Arabs and that import permits can be granted only to citizens. Indian merchants and businessmen, therefore, have 'silent' Arab partners who are paid a fee or percentage of the earnings.

Indian shopkeepers and traders have shared in the rising prosperity of the Gulf, but their prosperity is tempered by the anxiety that some day they may share the fate of the Indian trading and business communities of East Africa. Indeed, many of the Indian merchants in Oman and Dubai once ran businesses in Uganda, Tanzania, Zanzibar, and Kenya.

Finally, some Indians are directly employed by local Arab families as ayahs, cooks, sweepers, and gardeners. The ayahs are a particularly conspicuous part of the local scene in several Gulf states. In Kuwait, for example a thousand or more Indian ayahs can be seen on a Sunday evening in front of the city's Catholic church talking and strolling with one another and with young Indian boys.[20] A substantial part of the middle and upper classes in the Gulf rely upon India for household servants.

This brief account of Indian employment in the Gulf indicates not only how diverse the Indian labor force is, but also the extent to which Indians have become an inextricable part of the structure of the Arab labor market. The slack in construction has been more than filled by a growing demand for labor in other sectors of the economy – a demand linked to several fundamental changes in the economy of the Gulf.

THE DEMAND FOR MIGRANT LABOR

A major factor in the demand for migrant labor by the oil producing Gulf states is the decision by the Gulf governments to create welfare states. Governing elites in the Gulf are opposed to redistribution of political power, instead supporting policies to bring about a modest redistribution of wealth. With per capita incomes as high as US $17,100 in Kuwait (1979) and $14,400 in the United Arab Emirates (in 1978), these states are financially able to provide a range of social services equal to and often superior to those provided in advanced industrial countries. Free education from primary school through the university, free health care, free water, and low cost quality housing are provided by most of the Gulf governments. The Gulf not only needs a labor force to construct schools, hospitals and housing, it needs teachers, doctors, nurses, technical personnel, accountants, and managers to maintain these facilities. In the absence of local qualified personnel for these positions, the Gulf governments had little choice but to recruit outsiders. Social welfare policies necessitate labor imports.

A second reason for importing labor is that the Gulf governments are attempting to diversify their economies and reduce their dependence upon oil exports by investing in industry. Each of the Gulf countries has its own ambitious development program, with little in the way of regional coordination to minimize redundancy. Gulf governments have invested oil earnings in banking, aluminium plants, flour processing, drydocks, oil refineries, hotels, airports, roads and communications.[21] Initially, there was a massive need for construction labor. Now there is a persistent need for a labor force for maintenance and operation. As the demand for unskilled labor has declined, the demand for skilled labor has increased.

A third reason for importing labor is that the national populations of the Gulf states are small and labor force participation rates are low. The total population of the five states in 1975 was 2.8 million, but only 1.5 million were local citizens. Forty-five per cent of the local population is under age 15, and few women are in the labor force. Labor force participation rates are only about 20 per cent in each country. Moreover, a portion of the local labor force is not available at all for employment in the modern sector. In Oman, for example, much of the labor force is rural – 40,000 workers are in agriculture, leaving only 59,000 in what can be described as the 'modern' urban sector. Many Omani workers (as estimated 38,000) have also emigrated to neighboring states where wages are higher. In Kuwait and in portions of the Untied Arab Emirates the non-urban population is also sizable.

In addition, the skill quality of the local labor force is low. Less than half of the adult population in most of the Gulf states is literate. There is vocational education, but most students attend schools that follow the style and often the content of traditional Koranic schools, with a heavy emphasis on rote learning and recitations from the Koran. Higher education emphasizes literacy studies; Middle East universities are not known for preparing students for the needs of a modern industrial economy.

A substantial portion of the educated native labor force is siphoned into government administration and is not available for employment in either industry or social services. In Qatar, for example, half of the local labor force – 6,760 out of 12,500 – is employed by the government. Only 5,740 nationals are employed by the private sector which compensates for the labor shortage by employing 49,650 migrants.

Many Arabs view public employment as a sinecure where high incomes can be earned with little or no work. In addition to receiving high salaries, government employees may become lucrative silent 'partners' to foreign investors. Since the Gulf governments require that only citizens may own business, foreign investors often look within the government administration for such 'partners' a practice that is quite legal in the Gulf. Indeed, members of the emir families, including the rulers themselves, own hotels, banks, housing complexes, and factories with foreign collaboration.

Finally, government income distribution policies have stimulated the emergence of an economy and culture of consumerism. Since education and health care are provided free by the state, housing is given at low cost, and wages paid to government employees are high, the local population has a large disposable income. The souks, large multi-storied shopping centers, sell color television sets, stereo systems, video tapes, and a cornucopia of electronic equipment, automobiles and household furnishings. Import companies prosper, along with insurance agents, shipping companies, wholesalers, and retailers. As business expands, so too does the demand for a labor supply skilled in international trade, managing accounts, merchandising, and sales, a demand that can only be met partially in the local labor market.

In sum, with small populations, low labor participation rates, a substantial part of the local labor market in financially lucrative but non-productive positions in government, or in the traditional rural sectors, and with skill levels low, the need for migrant labor to meet the needs of expanding industries, social services, trade and construction has been high. Neither the local educational system nor the system of economic incentives has been adequate to produce a local skilled labor supply large enough to meet expanding demand.

The reliance upon expatriates for productive roles tends to reinforce many traditional features of nomadic Bedouin culture; lavish consumption when goods are available, the belief that subjects are entitled to benefits in the form of subsidies, grants, preferences and jobs from their rulers in return for loyalty; the notion that loyalty is contingent upon the receipt of benefits from rulers; the belief that prosperity is a matter of good fortune or cleverness; and the tradition of sharing within the tribe. Development in the Gulf appears to be taking place, in the sense that industries are established and incomes are rising, but the local population is not acquiring the values associated with modern productive life. A country with modern industries and other facilities is being developed, but largely through the efforts of expatriates. What has emerged is a social order in which the locals are consumers and the expatriates are the producers. Many young Arabs have been cut off from the traditional Arab way of life but have not acquired modern attitudes toward work, time, cause and result. They have as one Arab intellectual put it, become 'cultureless consumers'. The well known wry self-deprecating Arab proverb implicitly captures this distinction between temporary wealth that results from good fortune and wealth that comes through productive enterprise: 'My father rode a camel. I ride a Cadillac. My son flies a jet. My grandson will have a supersonic plane. But my great grandson, he will be a camel driver.'

ARAB VERSUS SOUTH ASIAN EXPATRIATES

In 1975 South Asians constituted 32.7 per cent of the labor force of the five Gulf states. Arab expatriates formed 25 per cent of the labor force. Throughout the Gulf there is an inverse relationship between the proportion of Palestinians – the principal Arab migrants –

and the proportion of South Asians. Bahrain, Oman and the United Arab Emirates, with 4 per cent, 4 per cent, and 8 per cent Palestinians in the migrant population respectively, have 63 per cent, 71 per cent , and 68 per cent South Asians. In Qatar the proportion of Palestinians is 18 per cent, and the proportion of South Asians drops to 57 per cent. In Kuwait, Palestinians form 40 per cent of the migrant population, and south Asians 11 per cent. In Saudi Arabia Palestinians are 34 per cent of the migrant population and south Asians are 5 per cent. Palestinians are among the most educated and skilled migrants. At the top of the labor market, a disproportionate percentage of the most educated manpower is expatriate and these jobs are held by Indians, Palestinians, Egyptians, and Lebanese. Where Arabs fill these positions, there are fewer Indians.

Publicly, officials in the Gulf states have expressed a preference for fellow Arabs over Asians and other foreigners. But Arabs (and Iranians) bring in the ideologies that pervade public life in Iraq, Egypt, Syria, Libya, Iran and Jordan. Both Bahrain and Oman restrict entrance of Palestinians. Bahrain's Sunni rulers are also concerned with the spread of Islamic fundamentalism from Iran among the local Shiite population and the rulers of Oman are fearful of influence from Communist Yemen. Kuwait fears domination from Iraq, which has made claims upon its territory, Bahrain fears Iran, which has also made territorial claims (and it turns an anxious eye toward Saudi Wahabi fundamentalism); and Oman is leary of Arab allies of the Soviet Union.

Another reason for not giving preference to Arab migrants is that it is difficult to reject their claims, as fellow Arabs, to the same medical benefits, free schooling, subsidized housing, and government employment that the state ensures the local Arab population.

In contrast, Asian migrants do not bear the baggage of political ideologies and make few demands. They do not interact with the local Arab population, do not make claims upon the state for benefits, do not expect to live in the country permanently, and can be expelled at will by the Gulf governments with far fewer political repercussions than would result from the expulsion of Arabs. Moreover, Asian migrants often have skills that are not so easily provided by migrants from Arab counties, and they are willing to engage in jobs that Arabs often will not accept.

South Asians also have advantages over Europeans and Americans. They need not be paid as much for the same work, and they do not require the costly housing and other amenities that must be provided to attract Europeans and Americans. South Asians are also more likely to stay as long as they are needed, since they are not attracted by job opportunities at home. And since middle class South Asian migrants speak English, they have an advantage over Thais and Koreans.

Gulf governments have little fear that any of the South Asian governments could do more than mildly protest mistreatment of migrants, nor would they be likely to suddenly withdraw migrants for political reasons or attempt to use migrants to extend their influence. India is dependent upon the Gulf for oil, exports, employment, remittances, contracts and for the good will that it seeks as counterweight in its relations with Pakistan. The Indian government is thus willing to tolerate conditions for Indians in the Gulf that it would not tolerate for its citizens elsewhere, and its interventions on their behalf are likely to be in a subdued and less public fashion.

INTERACTIONS OF MIGRANTS AND LOCALS, SELECTED STATES

United Arab Emirates

South Asian constitute the largest of the expatriate communities in the United Arab Emirates. In a total population in 1975, including migrants, of 656,000, 202,000 were Pakistanis and another 107,000 were Indians. The indigenous population numbered 200,000 and there were approximately 120,000 Arab migrants, including a large number of Palestinians. In 1979, with a population of 877,000, the Indian population was estimated by the Indian Ministry of External Affairs at 152,000.[22]

The UAE is a federation, the only functioning Arab federation, consisting of the oil-producing emirates of Abu Dhabi, Dubai, and the small emirate of Sharjah, together with the poorer 'village states' of Ras al Khaimah, Umm al Qaiwain, Ajman, and Al Fujairah. Social services are provided by the federal budget. Each of the emirates, however, is free to use its own oil surplus for development projects without approval from the central government. The result is often duplicate and redundant projects. Though Sharjah and Dubai are only a few miles apart, each has an international airport. Dubai and Bahrain have drydocks for the repair of tankers, and both have aluminum plants. The result is a conflict of interest between the emirates, each of which wants its own development projects, and the planning unit within the federal government which would prefer coordinated development and investment in capital intensive projects where less long term labor is required and indirect social costs are kept low.

Dubai. The Indian merchant community has long been associated with Dubai. Arab dhows, many Indian owned, regularly imported goods from South Asia and East Africa into Dubai from where they were shipped to other parts of the Gulf and throughout the Arabian peninsula. The Indian merchants and their Arab partners also established an extensive illegal trade (the euphemistic term is "re-export"), sending to Indian goods whose importation was restricted by the Government of India — gold, watches, tape recorders, and transistors.

An estimated 3,000 Indian merchant families live in Dubai, many having come well before the recent oil boom. The Sindhi Hindus dominate the textile trade and the Gujarati Hindus dominate the gold market. The merchants created an Indian Association as early as 1941. The association runs a club-house, organized in 1963, which maintains a bar, shows movies, organizes dances and other functions, and has its own restaurant. The association founded a school in 1962, which has a current enrollment of 3,800 children and a lengthy waiting list. The merchants also erected the Sri Krishna temple inconspicuously located in a small street near the Old Fort. The temple is well attended on Hindu Holidays, but members of the community avoid processions and other public observances that would call attention to their presence and offend the religious sensibilities of the Muslim population.

The 'new' migrants came to Dubai with the oil and construction boom. The Dubai Petroleum Company (DPC) employs 215 Indians in its central office, out of a staff of 596, and it is steadily replacing Americans and British on the staff with lower paid Indians and other Asians at the rate of 20 to 25 per year. Most Indian personnel at DPC have brought their families, and DBC employs many of the wives in clerical jobs. Indians, like other expatriates, are given three-year work permits by the government, which are easily renewed.

The Indian community provides trade expertise, skilled manpower, and its loyal support for the rulers of Dubai. In return the temple, the Indian club, the Indian school, the Hindu cremation grounds, and the many business interests of the merchant community are under the benign protection of the government.

The Indian community in Dubai is one of the most settled in the region. Indians constitute such a large proportion of the manpower in trade and commerce that Hindi is almost as widely used in the souk as Arabic. The new migrants have moved into supervisory jobs, staff the technical positions in the electric power plants, provide medical personnel for hospitals, and constitute the largest pool of office workers and store clerks. Cinema houses in Dubai regularly show Indian films in Malayalam and Hindi and there are numerous small Indian restaurants. As one Indian migrant noted, 'if there were elections here, Dubai would probably have a Malayalee mayor – his election campaign financed, of course by a Sindhi Merchant'.

Abu Dhabi. The employment situation for the Indian community in nearby Abu Dhabi is almost as favourable as in Dubai. Employment opportunities are so great that this emirate has drawn the largest number of Indians in the Gulf. The construction boom brought in unskilled and semi skilled construction workers and a large middle class of engineers, managers, doctors, nurses, and clerical workers.

Here too the Indian community has created a network of local associations to minister to its social needs: the Malayalee Samajam, the Indian Center, the Kerala Arts Center, the Indian Ladies Association, the Indian Islamic Center (an organization of Kerala Muslims), and St. Joseph's Club (attached to the Catholic Church). Hindu festivities are observed in the schools, the clubs, and in shrines at home since there is no public temple. The Indian Ladies Association runs a Kindergarten, and the Indian Center and the Catholic Church each run a school. The two schools are already overcrowded, and plans are underway to expand both and possibly start a third.

Members of the Indian middle class privately complain that they are paid less than the Europeans or the many Arabs from Egypt, Lebanon, and Jordan who have settled here. Wages paid to Indian and Pakistani workers on construction sites are also sometimes below market wages and even below those provided by contract. Accommodations and health facilities on some of the construction sites are inadequate. However, dissatisfied migrants have little recourse. Workers are legally tied to employers through the system of work permits[23] and a worker dismissed by his employer for whatever cause is legally required to leave the country. When a group of Indian workers in Abu Dhabi threatened to strike after contractors said that Muslim workers need only work six hours during Ramadan, but Hindus had to continue to work eight hours, the Indian Embassy reminded the workers that the employees were within their legal rights and that unions and strikes were illegal.

But such protests are infrequent. The differential between wages in India and wages in the Gulf for construction work is so great that workers migrate eagerly and, when jobs end, readily sign up for new construction projects. The large construction companies, such as Joannov and Paraskevaides (a Cypriot firm), Bernard Sunley (British), and Engineering Products India, obtain group visas from the UAE Labor Ministry, then recruit workers in India. They pay $6 to $7 a day to most construction workers, plus free accommodations, medical care, and subsidized food. It is common for unskilled workers to remit US $100 per month back to India, several times what their earnings would be at home.

Abu Dhabi officials are aware that they are more dependent upon expatriates than other states in the Gulf, and they would like to reduce the number of expatriates. But only 20 per cent of the local population is in the labor force. Moreover, perhaps a third of the population is outside the urban centers. (In fact the emirates encourage Bedouins to remain in the desert and smaller settlements by delivering medical and educational services to them.) Furthermore, educational levels are low in spite of a considerable investment in primary and secondary school education. The dropout rate is high, and only a few hundred students are enrolled in the secondary school in Abu Dhabi. Those who wish employment can readily join the Abu Dhabi army or government service without completing secondary school.

One official in the UAE Planning Ministry noted that every key sector of the economy of Abu Dhabi was dependent upon foreigners: Egyptians in the educational system, Omanis and Sudanese in the army, Palestinians in the Information and Planning ministries, and Indians in development projects and in the service sector. The same official questioned the strategy of investing in industrial projects that forced them to import foreign workers to run the new industries, build housing for the workers, and provide public services, all of which in turn required that they import still more foreign workers.

Bahrain

Expatriates form 40 per cent of the labor force in this state, a group of islands off the Arabian coast with a local population of 225,000. There are 30,200 migrant workers and 46,800 local workers.[24] Bahrain thus has the smallest proportion of foreign workers of any of the Gulf states. But paradoxically there is also more concern over the presence of foreigners than elsewhere and a greater governmental effort to reduce dependence upon expatriates.

Bahrain was the first country in the Gulf to develop oil (1932), and it has had the misfortune of seeing its oil resources depleted as prices have risen. It is expected to be the first state in the region to run out of oil. Production in 1978 was only 51 thousand barrels a day, compared with 2.5 million for Kuwait.[25] Still, its net earnings from oil leaped from $68 million in 1972 to $528 million in 1977. This phenomenal growth in revenues enabled Bahrain to expand production of electric power, water, and sewerage facilities, and to develop its port, airport, roads, schools, hospitals, and public housing. Living standards and personal consumption grew for the entire population, facilitated in part by generous food subsidies.

In an effort to reduce its dependence upon the sale of oil, Bahrain has developed an aluminium plant (Aluminium Bahrain, or ALBA), expanded its port facilities, built repair yards and drydocks, and created an 'off shore' banking industry (widely known as OBUs, or

Offshore Banking Units) to provide banking facilities for the entire region. Bahrain's development strategy is to become a service and entrepôt center for the Gulf. It provides generous incentives to investors, has attracted the international banks, is expanding investment in petrochemicals and steel, and proposes to become the trade and commercial outlet for Saudi Arabia—with which it expects to be connected by a Saudi-financed causeway.

Bahrain's labor supply has been insufficient to meet the demands of these new investments, the expansion or its social services, and the growth of its trade. Like other Gulf states, it imported a labor supply; unlike many other Gulf states it had a particularly strong preference for South Asians and a marked disinclination to admit many Arabs.

Bahrain's Indian connection is an old one. As early as 2000 BC Bahrain – or Dilmun, as the island was then called – was an important commercial center linking Mesopotamia with the Indus valley. Ships from Dilmun carried gold, ivory, timber, and lapis Iazuli from India to Babylonia, shipped copper from Oman to Mesopotamia in return for woolen goods and vegetables, and sold local pearls and dates. Excavations of ancient tumuli on the island reveal 100,000 grave sites, indicating the size of the population and the importance of Dilmun as a trade center.

In the first half of the twentieth century Bahrain was a British protectorate controlled by the Government of India with a political agent accountable to the Viceroy. Indian merchants established import business in rice, tea, sugar and shoes, subsidized Arab smugglers in gold and pearls, and managed the trade in hashish and opium, transshipping from Kabul to Bombay, then from Bombay to the Gulf and elsewhere in the Middle East. With the development of Bahrain Petroleum Company (BAPCO) in the 1930s and the establishment of refineries, Indians arrived as clerks and technicians, more merchants came from the Indian province of Sindh and from Gujarat, and nurses came from Kerala to work in hospitals. But the major influx, as elsewhere in the region, took place after 1972, only a year after Bahrain gained independence. Indians and others were imported for construction work and for employment in the aluminium plant, shipping, banking, and petrochemicals.

The government's Bahrainization policy specifies that employers try to hire qualified Bahrainis before importing foreign labor, that employers train and promote Bahrainis, and that expatriates be required to leave when Bahrainis are available to take their positions. The government has given considerable attention to vocational training and established training centers at BAPCO, ALBA, Gulf Air (which has its headquarters in Bahrain), and in the local hotels. There are also several technical secondary schools. During the boom years from 1974 to 1976 the rules on importing labor were relaxed, but thereafter the Labor Department tightened its control over the issuance of work cards to foreigners.[26]

The government has initiated a program to train 10,000 Bahraini nationals for positions currently held by expatriates. The Ten Thousand Scheme, as it is called, involves the training of employer-chosen applicants for the Bahrain Gulf Technical College. According to a report in the *Economist*,[27] the scheme has met with little success since 'companies claim they cannot find competent Bahrainis and are obliged to hire expatriates if they want things done efficiently. . . their lack of experience or formal qualifications, or their poor command of English, prevents their being promoted'. As for the retraining schemes, 'the employers objections are that their Bahraini employees do not take their training seriously but think that any certificate automatically entitles them to demand more money'. Bahrainis, say employers, are still illequipped for the jobs available in engineering, computers, accountancy, clerical work, and management and show little interest in government and employer-created training programs. Few Bahraini employees, they report, enrolled for training under the Ten Thousand Scheme.

While the Ten Thousand Scheme has proceeded slowly, the scheme it-self is an indication of how sensitive the government is to complaints by Bahrainis that too many expatriates are given jobs that Bahrainis should have. The Shiites in Bahrain, who constitute a majority of the population, have pressed hard for restrictions on the employment of expatriates since, some of them say, the ruling Amir has given preferences in employment to fellow Sunnis and to expatriates in an effort to limit the status of the Shiites. But the policy of Bahrainization is apparently widely supported by the entire middle class, who are resentful of the predominance of non-Bahrainis in the private sector. Educated Bahrainis are assured of positions within the government, and government employment according to one official estimate has increased at 10 per cent per year, enough to absorb the output of Bahrainis from schools and colleges. But the best jobs in offshore banking, in the dockyards, and in the recently established satellite communications facility continue to be held by expatriates.[28]

One reason educated Bahrainis do not move into these positions is that many have had their advanced education in Baghdad and Riyadh, in a system of education that does not adequately prepare them for the more skilled positions in the private sector, where as one British employer put it, 'a western work ethic and fluency in English' are required as well as technical and administrative skills.

Indians seem particularly able to compete for many of these positions. Their knowledge of English and their level and type of education and experience give the Indians an edge over most Arabs, and their willingness to work for lower wages gives them an edge over Europeans and Americans. In spite of the decline in the construction industry and the decrease in the number of unskilled workers entering the country, the Indian population is increasing. In the mid-1970s, there were 9,000 Indian workers in Bahrain, 6,700 Pakistanis, 6,200 migrants from other Arab countries, and several thousand Iranians. More recent figures on the composition of the non-national labor force are not available, but the Bahrain Sports Club, the largest single Indian institution in the country with a membership of 1,200 families and the Indian school with 1,800 children have both expanded rapidly in the last five years.

The comparatively liberal atmosphere of Bahrain makes it a more attractive place for Indians and other foreigners to live than other countries in the Gulf. There are more young educated Arab women and a larger middle class than elsewhere. Drinking is permitted, and Bahrain has a modest night life that is absent elsewhere in the Gulf or in Saudi Arabia. But precisely because there is a large, growing, secularized, and increasingly politicized middle class, there is more anxiety among the expatriate middle class Indians. With the prospects ahead of declining revenue from oil, and an indigenous middle class that views expatriates as a block to opportunities and income, Indian middle class migrants in Bahrain have more reason to be uneasy than Indians elsewhere in the Gulf.

Oman

Oman is both a labor-importing and labor-exporting country. Before the accession of the present Sultan in 1970, Oman was an isolated country, torn by tribal conflicts, sectarian clashes between Sunnis and Ibadi Muslims, and between the Sultan and supporters of the rival imam. Oman was nominally independent, but throughout the nineteenth century and in the first half of the twentieth British officials of the Government of India policed the region. Members of the Indian Political Service and the Indian Civil Service were posted in Muscat as Agents and Residents. The Sultan and his family, the British officials, the tribal leaders, and the merchant community constituted the politically important groups in the country.

In the nineteenth century Indian merchants dominated the economy of Oman. They were the import and export agents for Western companies, managed the wholesale and retail trade, and were bankers. 'By 1856,' writes the historian Robert Landen, 'few products were exchanged in the Omani empire . . . without an Indian merchant being involved in the transaction in some capacity.'[29]

The Indian merchants included Khojas, Muslims from the province of Sindh (now in Pakistan), sometimes called Hyderabadis, but most commonly known as Ismaelis; Baluchi Muslims from the Makran coast of Pakistan; and Hindu merchants from Kutch, on the Gujarat coast. Many of the Baluchis and Khojas were made Omani citizens 'diluted Omanis' they have been called[30] – but the Hindu merchants were not.

The domination of Oman by a fundamentalist regime in the 1860s threatened the Hindu merchants. 'Imam Azzan,' writes Landen, 'claimed he did not want to interfere with their religion, yet he objected to the use of drums, bells and cymbals in Hindu religious ceremonies.'[31] As Hindus were beaten, plundered, and murdered, many of merchants emigrated to Zanzibar and other trading centers along the East African coast. Another exodus took place in the early 1930s with a shift in trade from Oman to Dubai.

But the Hindu merchants held a secure place in the country's economy. They linked the coast and the interior when the government in Muscat was limited to a handful of coastal towns. Their financial position remained relatively secure, for even when the economy was relatively stagnant they continued to import food to Oman, export dates to India, manage the pearl trade from Bahrain, and link Oman to Zanzibar, Somalia, and Mozambique. Indian merchants worked closely with government officials, walis (provincial governors appointed by the Sultan), and the ruling family, often serving as their bankers. On the eve of World War II, a prominent Indian merchant family from Kutch became contractors for the RAF.

Notwithstanding the trade and the British and Indian presence, Oman remained one of the more isolated and underdeveloped countries of the world before 1970. There was no industrial development. There was only one major medical facility run by missionaries. The Sultan prohibited Omanis from leaving the country without his permission (though many slipped out to live in exile) and forbade them to wear western clothing. Movement within the country, even within the capital, was restricted. The gates to the walled town of Muscat were closed three hours before sunset. Fearful of a coup from his fellow Arabs, the Sultan encouraged Indian merchants to build their homes and shops around the palace. The Sultan recruited soldiers from Baluchistan, a process made easier by the fact that until 1958 Oman had possession of the port of Gwadar on the Makran coast. Even after Gwadar was sold to Pakistan, the Sultan continued to recruit Baluchis for his armed forces. The Sultan also turned to the Government of India for advisers, and some Indian officials were sent on deputation to the police and to the public works departments.

In 1970, the Sultan, Said bin Taymur, was overthrown by his son, the present Sultan, Qabus bin Said Al Bu Said, with the help of the British. The old Sultan moved to London where he lived in Claridges Hotel until he died a few years ago.

The development of oil production in Oman in 1967 and the change of government in 1970 initiated a new era in the country's modernization. Oil revenues were used to develop agriculture and animal husbandry. Refrigeration and processing facilities were built for the fishing industry. New industries were established in cement, petrochemicals, and oil refining. The port was upgraded. Roads were built, and the capital area, consisting of Ruwi, Muttrah, Muscat, a string of towns along the coast was linked with a single highway. There was much construction, including a large modern shopping area in Ruwi, hotels, movie houses, offices, a new palace in Muscat, and new government buildings. The demand for construction workers sharply declined after 1975, but a number of new projects, some already under way and others in advanced stages of planning, require expatriate labor – a refinery, glass factory, steel rolling mill, copper plant, new pipeline, and a new major road, Oman has little oil compared with the oil-rich states up the Gulf, and until recently it was believed that oil production would soon come to an end. But new reserves have been found, and it is now expected that Oman has enough oil to continue exports at least until the end of the century.

Since Oman's educational system was underdeveloped and so many educated Omanis had left the country, there was a shortage of trained manpower. In the early 1970s an influx of migrant workers began, mainly from Pakistan and India. By 1975, according to the Oman Labor Department, there were 70,000 foreign workers in Oman, as against 99,000 nationals in the labor force, but Birks and Sinclair put the foreign labor force at 81,000 and the World Bank at 104,000. It is also reported that an additional 38,000 Omanis are employed abroad. Since much of the Omani labor force is engaged in agriculture, it is very likely that a majority of the labor force in the urban areas, especially in the capital region, is foreign.

With its local Ibadi Muslim population, a Baluchi community, an African population made up of descendants of former slaves, Shi'as from Iran, two Sunni Arab tribal groups in the province of Dhofar, Arabs who had returned from Zanzibar where they formed the ruling class, Hyderabadi and Kuchi merchants from Pakistan and India, and now Indian and Pakistani construction workers and middle class technicians and managers, Oman has become one of the most culturally heterogeneous countries in the region. The Indian Embassy estimates that there were about 60,000 Indians in Oman in 1979. The largest numbers come from Kerala, and the remainder from Goa, Gujarat, and the Punjabi. Hindi, along with Arabic, is the language of the souks in Muscat, Ruwi, and Muttrah and other towns along the coast. Egyptians work as teachers, as they do in most of the Gulf states. The army consists of Omanis and Baluchis with some British officers.[32] The merchants are Khojas, Kutchis, and Baluchis. Engineers, managers, and technical and administrative personnel of all kinds are expatriates. One Indian is technical advisor to the Sultan, with managerial responsibilities for the Sultan's private properties. The palace itself was built by an Indian construction company from Bombay, which now has offices in Oman and a number of government contracts. Some police officers are recruited from India, and it is said that several regiments in the army are entirely Baluchis. 'Whatever is done here,' said one foreigner, exaggerating somewhat, 'is the work of expatriates, not Omanis.'

The small number of educated Omanis – and they are few in number – hold positions in government, but few Omanis have had opportunities to develop skills beyond agriculture, date cultivation, and fishing, Oman's traditional major economic activities. 'The pace of development has been too fast here,' noted an expatriate. 'The people here are unprepared. They want consumer goods, not education.'

Some of the Omanis who fled the country during the reign of Said bin Taymur, the father of the present Sultan, returned after 1970, but many continue to work outside. Many are employed in the armies of neighboring Gulf states: quite a few work in the nearby emirates of Dubai and Abu Dhabi where salaries are higher than in Oman.

Social life among the various communities in Oman remains highly segmented. The Indian middle class has some social contacts with English-speaking Lebanese, Jordanians, and Zanzibar Arabs, but almost no social contact with native Omanis. In 1974 the Sultan gave land to the Indian community to enable them to build a social center. There are now several schools for Indian children, a Roman Catholic Church, a few Protestant churches, and several temples, including a gurdwara for the Sikh community. The Sultan's government has a reputation for greater religious tolerance than is the case for most of the other Gulf states or for Wahabi-dominated Saudi Arabia.

The incident involving Indian labor for a Cypriot-owned construction firm, briefly mentioned earlier, indicates how powerful are the forces keeping Indians in Oman. Under Omani law an employer must provide a minimum wage of 3.6 rials daily, accommodations, and food – wages that are roughly one half of what is paid in other Gulf states. This large construction company paid its Indian workers only 2 rials, provided them with tents rather than wooden barracks for accommodations (with temperatures reaching 50 °C) and inadequate medical facilities, paid steamship rather than air transportation to India, and kept its workers on yearly rather than three-year contracts so it did not have to pay the annual increments required by law. The company, it was reported, regularly 'packed off' workers who protested. Several government ministers warned company officials that they were breaking Omani law, especially after there were reports of massive discontent among the workers. But even after the warning, the company called in the police, picked up 'trouble makers', and within a few hours had them on a plane to Bombay. Other workers then protested to the Indian Embassy, which informed the Omani government. The workers launched a slowdown, which came to an end when the Omani police arrested some 2,000 workers. Once again the Indian Embassy protested, but the police commissioner was 'out of town', and the ministers of external affairs and labor could not be reached. The Indian Ambassador arranged the release of most of the workers, but 200 were deported. The Government of India was outraged and halted the emigration of all workers to Oman effective February 1978. The Oman government requested that the ban be lifted so that relations between the two countries 'would not be spoiled'. 'It was just an incident,' said one Omani official. There were clamors in Kerala and elsewhere in India that the ban be lifted. In July 1978, the government ended the ban, but it refused to allow workers to emigrate for employment with the offending company.

Though salaries in Oman are lower than in other Gulf states, they remain attractive for South Asians, especially since the cost of living in Oman is lower than elsewhere in the region. Workers with minimal skills can earn from 80 to 100 rials a month ($240 to $300) plus food and accommodations. Workers can save 60 rials a month ($180 or Rs 1,400). More skilled workers such as mason helpers, carpenters, and drivers can save Rs 2,000 a month. Remittances to India from Oman run $100 million a year.

As elsewhere, immigrants cannot become citizens. A few exceptions have been made for a handful of Indian businessmen – an important privilege since it entitles them to own their own businesses without an Omani 'silent partner.' But the Indian business community, perhaps because it is well-entrenched in the local economy, is anxious about its future. In 1974, following talk in official circles of expelling Indian businessmen, the Sultan himself introduced the policy that required that 51 per cent of ownership of a business be Omani. In practice Omani agents – often government officials or members of the ruling family – simply receive a fee from Indian businessmen in return for registering as the owner. Indian merchants fear that Khojas and Baluchis who are Omani citizens will try to remove them by allying themselves with some of the Omani 'silent partners' in the government.

Kuwait

Does the overwhelming presence of a foreign population retard the movement toward parliamentary politics in the Gulf? The experience of Kuwait suggests that it may be a factor affecting the behaviour of the ruling Sheiks and perhaps even of sections of the middle class that elsewhere has been in the forefront of the attack against monarchies.

Kuwait has been governed by what one writer describes as a 'royal family-merchant oligarchy . . . and the armed forces',[33] a description that would apply to all the Gulf states. The royal family, the Al Sabahs, which informally shares its power with aristocratic merchant families, agreed to a constitution in 1962 that established an elected National Assembly. Of a total population of one million, only 472,000 were Kuwaitis, and of these only 50,000 were qualified to vote. The first assembly was elected in January 1963, and from the beginning there were sharp political cleavages between supporters of the amir and leftist opponents supported by the large Jordanian/Palestinian immigrant population. In 1967 unions went on strike against the government for not giving adequate support to front line Arab states in the war with Israel. Thereafter, the royal family took a more positive role in supporting the Palestinian cause. The Kuwait government funded the Palestine Liberation Organization and in the 1973 war sent troops to fight on the Suez Canal. The government permitted Palestinians to enter government service and gave them a voice in the news media. Palestinians sought a larger role in Kuwaiti affairs and objected to the Kuwaiti nationality law of 1966 that set an upper limit of 50 on the number of aliens that could become naturalized citizens each year.[34] They opposed Kuwait's relationship with Egypt and Kuwait's moderate position in advocating a cease fire in Lebanon in 1976. Members of the governing elite became alarmed at the increasing signs of militancy among the Palestinians and their Kuwaiti supporters. In August 1976 Amir Sabah prorogued the assembly and suspended the constitution, 'ending the fourteen years of Parliamentary experimentation in Kuwait'.[35] Strikes and public meetings were banned, the press was placed under tight control, and public opposition to the government was ended.

Kuwait is educationally the most developed country in the region. Fifty-five per cent of the Kuwait population are literate, well above the UAE (14 per cent). Oman (20 per cent), Iraq (26 per cent), Qatar (33 per cent), Saudi Arabia (33 per cent), and even Bahrain (47 per cent). Among the Arab states only Lebanon (68 per cent), and Jordan(62 per cent) have higher literacy rates. Kuwait's death rate is among the lowest in the region and life expectancy at birth is the highest. Its small national population and its extraordinarily high gross national product as a result of its high oil production (2.5 million barrels a day, about a tenth of the output in the Middle East) combine to give Kuwait the world's highest per capita income. It was $17,100 in 1979, well above that of the United States ($10,630), and even well ahead of Saudi Arabia ($7,280).[36] Kuwait began to export crude oil in 1946, and output accelerated in the 1950s at a rate of 17 per cent a year. Development projects were initiated in the early 1950s with the establishment of a water distillation plant, and there was a steady pace of new projects long before the great boom of the mid-1970s. The government of Kuwait moved more cautiously than did some of the other Gulf states. It did not suffer from the uncontrolled construction activities that look place elsewhere in the Gulf, and it avoided making many unproductive investments.

Nonetheless, the expansion of social services, the decision to make new housing available to the Kuwait population, and the construction of new industries led to a massive infusion of expatriates. Yet the mid-1970s this small country had imported a labor force that was twice as the national labor force, 211,000 to 87,000. The bulk of the migrant workers came from other Arab countries — Egypt, Jordan, Yemen, Syria, Lebanon, and Oman. Another 29,000 came from Iran, 21,000 from India, and 11,000 from Pakistan. With their dependents, the migrants totalled over half a million.

Indians and Pakistanis form a small proportion of the migrant labor force in Kuwait in part because there are so many Palestinians — about 200,000, or 40 per cent of the migrant population.

There were, 32,000 Indian and 23,000 Pakistani migrant workers and their dependents in Kuwait in 1975. In 1979 the Indian government estimated that the number of Indians had risen to 65,000. More than half of the Indian migrants are in unskilled occupations, either in construction or working as domestics. There are also many Indians in the health services as nurses and doctors.[37] Migrants from Kerala are the largest single ethnic group among the Indians and of these a higher proportion are Christian than elsewhere in the Gulf. Christian girls from Kerala and Goa work as nurses and ayahs. (The Catholic Church is the largest Indian institution in Kuwait, and its Bishop, a Spaniard, served in Kerala before coming to Kuwait.) Many of the migrants are Moplahs, or Malayalee-speaking Sunni Muslims from Kerala. Some of the professional businessmen and many of the construction workers are Hindu. The Indians have several social clubs and three schools. There are no Hindu temples – government permission has not been granted to build one – but there are Hindu shrines and Sikh gurdwaras at construction sites.

As elsewhere in the region, the Indian connection with Kuwait is an old one. In the days when Kuwait was little more than a small fishing and pearldiving town, dhows engaged in trade with India. Seals found in the nearby island of Failaka suggest that Kuwait was on the trading route from Mesopotamia to the Indus. Well before British rule, Arab traders visited Kerala, some settling in the Indian town of Calicut and intermarrying with the local population. Indians found work in Kuwait as pearl divers, and Indian merchants shipped tea and rope from Kerala in return for dates brought to Kuwait from Basra. With the establishment of a British presence in Kuwait, Indian influence grew. Indian officials lived and worked in Kuwait and the Indian rupee became the official currency. With the development of oil after the war, British companies moved into Kuwait, importing some personnel from India. In 1962 Kuwait became independent.

Migrants came to Kuwait in three waves. Iraqis, Saudis, and Omanis settled in Kuwait in the 1930s; in the 1950 came Palestinians, Iraqis, and Iraninans; a third wave came with the expansion of development activities in the late 1960s through mid-1970s, with an influx of South Asians, Egyptians, and Lebanese. Kuwait City itself, a settlement of 35,000 in 1907, had a population of nearly half a million in the 1975 census.

The expansion of social services resulted in a rapid increase in the number of expatriates. Kuwait developed one of the most extensive and expensive educational programs in the region with free public education from kindergarten through university for all citizens. As an incentive, parents were paid an allowance for each child in secondary school. The government also established unusually comprehensive medical facilities and funded a massive housing program to provide accommodations for Kuwait nationals. One of the largest housing projects, located in Ardiya, a suburb of Kuwait, was constructed by Engineering Projects India (EPI).

The government of Kuwait guaranteed employment to all Kuwaiti graduates of high schools and universities. A very substantial proportion of such graduates – one estimate places it at half – is in government service.

Expatriates receive some but not all of the benefits given to nationals. Non-Kuwaitis may send their children to Arab-medium schools free, from primary school through high school but not to the university. They may use the hospitals, but Kuwaitis are given preference, and employers of large firms are encouraged to set up their own medical facilities. Housing is provided to Kuwaitis only. Kuwaiti receive government-built homes on interest-free 30-year loans. Kuwaitis and non-Kuwaitis Arabs may build and own their own homes, but non-Arabs cannot. Only Kuwaitis can participate in public share-holding companies, and all business, including small shops, must have Kuwaiti partners owning 51 per cent.

The government of Kuwait encourages foreigners to live apart from the local population. Many Indian construction workers live at the EPI site in Ardiya, while most of the longer term Indian residents reside in Salmya, a section of Kuwait City, or near the oil refinery of Ahmady. Indians do not send their children to the Arab schools, but run a school of their own. The Indian middle class has a social club, the Indian Arts Circle whose 600 members are mainly executives, businessmen, doctors, and engineers and their families.

Unlike Oman, Kuwait has virtually no old quarters, and only one old souk (where Bedouin women sell imported goods). Today, Kuwait is a large modern city, with high rise buildings, large department stores, and traffic jams. The largest 'souk' is an airconditioned two-story building in downtown Kuwait with dozens of small shops selling watches, jewelry, cassettes, color televisions, stylish clothing, and furniture imported from Japan, Taiwan, south Korea, West Germany, Switzerland, and the United States. Houses built for Kuwaitis are spacious and well constructed. In the Indian-built project of Ardiya there are 3,500 homes, each with 3,000 square meters including a deewanya, the traditional men's sitting room, a large kitchen, three large bedrooms, a family room, an enclosed verandah, an open walled roof and a garage. Since mortality rates are low and birth rates very high, Kuwaiti families are large, and employment of imported servants, especially ayahs, is common among the middle class.

Though fewer Indians hold technical, administrative, and white collar positions in Kuwait than elsewhere in the Gulf, the Indians have a relatively secure position as domestics, in the hotel industry, and in the medical services. With the slowdown in construction, however, there has emerged a class of "floating" Indian workers who look for work illegally. Both government and employers have tried to prevent such a free labor market from developing. Efforts by EPI to stop their own workers from looking for jobs elsewhere provide one example of how an Indian firm and the government of Kuwait have worked together. EPI employs 6,000 Indians. Its unskilled workers are paid $200 to $250 per month, plus room (in barracks) and board (in mess halls), medical care, canteens, sports, and free movies. When workers discovered that they could earn higher wages with other construction companies, some changed their jobs or took leave to pick up higher day wages when other projects needed short-term labor. When EPI tried to halt the loss of its manpower its workers went on strike for higher wages. The director of EPI, a former Indian military officer, dismissed the union leaders and reported workers who had left in violation of their work permit. The government deported the union leaders and workers without appropriate permits, and the strike ended.[38] EPI subsequently raised its wages closer to prevailing market rates.

INTERNATIONAL MIGRATION POLICIES

Whether migrants will continue to be admitted into the Gulf states, in what numbers, what kinds of jobs they will get, and how long they will be allowed to remain are all matters of government policy of the Gulf states. India, Pakistan, or any other country could, of course, refuse to allow its workers to exit, but it is politically difficult for sending countries to halt emigration and in no case are they in a position to recall their workers. The Indian and Pakistani governments view emigration as desirable, and it is only at the margins that they try to influence the process. Whatever scholars may say about the social costs of emigration, sending countries are usually unwilling and unable to intervene in the process. For India and Pakistan, the greatest anxieties are over an end to emigration to the Gulf or, even worse, a forcible repatriation of migrants.

Gulf state migration policies must be understood not only within the economic and demographic context of rich countries with large government revenues, rapid investments, small populations, and low labor force participation rates, but also within the political context of autocratic regimes, politically nonparticipant populations, policymaking by a small group of men, and pan-Arab sentiments tempered by elite anxieties over the intrusion of political ideologies and influences from neighboring Arab countries. There are some variations among the Gulf countries, but in the main similar migration policies are pursued throughout the region.

1. All migrants are temporary, but the migration process is enduring. No Gulf state permits migrants to become citizens.[39] Even stateless Palestinians are denied citizenship though many spend their entire lives in a single country. Work and residence permits are given for limited periods, although they are renewable. In practice, an increasing number of migrants stay for extended periods, and some may remain for their entire working lives, but they always remain legally 'temporary' residents; with little notice, they may be asked by the government to leave. At the same time, the migration process is continuous and durable. As people leave, they are replaced by others. Foreign labor is required in so many sectors of the economy that no government in the Gulf could end migration – or expel the migrant population – without damaging the economy and reducing social services. It is

critical to distinguish between the insecurity of the individual migrant and the stability of the migration process.

2. Migrants are incorporated into the economic structure but are excluded from the social structure. Separation, not integration or assimilation, is the goal. As a matter of policy migrants are housed in separate communities away from the local population. There are no programs for incorporating migrant children into local schools. Social contacts between Arabs and expatriates are minimized. Migrants create their own infrastructures for community life – sports, clubs, restaurants, cinemas, schools, and, in a few places, their own religious institutions.

3. The political rights of migrants are restricted. Migrant workers may neither form nor join unions. Public meetings are prohibited. Associations must be confined to social functions. Religious life must be circumspect. Violation of these rules may lead to immediate expulsion from the country. Law-breakers, including those found guilty of traffic violations, may also be expelled. It should be noted, however, that political rights for the local population are also restricted. Elections have been permitted in Kuwait and in Bahrain, but, in the main, regimes throughout the Gulf are autocratic, and the freedom to organize unions, political organizations, the right of assembly, and a free press are either absent or carefully circumscribed.[40]

4. There is no free labor market. Migrants may receive work permits after obtaining No Objection Certificates from the government. Workers may not change employers without the consent of their original employer and the Ministry of Labor and Social Affairs. Workers can be deported if they accept employment with a second employer without obtaining the consent of their original employers and the ministry. They can also be deported for 'incitement of workers to strike or to refrain from working' or 'physical or verbal attacks on employers or supervisors'.[41] These legal provisions prevent trade union activities, force workers to remain with their original employer irrespective of alternative opportunities, and enable employers to arbitrarily set wage rates. Work permits are also of limited duration and must be renewed by the government at periodic intervals. The government may refuse to renew a work permit if the

employer fails to demonstrate that local workers are not available, or if the government concludes that the continued presence of the alien is no longer desirable. Several Gulf states require migrants to leave the country for at least one year before obtaining a work permit from another employer.

5. Governments provide substantially fewer benefits to migrants than to the local population. The Gulf governments provide health, education, and housing benefits to the native population but not to migrants. Construction companies provide dormitories and medical services to their workers, usually near the construction site. Most of the large firms arrange for rental housing on the open market or build their own housing facilities. Many also provide medical services. Hospital facilities are available to expatriates although preferences are given to natives. No arrangements are made to provide kindergarten or school facilities for the children of non-Arab-speaking migrants.

6. Expatriates may not own businesses, land, or property. Throughout the Gulf only citizens can own these assets. Similarly, import licenses and franchises are only given to citizens, although in practice many businesses are wholly financed and managed by foreigners.

7. In the allocation of work permits to foreigners, there is no evidence that preferences are given to migrants from Arab countries. Though leaders to Gulf countries speak of their preference for migrants from Arab neighbors, both Bahrain and Oman restrict the employment of Palestinians, including Jordanians of Palestinian origin. Both of these countries have imported more South Asians than Arabs. Kuwait and the United Arab Emirates have substantial numbers of Palestinians (204,000 and 36,000 respectively), and both have strong pan-Arab tendencies, but neither has restricted employers from freely hiring Indians or Pakistanis. As noted earlier, the disadvantage of Arab migrants is that they are inclined to demand equal rights with the local population in housing, education, and health facilities; they also bring to the Gulf the political ideologies and cleavages that characterize other countries in the region. Indians and Pakistanis, in contrast, see themselves as outsiders, do not make demands upon the state, are nonpolitical, and, given the

language differences, do not politically interact with the local population.

THE FUTURE POSITION OF EXPATRIATE COMMUNITIES IN THE GULF

A World Bank study of future manpower needs in the Middle East reports that the demand for professional and paraprofessional workers 'will more than quadruple over the ten-year period [from 1975 to 1985]' and that the proportion of professionals and paraprofessionals among the migrants is likely to increase from 17 per cent in 1975 to 27 per cent by 1985. 'This upward trend in skill requirements [is] combined with [an] overall increased flow of migrants demanded by the oil exporting states.'[42]

The number of migrant workers in the Gulf states in 1975, according to World Bank estimates, was 613,000, and it is expected to rise to 1.15 million by 1985.[43] The proportion of non-nationals in the labor force is thus expected to increase from 68 per cent in 1975 to 73 per cent in 1985. The local population constituted 54 per cent of the total in 1975; by 1979 it had already declined to 47 per cent; and it is likely to decline further by 1985.

One factor in the growth of the non-national population in the Gulf is the tendency of migrant workers to bring in their dependents. The World Bank estimates that in the Middle East and North Africa the Indian and Pakistani labor force will double within the decade, but there could be more than a fourfold increase in their population. By 1985 the Indian population is expected to reach a million and the Pakistani population 1,856,000. Even if the proportion of South Asians in the migrant labor force in the Gulf remained the same – about 48 per cent their proportion of the entire population will increase as their family members migrate.

If manpower requirements alone determined the fate of the migrants, one could predict with confidence that expatriate communities would remain in the Gulf states through the remainder of this century. One could also predict an increasing trend toward lifetime migration; the shift from short-term construction workers and other unskilled labor to semi-skilled and skilled workers and the growing proportion of professional and paraprofessional migrants make a high turnover rate increasingly inefficient and uneconomical.

In any country in which the majority of the working population is deprived of citizenship and lacks the limited rights given to the national population, one might expect the migrant population to become politically demanding. And yet, for a variety of reasons, this seems unlikely in the Gulf states. For one thing, the autocratic political environment makes any form of protest movement unusually difficult. In the liberal environments of Europe and the United States, temporary migrants and even illegal migrants know they have rights and that groups within the host societies will come to their defense. In the Gulf, expatriates know that protest will result in dismissal from employment and exile from the country, and that no courts, media, interest groups, or political parties will come to their defense.

Moreover, in the case of Indians and Pakistanis, their governments and their embassies are reluctant to seek any change in the status of migrants. Both countries are concerned that wages and working conditions be stipulated by contracts and that contracts be properly adhered to by employers and enforced by the government. But the embassies of the two countries are not equipped to monitor contracts nor to investigate complaints. Moreover, both countries accept the rights of the host country to restrict migrants from owning businesses and other properties, forming trade unions, or engaging in political activity.

Nor are there any indications that the migrants themselves are prepared to openly question the terms under which they work.[44] The migrants are reluctant to do anything that might endanger their opportunity to work in the Gulf at wages that exceed by many times what they could receive at home. They may privately complain that Europeans, Americans and Arab expatriates are paid more, or that local Arabs who are less qualified are employed for the same work, but collective action to remedy the situation is unthinkable.

The asymmetry between the sending and receiving countries on migration policies is thus matched by an asymmetry between the migrants and native populations on the question of who has the power to change the relationship. Though the Arab governments fear being overwhelmed by migrants, it is the migrants who have more to fear, for individually they can be forced to leave, and collectively all of the migrants from a particular country can be expelled. Indian and Pakistani migrants, familiar with what happened to their countrymen in East Africa, correctly consider their position precarious.

Any one of the several groups might want to expel foreigners.[45] The local middle class might seek a larger share of private sector employment, particularly in Bahrain or Kuwait where this class is growing. The Arab business community in Oman, Dubai, or Abu Dhabi might want to push out expatriate businessmen and take exclusive control of trading and selling. Expatriate Arab populations within the Gulf – Palestinians, Lebanese, Egyptians, and North Africans – competitors of the Indian business and professional communities, might want to turn out the south Asians. The growing presence of non-Islamic cultural and even religious institutions might fuel an anti-foreigner, anti-non-Arab movement. Gulf governments would be hard pressed to resist political demands couched in Arab nationalist, religious fundamentalist, or secular socialist terms, all three of which could be used against Indians, Hindus, and capitalists.

Finally, while the close association between the Indian community and the rulers in each of the Gulf states has provided the migrants with an important source of security, it is also a long-term source of danger. If the protection provided by the Sheikhs for the foreign community is withdrawn, if the rulers are overthrown, the expatriates would be threatened. Paradoxically, the 'democratization' of the region would endanger the migrants, even if and perhaps especially because the migrants form a majority of the working population.

It is this sense of the precarious political position of the Indian community rather than an assessment of long-term manpower requirements in the Gulf states that makes the Indian government reluctant to build remittances into their long-term economic projections of their foreign exchange, or to make any long term assumptions about the role of emigration in relieving unemployment in selected regions of the country. In the light of what happened to Indians in Burma in the 1950s, and in East Africa in the 1960s, and the political turmoil in Iran in the 1970s, the Indian government's view may be a prudent assessment of what lies ahead. Politics, not economics, will ultimately be decisive. How the Gulf governments and politically articulate groups within the Gulf feel about expatriates in general and Indian migrants in particular, and how the relationship unfolds between the Gulf governments and India, will decide the fate of this diaspora.

NOTES

* I am grateful to the Committees on the Near and Middle East and on South Asia of the American Council of Learned Societies and the Social Science Research Council for funding my work in the Gulf. I am also grateful for the assistance provided by the Indian and American Embassies and Consulates in Kuwait, Abu Dhabi, Dubai, Manama, Ruwi, and Muscat. Officials in a variety of businesses, government departments, and Indian social institutions throughout the Gulf generously agreed to be interviewed. They include officers of the Kuwait Development Fund, Holy Family Cathedral, Engineering Projects India, the Indian School, the Ministry of Electricity and Water, the Indian Arts Circle, the Kuwait Ministry of Planning, and the Commercial Bank of Kuwait, all in Kuwait; the Ministry of Labour, the Indian Association, the Indian Sports Club, International Trade, Ltd., Dubai Petroleum Company, and McDermett Ltd., in Dubai; the Ministry of Planning, the Ministry of Labour, the Indian Social Center, the Center for Documentation and Research, and Abu Dhabi Gas Liquification Company in Abu Dhabi; the Ministry of Information, the Bahrain School, Asia Trading Company, Department of Public Works, the Immigration Department, the Ministry of Labour and Social Affairs, Transcontinental Constructions, Ltd., and the Bahrain Sports Club in Bahrain; the Indian Cultural Association, the Pakistan Embassy, the Directorate of Properties for H.M., the Ministry of Labour and Ramdas Traders in Oman; the Passport Office of the Ministry of External Affairs in New Delhi, and representatives of the World Bank, the Ford Foundation, and USAID. I also thank Emile Nakhleh, William Quandt, Jairam Ramesh, Alice Ilchman, R.D. Sharma, Roberta Ornstein, Robert Franklin, David P. Good, Richard T. McGuerty, Amelia Leiss, Ambassador Robert Pelletreau, Ambassador Giteshwar Raj, Bishop Victor San Miguel, Ambassador A.K. Budhiraja, Consul Eric Weaver, Consul V. Venketaraman, Ambassador Hamid Ansari, Ambassador H.K. Mahajan, and Ambassador L.N. Rangarajan. This study was conducted under the auspices of the Center for International Studies at the Massachusetts Institute of Technology.

1. Among the alternatives to the use of expatriates are a slower rate of investment; a major effort to increase labor force participation rates

of women; and improving the quality of the labor force through a revised educational system. But none of these alternatives seems realistic within the framework of the Gulf political systems, prevailing ideologies, and cultural beliefs.

2. J.S. Birks and C.A. Sinclair, *International Migration and Development in the Arab Region* (Geneva: International Labour Office, 1980) and, by the same authors, *Arab Manpower: The Crisis of Development*, New York: St. Martin's Press, 1980. These two books provide the most authoritative data on migration to the Middle East, but the statistics should be treated as approximations. There are contradictions in statistics published by Gulf governments, disparities between data from countries of immigration and countries of emigration, and, for several Gulf states, no census against which statistics reported by ministries could be checked. The absence of reliable data partly reflects the underdeveloped statistical facilities but may also reflect the reluctance of some Gulf governments to fully report their dependence upon expatriate labor. For my data I have relied primarily upon the Birks and Sinclair studies, but I have also made use of data provided by the United States Economic Commission for Western Asia, the World Bank, the Indian Ministry of External Affairs, and the Gulf governments. The variations, though irritating, should not affect the central arguments of this article.
3. The Indian Ministry of External Affairs estimated in 1979 that there were 500,000 Indians in the Middle East, of whom 333,000 were in the Gulf states discussed here, estimates based partly on reports from Indian embassies and partly on the number of passports issued by the Ministry. In 1978 the government issued 1.2 million passports, compared with 900,000 in 1977. In all, 4 million passports, each for five years, are currently valid.
4. United Nations and World Bank data on population growth in the Gulf states indicate continued high immigration. According to these sources, the population of the five Gulf states reported here was 2,714,000 in 1975, 3,379,000 in 1978, and 3,515,000 in 1979. This represents an increase of 800,000 persons, or 29.5 percent, over four years. A growth rate of 3 per cent annually among the local population would produce an increase of 184,000. The remainder represents natural increase among the migrant population plus new migration. In 1975, the local population, constituted 54 per cent of the population of the five Gulf states; in 1979, they had dropped to 47 per cent. The most significant changes were in Kuwait, where the local population declined from 47.4 per cent in 1975 to 41.7 per cent in 1979; and the United Arab Emirates, where the local population declined from 30.5 per cent to 25.6 per cent.

5. Figures on remittances from *Times of India*, 17 November 1979, 'Remittances from abroad increase'.
6. The Indian government does not publish data on what proportion of annual remittances comes from the Gulf states. For estimates see Z. Ecevit, 'International labor migration: Economic implications for less developed countries,' Development Economics Department, Population and Human Resources Division, World Bank, ms., 1977; and Mark Baird, 'India's balance of payments: Invisibles on current account', World Bank, ms., 1978.
7. A study of Pakistani migrants to the Middle East estimates that the average annual remittance per migrant is Rs 31,000, of which Rs 21,000 is sent in cash, Rs 7,500 brought by migrants on home visits and Rs 2,500 remitted in kind. The Pakistani data are based upon an extensive survey of migrating Pakistanis, returning migrants, and their families within Pakistan. See Ijaz Gilani, *Pakistani Emigration to the Middle East: A Cost Benefit Analysis*, Islamabad: International Migration Project, Pakistan Institute of Development Economics 1980. The study was conducted for the World Bank. If Indian per capita remittances are comparable, then the addition to India's balance of payments would range from $1.2 to $2 billion per year.
8. Raju Kurian and Dilip Thakore, 'Gulf money in Kerala: Coping with the problems of plenty', *Business India*, 25 June 1979.
9. According to a 1979 report of the Government of India Ministry of External Affairs there are 10,657,000 persons of Indian extraction living abroad of whom 6.6 million have foreign citizenship. Less than a million live in Great Britain, the United States, and other developed countries. Of the remaining 9.2 million, the largest numbers are in Malaysia, Nepal, Sri Lanka, Surinam, Singapore, Guyana, Fiji, and Trinidad. Most of these settlers have lived in the Diaspora for one or more generations, have settled with their families, and, with the exception of tea plantation workers in Sri Lanka and some of the settlers in Nepal, now have citizenship in the country in which they live. Approximately half a million Indians reside in the Middle East, all with Indian citizenship, and most are migrants. In addition to the 333,000 residing in the Gulf states reported here another 100,000 live in Saudi Arabia, 21,000 in Iran, 20,000 in Iraq, 17,000 in Yemen (PDR) and 10,000 in Libya.

   For a comprehensive account of the history of the Indian diaspora during the era of British rule, see the trilogy by Hugh Tinker, Director of the Institute of Race Relations in London. The first volume, *A New System of Slavery: The Export of Indian Labour Overseas, 1830-1920* (London: Oxford University Press, 1974) describes the export of

Indians to the sugar, coffee, tea and rubber plantations in Mauritius, South and East Africa, the Caribbean, Guyana, Ceylon, Malaya, and Fiji. The second volumes *Separate and Unequal: India and the Indians in the British Commonwealth, 1920-50* (Delhi: Vikas Publishing House, 1976), deals with the political struggles of the overseas Indians. The third volume, *The Banyan Tree: Overseas Emigrants from India, Pakistan and Bangladesh*, New York: Oxford University Press, 1977, describes the expulsion of South Asians from many of the former British colonies — ending, in some instances, a diaspora 100 years old.

10. Data on emigration from India by state of origin are not available. But one indication of the order of magnitude is the number of passports issued by each of the regional passport offices. In 1977, the two passport offices in Kerala issued 170,000 passports and in 1978, 300,000. *The Hindu Overseas Edition*, 9 February 1980.
11. Mathew Abraham, 'Kerala unemployment zooms', *India Abroad*, 21 November 1980.
12. Among the few studies of the impact of migration on Kerala are: B. A. Prakash, 'Impact of Foreign Remittances: A Case Study of Chavakkad Village in Kerala', *Economic and Political Weekly*, vol. 13, no. 27 (8 July 1978) and E.T. Mathew and P. R. Gopinathan Nair, 'Socio-economic Characteristics of Emigrants and Emigrants' Households: A Case Study of Two Villages in Kerala', *Economic and Political Weekly*, vol. 13, no. 28 (15 July 1978) Migrants from Kerala are criticized for their failure to put remittances into productive investment at home, but few investors in India have found Kerala an attractive place to invest. Banks, private firms, and the government of Kerala have not developed any incentives for migrants to invest their savings. Critics of the Marxist-led government of Kerala have said that the government has been more concerned with questions of income distribution and mobilizing political support than with marshaling resources for the development of the economy.
13. Some observers have noted that the improvement in the financial and social status of returning Muslims in Kerala has contributed to the growth of Islamic schools, mosques, and other Muslim institutions in the state. How much of the increasing political awareness, militancy, and, in some localities, fundamentalism on the part of Muslims is a result of return migration is unclear. Still other critics point to the "deradicalizing" effects of migration, arguing that improving the income and status of migrants, increasing the wages of local people, and siphoning off those who might join protest movements weaken leftist political groups.
14. Under a Kuwaiti regulation, an immigrant may bring his family in only

if he earns at least US $1,500 a month. Most Gulf states have similar regulations.

15. Lower income migrants who leave their families in India are also demanding more educational opportunities for their children within India. In a memorandum to the Indian government, representatives of the Kerala Muslim Cultural Centres in Qatar, Kuwait, and the United Arab Emirates called on the government to reserve admission for the children of migrants in educational institutions in India. See 'Gulf Indians plead for more attention', *Hindustan Times Overseas Edition*, 9 April 1981.
16. In 1977 Bahrain imported 130 films from India, compared with 108 in 1976 and 52 in 1975. *Statistical Abstract, 1977*, Directorate of Statistics, State of Bahrain, 1978.
17. Upon the arrival of 60 illegal immigrants expelled from the United Arab Emirates, the alarmed Kerala Chief Minister, E.K. Nayanar, sent a message to Prime Minister Indira Gandhi urging her to negotiate with the Gulf government to avoid a sudden return of more migrants that would swell the large army of the unemployed in the state. A Government of India delegation was subsequently sent to the Gulf and the number of Indians repatriated remained small.
18. After the new emigration to the Gulf began in 1973, the Government of India chose the Labor Ministry to handle emigration procedures. The Ministry licensed agents to engage in bulk recruiting. The Labor Ministry was responsible for reviewing a contract and referring the agent to the Ministry of External Affairs to register the contract and obtain final government permission for workers to leave. After protests from agents, who found the process time consuming, and a challenge to the constitutionality of the procedure, the Supreme Court issued a judgment (in March 1979) declaring that the procedures established by the Labor Ministry were technically flawed. The responsibility was then transferred to the Ministry of External Affairs, which had had responsibility for migration since the Emigration Act of 1922. The Ministry of External Affairs established a procedure under which it examined all labor contracts but did not license agents. The Ministry relies on the Indian embassies in each of the Gulf countries for guidance as to an appropriate wage rate and for assurance that the facilities provided the workers are satisfactory. In practice, however, few Indians are refused permission to emigrate to the Gulf.
19. Physicians in the Gulf reportedly earn from US $50,000 to $200,000 per year. West Asian countries select doctors from a panel submitted by the Foreign Assignment Section of the Union Home Ministry of the

Government of India. Under Indian law, no Indian doctor can take employment outside the country without permission of the government, although, of course, many do.

20. In *Pastor in Kuwait* (Kuwait: Bishops Houses, 1978), Mgr. Victor Sanmiquel, the Bishop of Kuwait, estimates that there are 40,000 domestic servants in Kuwait, half of whom are from India and Pakistan.
21. To what extent the various investments made by the Gulf governments will become profitable is another matter Redundant investments (e.g. international airports at Dubai and at Sharjah, 20 minutes apart by car) are likely to be unprofitable, but there are also doubts about the long-term profitability of some of the industrial investments.
22. *The Times of India* (14 February 1980) reports that 250,000 Indians reside in the United Arab Emirates, but no source is given. One reason for the considerable variation in estimates is that the UAE reportedly has a substantial number of illegal migrants.
23. A new labor law passed in the United Arab Emirates in 1979 barred foreign workers from changing their jobs unless they left the country for a year. The provision ended the casual labor pool used by local contractors. The law was in part designed to curb the increasing number of unemployed foreigners in the country. When the law was passed, the Gulf Indian Welfare Association in the UAE expressed concern that thousands of Indians who had changed jobs illegally would be forced to leave the country. They also expressed the fear that employers would be able to reduce salaries, benefits, and other privileges at will since the employee would be totally dependent upon his initial sponsor for permission to remain in the country. See 'UAE decree hits hard 70,000 Indians', *Times of India,* 20 January 1980.
24. According to a report by the Population Division of ECWA, 'An overview of the population situation in Bahrain', *Population Bulletin of the United Nations Economic Commission for Western Asia,* no. 14, June 1977, one out of every five persons living in Bahrain is an immigrant, but 37 per cent of the labor force is non-Bahraini. The report concludes that 'considering the degree to which the Bahraini economy is dependent upon its foreign workers, the time required to educate and train sufficient numbers of native Bahrainis, and the number of trained Bahrainis remaining abroad, it seems unlikely that the proportion of non-Bahrainis among the total population will be reduced to any great extent in the near future' (p. 68).
25. Data on oil production from *Middle East Oil,* Exxon Background Series, Public Affairs Department of Exxon Corporation, New York, September 1980.

26. Bahraini employers wishing to import expatriates must obtain No Objection Certificates (NOC) and work permits from the Labor Department. Some Bahraini employers then permit their workers to take employment with another employer in return for a 10 per cent kickback on wages. One Bahraini, it is said, collects 10 per cent from 50 to 60 expatriates each month. Some employers may also take kickbacks from their own expatriate labor, by paying a lower wage than is provided by the contract. The Bahrain Immigration and Labor Department restricts the number of NOCs and work permits and attempts to prevent their misuse, but it is limited by the inability of workers to protest abuses since a worker knows that if he reports the holder of his NOC he would lose his job. Once a permit holder loses his job he is, under Bahraini law, prohibited from entering the labor market.
27. 'Gulf survey', *Economist*, 13-19 December 1980, p. 51.
28. The occupational distribution of non-Bahraini is indicated by the allocation of labor permits. The government issued 26,267 permits to non-Bahrainis in 1977: 8,416 to crafts and production process workers, 2,103 for services, sports, and recreation workers, 1,563 for administrative, executive, and managerial workers, 1,460 for sales workers, 1,046 for transport and communications workers, and 1,342 for professional technical, and related workers. *Statistical Abstract*, 1977, Directorate of Statistics, State of Bahrain, October 1978.
29. Robert G. Landen, *Oman since 1856: Disruptive Modernization in a Traditional Arab Society*, Princeton: Princeton University Press, 1967, p. 134.
30. Ian Skeet, *Muscat and Oman: The End of an Era*, London: Faber and Faber, 1974, p. 192.
31. Landen, cited in n. 29, p. 309.
32. David Smiley, *Arabian Assignment*, London: Leo Cooper, 1958. Smiley, one-time chief of staff for the Oman military, reported that the Baluch constituted 70 per cent of the army, 'for the Sultan never really trusted his Arabs' (p. 24).
33. David E. Long, *The Persian Gulf: An Introduction to Its People, Politics, and Economies*, Boulder, Colorado: Westview Press, 1976, p. 32.
34. George Dib, 'Migration and Naturalization Laws in Egypt, Lebanon, Syria, Jordan, Kuwait, and the United Arab Emirates, Part II: Naturalization Laws', *Population Bulletin of the United Nations Economic Commission for Western Asia*, no. 16, June 1979, p. 8.
35. *Area Handbook for the Persian Gulf States*, ed. Richard R. Nyrop, Washington, D.C.: US Government Printing Office, 1977, p. 172.

36. The World Bank, *World Development Report, 1980*, New York: Oxford University Press, 1981, p. 135.
37. *The Population Census of 1975*, Central Statistical Office, Census Division, Ministry of Planning, State of Kuwait, June 1977 reports that there are 21,475 Indians and 11,038 Pakistanis in the labor force. Half of the Indians are in services; 2,600 are in professional, technical, and related work; 3,700 are in transport and production; 1,700 are in sales.
38. In Kuwait an alien who comes for the purpose of working with a person or company must present a (NOC) from the Ministry of Labour and Social Affairs to the passport control officer at his point of entry. NOCs are granted to employers if they can demonstrate that Kuwaiti workers are not available. Work permits are subject to approval of the Ministry of Labour and Social Affairs. Contracts must be of limited duration, not to exceed five years. Regulations prohibit foreign workers from changing employers during the term of their contracts without the consent of the original employer and the Minister of Labour and Social Affairs. Workers can be deported if they accept employment with a second employer without obtaining the consent of their original employer and without the knowledge of the Ministry of Labour and Social Affairs. They can also be deported if they are convicted of 'incitement of workers to strike or to refrain from working' or physical or verbal attacks on employers or supervisors. Since workers can only remain in the country while working for their employer, and since they cannot seek employment on the open market without having been released by their employer, in effect, an employer can seek the deportation of any of his employees—a provision of the law that discourage workers from trade union activities and ensures a politically docile labor force.
39. Dib, op. cit., n. 34. According to Dib, a Professor of International Law at Lebanese University, Islam distinguishes between Muslims, dhimmies or Peoples of the Book (Christians and Jews), and musta-minun or persons temporarily residing in the Islamic world (Dar al-Islam) as a result of agreements between an Islamic and non-Islamic government or between individual Muslims and a national of a non-Muslim 'pagan' country. Under Ottoman rule a system of "capitulations" was established under which concessions were made relating to the religious affairs of Christian subjects. In the post-Ottoman period, each Arab state set its own rules with respect to aliens and non-Muslims living within its territory. The 1963 Citizenship Law of Bahrain says that citizenship may be granted by naturalization to an applicant who has resided in Bahrain for at least 25 consecutive years, but only if he is an Arab. Apart from the Law, the ruler may grant citizenship to anyone he choses. See Emile

A. Nakhleh, 'Labor Markets and Citizenship in Bahrayn and Qatar', *Middle East Journal* (Spring 1977), p. 150.

40. For an account of the demand by local workers for the right to unionize, and the government's opposition to unionism in Bahrain, see Nakhleh, cited in note 39. Bahrain's constitution guarantees the right to form guilds and unions, but no law was written to implement the article, and the subsequent freezing of many constitutional provisions killed the issue of unionism. The 1976 Labor Law, notes Nakhleh, does not mention labor unions.
41. Dib, op. cit., n. 34, p. 8.
42. 'International labor migration in the Middle East and North Africa', Technical Assistance and Special Studies Division, World Bank, Washington, D.C., March 1981, p. 10.
43. The World Bank estimates that manpower demand in each of the Gulf states will increase as follows between 1975 and 1985:

	1975	*1985*
Kuwait	297,000	414,000
Oman	192,000	257,000
UAE	292,000	632,000
Bahrain	79,000	150,000
Qatar	74,000	136,000
Total	934,000	1,589,000

This projected 70 per cent increase in the labor force by 1985 is consistent with the actual population increase of 29.5 per cent that took place from 1975 to 1979. See 'International labor migration in the Middle East and North Africa', op. cit., n. 42, p. 3.

44. However, Gulf Indians have made demands upon the Government of India. Representatives of the Kerala Muslim Cultural Centers in Qatar, Kuwait, and the United Arab Emirates submitted a memorandum to the Indian government calling for a reduction in air fare, the establishment of an additional international airport in Kerala, and the lowering of customs duties. They also asked the government to create facilities for them in the Gulf cultural centers, libraries, a community hall. They wanted the embassy to negotiate compensation for workers in the event of premature termination of services, and they requested a separate ministry to deal with Indian immigrants. And they wanted more favourable banking arrangements so that they could send remittances home; they asked the government to allocate cement to them for housing construction, against remittances; and they called for

reservations of places for their children in schools. See 'Gulf Indians plead for more attention', *Hindustan Times*, Overseas Edition, 9 April 1981.

45. Opposition to migrants has been openly expressed in the Gulf press. The Abu Dhabi magazine, *Al Azmena al Arabiya*, published an article (4 July 1979) by its chief editor, Mohammad Obeid Ghobash, calling upon Sheikh Rashid, the ruler, to terminate projects that require the importation of foreign workers 'even though these projects could be of economic benefit'. An editorial in the 8 August issue of the journal said that UAE citizens were not getting the full benefit of such services as health, education, housing, and commerce because of 'foreign competition'.

CHAPTER 8

An 'Incipient' Diaspora: Indians in the Gulf Region

PRAKASH C. JAIN

Writing in the mid-1980s Myron Weiner described the migration and temporary settlement of Indian workers in the Middle East as 'incipient' diaspora. The description still appears to be relevant. Following Weiner (1986: 47), an 'incipient' diaspora can be defined as a relatively sizeable group of foreign workers in industrial or oil-producing economies who are ethnically distinct from the host population and who are 'allowed to remain in their host country only to work' but are not entitled to become citizens. As such they live in 'a state of legal and political ambiguity, economic insecurity and as social outsiders'. Though these workers are not 'immigrants' in true sense of the term, a large number of them 'continues to remain indefinitely in the host country'. The 'incipiency' of the diaspora obtains from the fact that naturalization and citizenship laws in all the Persian Gulf Arab countries to which Indian migration has taken place are extremely stringent and it is almost impossible for the migrants to have permanent resident status. Often work contracts are time-bound and even otherwise the migrants desire to return home after a few years of stay. This migration is therefore transitory as well as circulatory in nature.

Before we further elaborate on the volume and sociological characteristics of Indian migration to the Persian Gulf region it would be useful to point out at the outset that incipiency is not only the hallmark of this particular form of the Indian diaspora but also of the available literature on the subject. To the best of my knowledge no systematic work has so far been done from the Gulf end, that is on the Indian diasporic aspects, though considerable empirical work is available on the Gulf returnees in Kerala from where a large-scale Gulf migration has taken place (Prakash 1998; Zachariah 2002).

FORMATION OF THE DIASPORA

Although Indo-Gulf trade relations existed even during the Indus Valley civilisation, modern historical evidence of Indian settlement in the Gulf area dates back to only the sixteenth century A.D. The Portuguese relied heavily on Hindus in their attempt to secure a monopoly of the Indian Ocean/Arabian Gulf trade (Allen, Jr. 1981: 39). During the nineteenth century when the region came under

TABLE 8.1: ANNUAL LABOUR OUTFLOWS FORM INDIA TO WEST ASIA, 1976-2003

Year	*Number of Workers*	*Year*	*Number of Workers*
1976	4,200	1990	143,565
1977	22,900	1991	197,889
1978	69,000	1992	416,784
1979	171,800	1993	438,338
1980	268,200	1994	425,385
1981	272,000	1995	413,334
1982	224,257	1996	414,214
1983	217,971	1997	416,424
1984	198,520	1998	355,164
1985	160,396	1999	199,552
1986	109,234	2000	243,182
1987	121,812	2001	278,664
1988	165,924	2002	367,663
1989	125,786	2003	466,456

Source: Ministry of Labour (2002 and 2003).

Note: The figures given in the above tables do not include the persons who are running the business in partnership with foreign nationals; those who emigrated on visit visa and stayed on to get a job and those skilled workers and professionals (like doctors, engineers, chartered accountants, computer specialist etc.) in whose case emigration clearance is not necessary.

the British influence and/or administration the Indian merchant communities flourished in a number of towns in the Gulf countries. In Oman until 1970 commerce was dominated by Hindu banias who enjoyed considerable religious freedom. They served as bankers, importers and exporters, agents for local merchants, and government contractors (Allen, Jr. 1987: 12). More or less similar situation existed in Aden (Yemen) where the Indian community numbered 8,563 in 1856; 7,387 in 1931; 9,452 in 1946 and 15,817 in 1955 (Gavin 1975: 445). Among other Gulf countries the Trucial States Sheikhdoms (UAE) comprising Abu Dhabi, Dubai, Sharjah, Ras-al-Khaimah, Umm-al-Quaiwain, Ajman and Fujairah had extensive trade relations with India during the late nineteenth and early twentieth centuries. Dubai served as the major centre of Indo-UAE trade. Since India's independence, 'the Indian merchants and their partners also established an extensive illegal trade, sending Indian goods whose importation was restricted by the Government of India – gold, watches, tape recorders, transistors' (Weiner 1982: 13).

A number of these merchant communities continued to operate on a much larger scale in the entire region even after the independence of the various Gulf countries which not only denied citizenship to non-natives, but also implemented trade licensing systems in favour

TABLE 8.2: THE DISTRIBUTION OF ANNUAL LABOUR OUTFLOWS FROM INDIA TO WEST ASIA BY COUNTRY OF DESTINATION, 1982-90

Country	*1982*	*1983*	*1984*	*1985*	*1986*	*1987*	*1988*	*1989*	*1990*
Bahrain	17,069	18,894	15,514	11,246	5,784	6,578	8,219	8,520	6,782
Iraq	35,268	13,001	11,398	5,855	5,040	2,330	4,284	5,085	1,650
Kuwait	9,764	11,490	5,466	5,512	4,235	7,354	9,653	5,679	1,077
Libya	10,433	5,900	5,179	2,449	2,552	2,272	593	632	305
Oman	39,792	49,120	43,228	37,806	22,417	16,362	18,696	16,574	34,267
Qatar	14,357	7,772	4,362	5,214	4,029	4,751	4,654	7,991	3,704
Saudi Arabia	78,297	83,235	88,079	68,938	41,854	57,234	85,289	49,710	79,473
UAE	19,297	25,559	24.286	21,286	23,323	24931	34,029	26,189	11,962
Others	15,288	7,024	8,410	4,729	4,415	3,544	4,471	5,406	4,345
Total	239,545	224,995	205,922	163,035	113,649	125,356	169,888	125,786	143,565

Source: Ministry of Labour (different years).

of their own citizens. Moreover, at the same time the emergence of Gulf countries as oil-producing and exporting economies and the consequent demand for labour since at least the 1970s changed the size and complexion of the Indian as indeed of all other expatriate communities in the region.

Large-scale Indian labour migration to the Gulf countries is however a recent phenomenon (See Tables 8.1 to 8.4). In 1948, for example, there were only 14,000 Indian workers in the West Asian countries. Of these 5,594 in Aden, 1,138 in Bahrain, 1,000 in Egypt, 2,500 in Iran, 650 in Iraq, 1,250 in Kuwait, 1,145 in Muscat, and less than one hundred each in Jordan, Lebanon, Palestine, Syria and

TABLE 8.3: THE DISTRIBUTION OF ANNUAL LABOUR OUTFLOWS FROM INDIA BY DESTINATION, 1991-6

Country	*1991*	*1992*	*1993*	*1994*	*1995*	*1996*
Bahrain	8,630	16,458	15,622	13,806	11,235	16,647
Kuwait	7,044	19,782	26,981	24,324	14,439	14,580
Oman	22,333	40,900	29,056	25,142	22,338	30,113
Saudi Arabia	130,928	265,180	269,639	265,875	256,782	214,068
UAE	15,446	60,493	77,066	75,762	79,674	112,644
Others	7,121	13,974	19,974	20,476	28,866	26,162
Total	191,502	416,784	438,338	425,385	413,334	414,214

Source: Ministry of Labour (2002).

TABLE 8.4: THE DISTRIBUTION OF ANNUAL LABOUR OUTFLOWS FROM INDIA BY DESTINATION, 1997-2004

Country	*1997*	*1998*	*1999*	*2000*	*2001*	*2002*	*2003*	*2004*
Bahrain	17,944	16,997	14,905	15,909	16,382	20,807	24,778	22,980
Kuwait	13,170	22,462	19,149	31,082	39,751	48,549	54,434	52,064
Oman	29,994	20,774	16,101	25,155	30,985	41,209	36,816	33,275
Saudi Arabia	214,420	105,239	27,160	59,722	78,048	99,453	121,431	123,522
UAE	110,945	134,740	79,269	55,099	53,673	95,034	143,804	175,262
Qatar	–	–	–	–	13,829	12,596	14,251	16,325
Others	29,951	54,952	42,968	46216	45,996	50015	44,044	20,068
Total	416,424	355,164	199,552	243,182	278,664	367,663	466,456	474,960

Source: Ministry of Labour (2003:117 and 2004-5: 93).

TABLE 8.5: ESTIMATES OF INDIAN IMMIGRANTS IN WEST ASIA, 1975-2004

Country	*1975*	*1979*	*1983*	*1987*	*1991*	*2004*
Bahrain	17,250	26,000	30,000	77,000	100,000	150,000
Iraq	7,500	20,000	50,000	350,000	–	–
Kuwait	32,105	65,000	115,000	100,000	88,000	400,000
Libya	1,100	10,000	40,000	25,000	12,000	20,000
Oman	38,500	60,000	100,000	184,000	220,000	450,000
Qatar	27,800	30,000	40,000	50,000	75,000	150,000
Saudi Arabia	34,500	100,000	270,000	380,000	600,000	1,500,000
UAE	107,500	152,000	250,000	225,000	400,000	1,000,000
Others	–	68,000	21,000	21,000	10,000	200,000
Total	266,255	501,000	916,000	1,096,000	1,505,000	3,870,000

Source: For 1975 figures see Birks and Sinclair (1980: 39) and for 1979, 1983, 1987 and 1991 figures Nayyar (1994: 32). The 2004 figures are eastimates by the author. 'Others' include Yemen and Israel.

Palestine, Syria and Turkey (Kondapi 1951: 528). In the next two decades the Indian population in West Asia almost tripled. Thus in 1970-1 there were a little over 40,000 Indians – Aden 2,000, Bahrain 5,500, Iran 1,000, Iraq 12,000, Kuwait 12,000, Muscat 4,500, Qatar 2,000 and Saudi Arabia 1,000 (Tinker 1977: 12). Since then as a result of the booming oil economy and the shortage of labour in the Gulf countries, there has been a phenomenal increase in the number of Indians working in the Gulf countries. In 2004 there were about 3.9 million Indians in the Gulf and other West Asian countries. Of these about 1.5 million were in Saudi Arabia, about a million in the UAE, about half-a-million in Oman, 400,000 in Kuwait, 150,000 in Qatar and 150,000 in Bahrain (see Table 8.5).

SOCIO-ECONOMIC CHARACTERISTICS OF MIGRANTS

Region and Religion

About 40 to 50 per cent Indian migrants to the Gulf countries originate in Kerala; the rest come from Andhra Pradesh, Tamil Nadu, Karnataka, Goa and other Indian provinces. A Survey conducted in the UAE, found that 35 per cent of the Indian community hailed from Kerala, followed by Maharashtrians, Gujaratis and Goans. The majority of Indians were Sunni Muslim (56 per cent) followed by Christians (26 per cent) and Hindus (16 per cent).

Gender

The overwhelming majority of Indian migrants to the Gulf countries is male. The simple reason for this situation is the fact there are very few job opportunities for women in the Gulf countries. Nursing, school teaching and domestic service are some of the few vocations which are open to women and even for these the competition among potential migrants from different countries is intense. Moreover, Indian society still does not favour independent female migration abroad. Thus, studies conducted in Kerala villages in the 1970s found that not more than 2 per cent of total number of migrants to the Gulf countries were women (see Commerce Research Bureau 1978; Mathew and Nair 1978; Prakash 1978). The 1987 state survey of Kerala, however, found this figure to be 7.5 per cent (DES 1987).

The proportion of women among the Indian population in the Gulf countries is also very low as the majority of Indian migrant workers do not take their families with them. It was estimated that not more than 10 per cent of the total Indian migrant workers in 1983 for example lived with their families (Gulati 1986: 197). This phenomenon can partly be explained by the fact that only those workers who earn a minimum prescribed salary are entitled to take their families along with them. Obviously, many eligible workers do not exercise this privilege. High cost of housing, lack of educational facilities for children, desire to save as much money as possible and inability of Indian women to adjust in the socio-cultural milieu of the Gulf countries are some of the factors which may account for this phenomenon.

Age and Marital Status

A majority of migrants to the Gulf countries happen to be young in age. According to a study conducted by Commerce Research Bureau (1978) in Kerala it was found that 79 per cent of the migrant workers were 35 years of age or younger. Another study found that as many as 84 per cent of migrants were under 35 years of age and that about 50 per cent of the workers were unmarried.

Educational and Skill Levels

Educational and skill levels of the migrants to the Gulf countries appears to have been rather low. Data from Kerala state suggests that over two-thirds of the migrants to the West Asian countries in the late 1970s had completed less than ten years of schooling. The same study also found that about 62 per cent of emigrants were unskilled workers (see Gulati 1986: 199). On the basis of a few sample surveys done in Kerala in the late 1970s, Nair (1986: 71) suggests that by and large the Gulf migration from India represented 'predominantly a flow of excess operative and manual labour' and as 'the proportion of highly qualifieid personnel was small, not exceeding 10 per cent for most of the region' it did not constitute a serious problem of brain drain.

Occupational Status

A significant proportion of migrants from Kerala (ranging from 33.8 per cent to 69.4 per cent) were unemployed at the time of migration. The proportion of unemployed was found to be low in relatively poor areas where income and educational levels were also low. Conversely, areas with high income and educational levels were the areas from where white collar workers (clerks, typists, teachers, nurses, etc.) as well as professionally qualified persons migrated. In this connection, Nair (1986: 73) observed that this is 'a specific area that has sent similar migrants to countries in the West and to Africa'.

ECONOMIC STATUS

The Indian diaspora in the Persian Gulf region is in constant flux for two important reasons – continuous 'circulation' of migrants, and the upgradation of the skill composition of the workforce. The unique nature of the diaspora and the fact that there is hardly any social scientific study on the subject makes it difficult to comment authoritatively. In the absence of systematic studies, it is only natural that newspaper reports should come handy. These sources clearly suggest that the vast majority of Indians in the Gulf countries have been earning their livelihood honestly and in legal manner, while a very small minority of them is involved in illegal economic activities such as smuggling, extortion and even begging. Interestingly, the latter reports are more numerous and precisely documented than the former.

Indian immigrants in the Gulf region constitute two major class segments (a) skilled, semi skilled and unskilled workers, and (b) professionals and entrepreneurs. The proportion of each class segment in the Gulf countries varies from country to country. Nevertheless it is widely believed that labour constitutes about 60-70 per cent of the total migration outflow from India to the Middle East. As an economist put it,

> It is striking that an overwhelmingly large proportion of the out migration, whether in construction or in other activities, was made up of workers employed in the service sector, so much so that the proportion employed in the manufacturing sector was small while that in the agricultural sector was negligible. Given that such emigration from India to the Middle East is temporary, it would seem to provide an example of international trade in services (Nayyar 1994: 30).

This situation is sociologically akin to the earlier ones in South Africa, Fiji, Malaysia and Burma where indentured and/or *kangani* labour and petty bourgeoisie consisting of a variety of skilled personnels and traders migrated simultaneously and yet remained apart from one another (see Jain 1990; 1999).

The available data on the occupational status of Indian workers in the Gulf countries suggest that until 1980s about 40 per cent of them were employed in the construction and transport industries. Utility and maintenance constituted another important category of employment followed by office and paramedical services. Table 8.6 provides data about the skill composition of labour outflows from India to the Middle East for the mid-1980s – a period characterised by declining labour export.

Since the late 1980s there has been a gradual shift in the socio-economic profile of the Indian migrants to the Gulf. The preponderance of workers in the construction industry and other skilled and semi-skilled sectors has been slowly reversed. A recent demographic study done in the UAE indicated that there has been an upward flow in white collar jobs. Indians have a stranglehold on textile, gold, electronics and construction industries. A sizable number also operate hotels and restaurants (Chandran 1993). According to the figures provided by the Indian Ministry of External

TABLE 8.6: THE SKILLS COMPOSITION OF LABOUR OUTFLOWS FROM INDIA TO THE MIDDLE EAST, 1984-6

Skill Category	*1984*		*1985*		*1986*	
	Number	*Percentage*	*Number*	*Percentage*	*Number*	*Percentage*
1. *Unskilled workers*	88,575	43.0	55,710	34.2	45,577	40.1
Construction Labour	85,797	41.7	51,330	31.5	39,314	34.6
Farm labour & Household workers	2,778	1.3	4,380	2.7	6,263	5.5
2. *Skilled workers*	86,014	41.8	86,037	52.8	53,432	47.2
Construction sector	45,882	22.3	46,318	28.4	24,485	21.5
Other activities & services	40,132	19.5	39,719	24.4	28,947	25.5
3. *White-collar workers*	7,477	3.6	5,753	3.5	7,351	6.5
4. *High-skill workers*	6,495	3.2	7,378	4.5	5,958	5.2
Para-medical staff	2,630	1.3	1,205	0.7	1,175	1.0
Technical & supervisory personnel	3,865	1.9	6,173	3.8	4,783	4.2
5. *Others*	17,361	8.4	8,157	5.0	1,331	1.2
Total	205,922	100.0	163,035	100.0	113,649	100.0

Source: Nayyar (1994: 28).

Affairs, skilled and unskilled workers accounted for about 70 per cent of the Indian migrants, white collar workers for about 20 per cent and professional had a 10 per cent share in 1998. The study referred to above had also found that in the early 1990s approximately 57 per cent of the Indian population earned less than 5,000 Dirham a month (3.6 Dirham to a dollar) whilst those earning above 25,000 Dirhams a month was about 10 per cent. The rest figured in between these income brackets. In effect, more than three-fourths of the

Indians in the UAE earned less than 10,000 Dirhams a month (Chandran 1993).

A good number of Indian immigrants in the Gulf countries, particularly in the UAE, Oman and Kuwait are involved in a variety of business activities. Some of the business houses such as Jashanmal in the UAE and Khimji Ramdas in Oman have since long been there. Many others are of more recent origin. Major Indian business houses have their operations in Dubai after the establishment of the Jebel Ali Free Zone, Dubai Cargo Village and Dubai Airport Free Zone. By 1996 at least 150 Indian companies were operating in the Jebel Ali Free Zone alone. The Indian entrepreneurs are particularly attracted to such features of Free zones as no income or corporate taxes, no trade barriers, no control on foreign exchange, 100 per cent foreign ownership, negligible bureaucracy, and above all an internationally competent infrastructure. Apart from individual entrepreneurs, a considerable number of Indian immigrants are involved in joint ventures between India and Gulf countries.

Another class segment of the Indian petty bourgeoisie in the region consists of professionals such as engineers, doctors, management executives, chartered accountants, bankers, architects, lawyers, teachers, etc., who constitute about 10 per cent of the Indian immigrant workforce. The professional migrants are drawn from all over the country.

The NRI remittances and investments have played an extremely important role in India's economic development. India's foreign exchange receipts from remittances have increased several fold during the past three decades or so. According to one estimate whereas India's forex receipts totalled less than $300 million in 1974-5, by 1984-5 this figure had increased to $2,500 million. The West Asian share in the country's total receipts was 12 per cent in 1974-5 and 58 per cent in 1984-5 (Nayyar 1989). According to estimates made by Gulati and Mody (1983), Kerala accounted for 42 per cent of the country's remittances receipts from West Asia in 1981-2.

NRI deposits have immensely helped India in averting its balance of payment crisis. A time series data compiled by the Department of Economic Analysis and Policy of the Reserve Bank of India on India's balance of payment trends since 1948-9 shows that Non-

Resident Indian Deposits (NRD) have risen continuously since the mid-1970s. The data further suggest that the dependence on NRDs was negligible up to 1974-5. After touching $40 million in 1974-5, these deposits rose steadily to $1.04 billion in 1979-80. The dependence on NRDs grew substantially in the 1980s from $1.8 billion in 1980-1 to $10.4 billion in 1989-90 and $10.6 billion in 1990-1, before falling for the first time in 1991-2 to $7.8 billion. The reversal in the rising trend of NRDs was clearly linked to large-scale withdrawal of such deposits by NRIs following the outbreak of Gulf War in late 1990. Since then the NRDs have picked up again and India's forex reserves, excluding gold and SDRs, were estimated to be $10.2 billion by January 1994, and over $100 billion by 2004.

It goes without saying that Indian workers who generally migrate without their families for a number of reasons, save most of their earnings as they get free food, accommodation and transport during their stay in the Gulf countries. The remitted money is mostly spent on the up-keep and maintenance of the households, paying out-standing debts, purchasing land and building houses, and buying consumer durables. Lavish expenditures on marriage and other festive occasions have also been reported from the Gulf migration areas in Kerala and elsewhere. It appears that very little amount of remittances is used for economically productive purposes. As Nair (1989: 344) put it:

> The available evidence suggests that migration and the resultant receipt of remittances do not seem to have made any significant impact on economic growth rate of the state economies. Nor did they have substantial effect on employment rates, labour market conditions, agricultural development and industrialisation. It would appear that the major part of the remittances which flowed into Kerala seeped into other regions of India through the mechanism of trade in consumption goods and construction materials caused by the changes in consumption patterns and the boom in the house construction sector.

Although most of the Gulf workers send their remittances through official channels, a considerable number of them also send their money through *hawala* and other illegal channels. These channels usually offer Rs.10 as commission for every dollar. Attempts to curb such transactions have not been successful in the past. However, if the government can pay competitive premium on workers' remittances, a considerable amount of foreign exchange can be attracted by diverting unofficial transaction through official route. This would also help curb smuggling of gold, gems, jewellery, electronic and textile goods and life saving drugs, etc. to India as the Gulf *hawala* dealers would have less foreign exchange at their disposal from this source.

Regarding NRI investment in India it can be effectively argued that the desire on the part of the Gulf and other NRIs to invest in India and to retain their Indian citizenship should be seen not so much as an expression of their patriotism but as pure and simple economic calculations. If India provides competitive advantage in business operations for the NRIs they would be more than willing to invest in India; if not, they might go elsewhere. This was seen during the 1990-1 Gulf crisis when Indian economy began to show the balance of payment crisis. The NRI investment in India had begun to decline and a considerable number of NRIs did not renew their FCNR deposits on maturity: instead they preferred to invest the money abroad. The successful subscription of the Resurgent India Bonds by the NRIs in 1998 which fetched $4.16 billion was mainly due to the scheme's favourable price to the NRIs. It is significant to note that the contribution of the NRIs in the Middle East accounted for about 50 per cent of the total receipts.

A small number of Indian immigrants in the Gulf countries particularly in the UAE are involved in such criminal activities as smuggling, trade in narcotics and arms, extortion, and other subversive activities. Dubai has long been associated with smuggling of gold, silver, precious metals, and electronic goods. A number of Indian and Pakistani smugglers live and work in Dubai. Until recently about 150 tons of gold and 1,300 tons of silver used to be smuggled into India from the UAE, mainly Dubai. This is mostly done by *dhows*, 'each of which normally carry 8 tons of cargo. At that rate, it works out to 150 landings on the Indian coast every year – almost one every alternate day' (Tellis 1991). Profits from smuggling were huge ranging from Rs. 40,000 to 50,000 per kg. after deducting landing cost, *hawala* transaction charges, bribes, salaries/commissions, etc. Of all Dubai smugglers, Dawood Ibrahim who has been residing in Pakistan since 1993 was the biggest. He alone reportedly smuggled between 25 to 30 tons of gold to India annually. The rest was farmed out to other smugglers with Ibrahim acting as a commission agent who charged a fee from them for making available landing facilities on the Indian coast.

The Emirate policy in regard to smuggling appears to be the one of turning a blind eye to such activities, of course, so long as there is no breach of peace. Otherwise the local authorities are known to come down with a heavy hand on trouble makers. Thus about three thousand Pakistani and five hundred Indian Muslim immigrants (mostly illegal) had to face deportation for their involvement in a demonstration against the demolition of the Babri Mosque in Ayodhya in December 1992 (Chandran 1993).

One major irritant in Indo-UAE relations involving some NRIs was the March 1993 Bomb blasts in Bombay in which 257 persons were killed, over 700 injured and property worth Rs. 27 crore destroyed. Whether this was a reaction to the demolition of the Babri Masjid in Ayodhya in December 1992 is not known, but the fact remains that the Government of India had carried out a massive crackdown on Dawood Ibrahim's cartel (Ghosh 1993). Search was particularly on for the Memon brothers – Yakub and Ismail – who reportedly had slipped to Karachi via Dubai.

Smuggling of South Asian children for camel races in the Gulf countries, Arab marriages to poor, young Muslim girls and clandestine flesh trade are some other dimensions of undesirable Indo-Gulf trade which are carried out by a few Indian migrants. 'Arab visitors known for their wealth, lure through unscrupulous agents young girls into so-called "marriages" where *kazi* and the agent are in league with the Arab buyer' (Gogate 1986: 50). Some of these Arab men happen to be quite old and already married several times over. Cases of such marriages are often reported from Hyderabad and Mumbai.

In recent years extortion has emerged as another 'industry' for some Gulf-based Indian 'entrepreneurs'. This enterprise is thriving in some metropolitan cities of India, especially in Mumbai. Its conspicuous presence has been particularly noted in Bollywood – the Mumbai film industry which annually produces about 800 films. 'It is well-known that the Abu Salem faction of the Dawood Ibrahim gang has been behind extortion threats to film personalities for the past ten years. Film producers admit that extortion threats are common and that most of them pay up quietly after a bit of haggling over the sum' (Singh 2000). As a noted film journalist put it, 'any and everybody who is seen as a moneybag in the moviemills becomes a potential target of the extortionist's bullet' (Kazmi 2000). Between January 1995 and January 2000 ten well-known film personalities were gunned down or shot at.

Apart from extortion, some Dubai-based gangsters have also infiltrated the Mumbai film industry. Globalisation of the entertainment industry, competition from cable television, piracy through the influx of DVDs and VCDs in the market, and unlawful private screening of films – have all given a blow to the Indian film industry. It is against this backdrop that the infiltration of the underworld black money has occurred in the film industry.

The Mafia is not only interested in producing films but also in grabbing distribution rights of films in the blossoming overseas market. The overseas market, which until recently, was a 'mere pocket money' option for Hindi film makers is now emerging as the big factor. 'So from selling films for the overseas market for paltry sums, the makers have graduated to asking for minimum guarantees (apart from paying a fixed sum, the distributor also shares a part of the profit with the producer) for their films'. Not surprisingly, 'the overseas territory started becoming a favourite demand of extortionists' (Bhatt 2000). It gives 'the gangsters an added advantage. Using a dummy distributor as a front, he can launder the money under the guise of bringing in forex. This white money is used to finance his *benami* but legitimate businesses in the construction, transport and hotel industries' (Singh 2000).

If Dubai provides a safe haven for a variety of criminals, the pilgrimage cities of Mecca and Madina, have emerged as child beggars' paradise. Estimatedly about 1,000 to 1,500 Indian children (both boys and girls) are annually involved in this begging racket, especially during the *Haj* time. About 400 of them are sent from Murshidabad district of West Bengal alone. Estimates suggest that the mafia running this racket earn about Rupees Five lakh per child annually (after deducting the expenditure). Depending on the number of children involved in the racket, the economics of begging in Saudi Arabia by the Indian children run into multi-crore rupees business (Mohan 1997).

SOCIAL ORGANISATION

The layman notion of social organisation among overseas Indian communities is represented in Tagore's analogy of the Banyan Tree. Tagore held the view that Indian settlement abroad is akin to the spread of grand old Banyan Tree. Implicit in this analogy is the assumption that Indian culture as well as social organisational patterns can be transplanted overseas. This view obviously does not correspond with the reality. The nature and patterns of social organisation among overseas Indian communities have varyingly been affected by numerous local factors. Perhaps the most generic among them was the nature and conditions of employment. The kind of initial employment (e.g. indentured or wage labour, trade or profession, etc.), and the socio-political conditions in the colonial/metropolitan societies under which such employment was taken up constitute the broad parameters of the evolution of varying social organisations and community life among overseas Indians. Transformation in such social organisational elements as caste, kinship and family, religion, etc., obtained due to the politico-economic conditions in different places. Hypothetically, it would seem that the degree of freedom of immigrant Indians in various colonial societies was a major factor in transforming the indigenous patterns of social organisation among the overseas Indians. Thus overseas Indian communities in the West Indies, Mauritius and Fiji which were primarily formed due to the slavery-like indentured labour migration exhibit more radical transformation in their social organisational aspects than in the overseas Indian communities in Burma, Malaysia, Singapore and Sri Lanka that were mainly formed from less coercive Kangani/maistry system of recruitment. To countries where Indians migrated more freely under 'passage' or 'free' migration system (e.g. Kenya, Uganda, Tanzania), social organisation among them shows least transformation. Similar argument can be advanced in relation to the more recent 'brain drain' emigres and their communities in Britain, Canada and the US. This remains an empirical issue whether the above mentioned hypothesis is also applicable to the Indians in West Asia. The purpose of this brief discussion is to show that compared to the 'Banyan Tree' view of the overseas Indians, it is far more fruitful to study the emerging patterns of social organisation among them from the political economy perspective.

The Banyan tree view presumes that transplantation of socio-cultural patterns abroad is an unhindered exercise. This however, has never been the case. The migration process itself sets the limits on this presumption in terms of selectivity of migrants, their motivation and destination of migration, etc. The working and living conditions of Indians in the Persian Gulf region amply demonstrate this. To begin with Indian migration to the Middle East is a male-dominated migration. A great majority of Indian migrants to the Gulf either cannot afford or do not want to take alongwith them their wives, with the result that there is an extreme sex imbalance in the diaspora, particular among the workers. This seriously hampers the formation of Indian 'community' in the Gulf countries. Middle class comprising professionals and entrepreneurs are an exception but even here all family members are not there for a variety of reasons. Grown up children seldom live with their parents as most of the time they are in India or abroad for their higher education which is expensive or lacking in most Gulf countries.

Short-term stay and inevitability of returning home is the hallmark of the Indian migration to the Persian Gulf region. A recent study in Bihar found that about two-thirds of the working class migrants to the Gulf stayed between 2 to 6 years, and 85 per cent between 2 to 8 years. The same study also found a high degree of circularity among the migrants: 25 per cent were once migrants, 42 per cent twice migrants, 21 per cent thrice migrants and 12 per cent had migrated four times or more (Rahman 2001). We do not have comparable data about the middle classes. Thus short-term stay and circularity, both these factors keep the 'community' in a flux.

The attitude of the host society is another factor in any consideration of a community life among the immigrants. The Gulf countries are absolutely clear on this count. As Weiner (1982: 26) put it,

> Migrants are incorporated into the economic structure, but are excluded from the social structure. Separation, not integration or assimilation, is the goal. . . . Social contacts between Arabs and expatriates are minimized. . . . An increasing number of migrants stay for extended periods, and some may remain legally 'temporary' resident, with little notice they can be asked by the government to leave.

The above-mentioned quotation underlines a number of pertinent issues regarding the attitude of the host countries of the Middle East. Legally, there is no question of permanent resident status, naturalisation and citizenship for the Indian migrants. Politically, the Gulf regimes are authoritarian – no political or trade union rights. Economically, market forces and a bit of anarchy (split labour market in wage structure, coercion in domestic service sector, etc) is the norm. Socially, the Gulf societies are patriarchal in ethos and practise. There is a certain social duality in terms of Arab *vs.* non-Arab in the Gulf countries. Fortunately, there is no racism in the Gulf societies but ethnic articulations in terms of *watni* vs. *non-watni* (native *vs.* non-native), and Muslim *vs.* non-Muslim are rather strong. Finally, Islam is the state religion in all the Gulf countries and any criticism – direct or indirect – is absolutely prohibited and can be severely punished.

The above discussion suggests that for a vast majority of Indian immigrants, particularly the working class, there is no organised community life in the Persian Gulf countries. Some degree of community life can be said to exist among the middle classes. To what extent this community life is based on traditional Indian social structure and institutions such as caste system, family and kinship, village and caste *panchayats* (agencies of social control), religion and festivals, regional-linguistic ties, etc. is difficult to tell for lack of any study on the subject. In fact we do not know even the social origins of the contemporary professionals, traders and other entrepreneural groups working and living in the Persian Gulf region. However, newspaper reports and knowledgeable people about the region suggest that regional-linguistic ties are particularly strong among the immigrants in the Gulf. These ties probably supercede religious ties. Thus community life appears to be organized in the form of regional/linguistic associations. It would not be out of place to suggest that the reproduction of the 'community' among the Gulf Indians is perhaps done more through fresh immigration and less through procreation.

The vast majority of Indian immigrants in the Gulf countries continue to hold more or less the same identities and patterns of cultural consumption as in India. Perhaps it would not be an exaggeration to say that for all practical purposes the Gulf countries are an extension of India. Most migrants to the Gulf return to India within two to six years and the non-labour migrants who visit India for attending marriage of relatives and for doing business, pilgrimage and sight seeing do so more often than any other groups of NRIs. There is also an impression that most Gulf NRIs seek spouses in India itself which further strengthens the bonds of family and kinship across the Arabia Sea.

Indian immigrants in the Gulf countries suffer from a number of discriminations – political, economic and socio-cultural. The patriarchal nature of the social structure and the rentier nature of the economy and state of the Gulf countries have effectively curtailed freedoms of political expression, occupational choice and recreational and formal religious activities of the Indian immigrants, and particularly of the non-Muslim immigrants.

As already pointed out, naturalisation and citizenship laws in the Gulf countries are extremely prohibitive for the immigrants. It requires some 15-30 years of continuous residency in addition to other personal qualifications to be considered for naturalisation. Moreover, naturalised citizens in all the Gulf countries continue to varyingly suffer from a number of political disabilities which prevent them from fully integrating into the life of their adopted country. In Bahrain, for example, a naturalised citizen may not vote or run for an elective post until 10 years after naturalisation. A naturalised Kuwaiti is ineligible for nomination or appointment to a representative body and does not have voting rights for 20 years after acquiring citizenship. In the UAE naturalised citizens, with the exception of those of Bahraini, Omani or Qatari origins, do not enjoy any of the political rights mentioned above (Russell 1988).

Trade unionism and strikes are illegal in all the Gulf countries, even in the UAE which is considerably liberal towards the Indians. The system of work permit legally ties Indians to their employers and a worker dismissed by his employer for whatever cause is legally required to leave the country.

Among all categories of workers the plight of housemaids is perhaps the worst. Lured to the Gulf by dreams of prosperity, the so-called governesses from India find themselves trapped in a vicious net of degradation and torture. In the UAE where this problem is acute, there is no law providing protection to these hapless victims of the recruiting agents as well as the employers. In the majority of cases, overwork, low wages, sexual exploitation, rape and torture are the broad parameters of their working and living conditions. Driven to despair these women sometimes have no option but to commit theft, which is often an attempt to retrieve their passport and some cash to run back home, or abscond or end up in vice dens to make both ends meet. In most desperate situations, they are left with no option but to end their lives. Reportedly, even the Indian Embassy, unlike some other embassies which have separate cells devoted to look after the welfare of the maids from their country, provides no recourse to them except promising to take up the matter with the local authorities which it never does. In this regard the position of India as indeed of most Asian countries vis-à-vis the Gulf countries can well be appreciated if we keep in mind the reality of asymmetrical relationship between these labour sending and labour receiving countries. As Weiner (1982: 12-13) put it:

> Gulf governments have little fear that any of the South Asian government could do more than mildly protest mistreatment of migrants, nor would they be likely to suddenly withdraw migrants for political reasons or attempt to use migrants to extend their influence. India is dependent upon the Gulf for oil, exports, employment, remittances, contracts, and for the good will that it seeks as a counterweight in its relations with Pakistan. The Indian Government is thus willing to tolerate conditions for Indians in the Gulf that it would not tolerate for its citizens elsewhere, and its intervention on their behalf are likely to be in a subdued and less public fashion.

Social life of Indians in most of the Gulf countries is highly segmented. They are required in most cases to live away from the areas of native Arabs in the camp sites where the workers have to live a regimented life. There is therefore little scope for building a 'community' among the working class Indian immigrants in the Gulf countries. However, many middle class Indian migrants who expect to remain in the Gulf for many years live with their families and have begun to evolve a network of socio-cultural associations which cater to their needs. These include schools, sports clubs, art centres, ladies associations, etc. In this connection Weiner (1982: 6) wrote in the early 1980s:

> The process has only recently started, and it is done with a minimum of conspicuousness. Indian sports clubs in Kuwait, Bahrain, Dubai, Abu Dhabi, and Oman – places in which the middle class can meet, eat, engage

in sports, and conduct their social life – now have long waiting lists for membership.

In Oman land was given by the Sultan in 1974 to enable the Indians to build a social center. 'There are now several schools for Indian children, a Roman Catholic Church, a few Protestant churches, and several temples, including a Gurudwara for the Sikh community' (Weiner 1982: 21). Similarly, Bahrain and Dubai also have one temple each; the Bahraini temple being over 100-years old. Elsewhere 'Hindus must observe their festivals in less conspicuous locations, or in private.' Non-Muslim Indian immigrants in Saudi Arabia are not allowed to take along with them any religious books or idols. Any negative reference to Islam – even if mild or indirect – is considered blasphemy. Thus in 1992 a Sharjah court awarded six-year jail-term to eleven Indian theatre activists (all from Kerala) for staging a play *The Ants That Feast on Corpses*.

Death is a nightmare for Indians working in the Gulf countries. The biggest problem of course is bringing home the body by the next of kin for funeral rites. In 1996, for example, 2,877 Indians had died in the Gulf countries including 1,461 in Saudi Arabia and 785 in the UAE. In Saudi Arabia non-Muslims are not allowed to be buried. Their bodies cannot be claimed until the responsibility of death (in the case of an unnatural one) had been fixed, and the wages and death compensation due to the deceased have been paid to the next of kin. The whole procedure takes, usually one to two months, and in complicated cases even longer.

Thanks to globalisation, the Indian entertainment industry which includes film, musical concerts, fashion shows, theatres, etc. has expanded tremendously in the 1990s. The Middle East connection through underworld and/or otherwise is well known. Regular shows of films, music concerts and plays are organized in major cities of the region to packed houses. The audience include not only the non-resident Indians but also the Arab masses. Perhaps this has something to do with cultural and civilizational affinity between India and the Middle East. A *Newsweek* report suggests that for millions of movie fans around the world, it is Bollywood, not Hollywood that spins their screen fantasies 'Given the chance between a Steve Martin divorce comedy and a (Indian) musical about the virtues of God and family, Arabs, Africans and South-East Asians often choose the latter', the report notes. Citing an incident the magazine says that when a famous Hollywood film star, Sylvester Stallone, showed up at a film festival in Dubai in 1998, unfortunately for him, so did Bollywood's biggest superstar, Amitabh Bachchan. While Bachchan was mobbed by his fans, Stallone was 'pretty much ignored'.

Sports and particularly Cricket is another Indian industry which has been expanded and extended to the Gulf region. Although the favourite sport of Arabs is football, cricket matches are particularly popular in the Gulf region, particularly in the UAE. The World cup cricket matches hosted at Sharjah have acquired considerable prestige and popularity. Similarly, Indian food, fashion and jewellery are some of the other items that are gaining ground in the Middle East in a big way. As Jain (1998: 357) put it in the wider context, 'the diasporic Indians display a dogged attachment to religious, linguistic, culinary and performative aspects of Indianness.' Additionally, in the Arab/Islamic context the Indian expressive and performing arts serve as complementary items to art forms which cannot develop there due to religious sanctions.

FUTURE PROSPECTS

In spite of drastic reduction in the pay and perks, humiliating working conditions, changing requirements of manpower, and increasing emphasis on Arabisation of work-force in the Gulf countries, an increasing number of Indian migrants have been marking a beeline to desert destinations for jobs. In the period between April 1992 and May 1993 about 372,000 migrants froms Kerala alone had reportedly flown out to the Gulf countries. The phenomenon, however, appears to be understandable given the fact that there are very few employment opportunities left in Kerala. In 1994 the number of unemployed in the state was reckoned to be around 4 million. In other regions of India which send migrants to the Gulf countries the economic situation may not be any different. Be that as it may, the Gulf migration is still an attractive proposition to the country as well as the individual emigrants and their families. As such the Gulf countries continue to remain the *El Dorado* for an overwhelming number of Indian migrants. Not surprisingly, in 2005 about half-a-million Indians migranted to the Gulf countries.

The importance of manpower export and reexport for India is underscored by the fact that remittances from abroad constituted 25 per cent of its export earnings in the mid-1980s. According to an International Labour Organization (ILO) report released in late 1988, the remittance inflows were 1.5 per cent of India's gross domestic product, 6 per cent of gross domestic savings, and 7 per cent of gross domestic capital formation. In spite of this, however, as the ILO report itself pointed out, India had not made serious efforts to 'manage, plan or channelise' manpower export to West Asia which accounted for 95.2 per cent of the country's total labour emigration during 1982-6.

The study states that the export of workers from India is largely left to recruiting agents and that the government's intervention is limited to ensuring that the terms and conditions of employment conform to the specified minimum norms. Similarly, regarding financial flow of remittances, deposits and investments, the Indian government offers no incentives in the form of premium exchange rates or the use of proportion of remittance for imports, the study points out. Also, there is no obligation on the part of migrant workers and their employers to remit any portion of their earnings to India. Foreign exchange control regulations only stipulate that remittance should be channeled through the official banking system and that balances held abroad be repatriated when the migrants return. Such balances can be kept in a special account and the migrant can claim 50 per cent of the amount within a period of 10 years. The study further points out that the Indian government tries to induce only the high skilled and income people living or working abroad to provide repatriable financial resources.

Besides sending remittances which had averted India's balance of payment crisis during the early 1990s, and have raised the level of forex reserves to a respectable level, Indian emigrants' role in boosting up Indo-Gulf trade is equally important. The latter role is even more admirable given the fact that the expatriates in the Gulf countries are allowed to do business only under the sponsorship of a local citizen. Nevertheless, if India benefits from such a migration, the Gulf countries too find it equally beneficial. These benefits are derived from the fact that Indian immigrants are generally hard-working, sincere, efficient, low-paid and law-abiding.

Finally the question of rehabilitation of Gulf return migrants is important given the fact that labour migration to West Asia is not a permanent phenomenon as the migrants are not given immigrant status in the receiving countries. Ideally, there is a need to transform and sustain this one-time or two-times migration-return migration process into what is known as 'circular migration' which is characterised by short term, transitory, repetitive or cyclic movement of people in which the migrants lack any declared intention of permanent or long-lasting change in residence. The smoothness and efficiency with which this process of circulation operates would largely determine the success or otherwise of India's manpower export policy.

CONCLUSION

The six GCC countries, namely, Saudi Arabia, Oman, United Arab Emirates, Kuwait, Qatar and Bahrain jointly host over 95 per cent of about four million Indian immigrants in the Middle East and North Africa. Large-scale Indian migration to these countries is relatively a recent phenomenon – about 30 years old. Oil economy and the scarcity of native workforce there and historical factors largely determined the patterns of this form of migration from India. Most migrants originate in Kerala and other south Indian states and happen to be young, unmarried, less educated and unemployed or underemployed. The migration is 'circular' in nature – migrants preferring to stay only for a few years at a time and looking for an opportunity to migrate again.

Given the stringent naturalization and citizenship laws prevalent in the Gulf countries it is almost impossible for any immigrant to become a citizen of any Gulf country. Lack of any political rights for non-citizens, vast gap between host society and foreign workers, fear of cultural pollution on the part of the ruling Arab elites and patterns of dualism (Arab *vs.* non-Arab, citizen *vs.* non-citizen, etc.) rather than pluralism renders the Indian immigrants as 'separate and unequal' in all the Gulf countries. It may not be an exaggeration to describe these Indian immigrants as 'social pariahs'.

On the contrary, the economic relationship between the Indian immigrants in the Gulf and the host countries can best be described as 'symbiotic'. The Indians are always in need of those extra bucks and the Arab regimes find in Indian immigrants a hardworking, disciplined and docile manpower. At the same time the Indian government is equally pleased to have in Gulf migrants a secure source of remittances and some economic investment.

Geographical proximity as well as a degree of socio-cultural affinity characterized by patriarchy provides enough room for Indians in the Gulf countries to transplant their socio-cultural habits and artifacts. Not surprisingly, Indian movies, music shows, cricket matches and certain food items are exceedingly popular not only among the immigrants but also the Arab masses. Gold being the most favourite metal of Indians provides another reason for them to go to the Gulf countries which have emerged as major centres of gold transaction.

In the mid-1980s Myron Weiner described the Indian Diaspora in the Middle East as 'incipient'. The situation probably has not changed since then and is not likely to change in near future. An overwhelming majority of Indian immigration in the Gulf countries would continue to remain as pure and simple 'non-resident Indians'.

REFERENCES

Adhikari, Anand, 'Resurgent India Bonds: Well Priced, Timed and Executed', *The Hindustan Times*, New Delhi, 27 August 1998.

Allen, Jr., Calvin H., *Oman: The Modernization of the Sultanate*, Boulder, Colorado: Westview Press, 1987.

———, 'The Indian Merchant Community of Masqat', *Bulletin of the School of Oriental and African Studies*, 44 (1), 1981, pp. 39-53.

Amjad, Rashid (ed.), *To the Gulf and Back: Studies on the Economic Impact of Asian Labour Migration*, Geneva: United Nations Development Programme, 1989.

Bhatt, Mahesh, 'Dard, Darr and Déjà Vu', *The Sunday Times of India*, New Delhi, 30 January 2000.

Birks, J.S. and C.A. Sinclair, *International Migration and Development in the Arab Region*, Geneva: International Labour Office, 1980.

Birks, J.S. et al., *GCC Market Report*, Durham: Mountjoy Research Centre, 1992.

Brochmann, Grete, *Middle East Avenue: Female Migration from Sri Lanka to the Gulf*, Boulder, CO.: Westview Press, 1993.

Chandran, Ramesh, 'India-UAE Relations Multi-Faceted, Growing', *The Times of India*, New Delhi, 26 November 1993.

Commerce Research Bureau, *Emigration, Inward Remittances and Economic Growth of Kerala*, Bombay: Commerce Research Bureau, 1978.

Department of Economics and Statistics, *The Report of the Survey on the Utilization of Gulf Remittances in Kerala*, Trivandrum: Department of Economics and Statistics, Govt. of Kerala, 1987.

Economic and Social Commission for Asia and the Pacific (ESCAP), *Returning Migrant Workers: Exploratory Study*, Bangkok: ESCAP.

Gavin, R.J., *Aden Under British Rule, 1839-1967*, London: C. Hurst and Co., 1975.

Ghosh, Soumya K., 'Crackdown on Dawood Cartel', *The Hindustan Times*, New Delhi, 22 March, 1993.

Gogate, Sudha, 'INDIA', in Manolo I. Abella and Yogesh Atal (eds.). *Middle East Interlude: Asian Workers Abroad*, Bangkok: UNESCO Regional Office, 1986, pp. 25-105.

Gulati, I.S. and Ashok Mody, *Remittances of Indian Migrants to the Middle East: An Assessment with Special Reference to Migrants from Kerala*, Trivandrum: Centre for Development Studies (Working Paper 128), 1983.

Gulati, Leela, 'The Impact on the Family of Male Migration to the Middle East: Some Evidence from Kerala, India',. in Fred Arnold and Nasra M. Shah (eds.), *Asian Labour Migration: Pipeline to the Middle East*, Boulder and London: Westview Press, 1986, pp. 194-212.

———, *In the Absence of Their Men: The Impact of Male Migration on Women*, New Delhi: Sage, 1993.

Jain, Prakash C., 'Indians Abroad: A Current Population Estimate', *Economic and Political Weekly*, 17(8): 1982, pp. 299-304.

———, 'Emigration and Settlement of Indians Abroad', *Sociological Bulletin*, 38(1): 1989, pp. 155-68.

———, *Racial Discrimination against Overseas Indians: A Class Analysis*, New Delhi: Concept, 1990.

———, 'Rehabilitating the Returning Migrants from the Gulf', *International Studies*, 28(3): 1991a, pp. 307-15.

———, 'The Social Implications of the Gulf Crisis: Refugees, Returnees, and Peripheral Changes', in A.H.H. Abidi and K.R. Singh (eds.), *The Gulf Crisis*, New Delhi: Lancers Books, 1991b, pp. 156-76.

———, 'Gulf Migration and its impact on India and Indo-Gulf Relations', *Journal of Peace Studies*, 5(1): 1998, pp. 12-28.

———, *Indians in South Africa: Political Economy of Race Relations*, New Delhi: Kalinga Publications, 1999.

———, *Population and Society in West Asia*, Jaipur: National Publishing House, 2001.

Jain, Ravindra K., *Indian Communities Abroad: Themes and Literature*, New Delhi: Manohar, 1993.

———, 'Indian Diaspora, Globalisation and Multi-culturalilsm: A Cultural Analysis', *Contributions to Indian Sociology* (n.s.), 32(2): 1998, pp. 337-60.

Kapoor, Pankaj, 'To NRI Market, to Bag a Big Hit', *Delhi Times*, 7 October 1999.

Kazmi, Nikhat, 'Bhai, Why Shoot a Dead Duck?', *The Sunday Times of India*, New Delhi, 30 January 2000.

Kondapi, C., *Indians Overseas, 1838-1949*, Madras: Oxford University Press, 1951.

Kurian, Raju, 'Patterns of Emigration from Kerala', *Social Scientist*, 7(6): 1979, pp. 32-53.

Mathew, E.T. and P.R.G. Nair, 'Socio-Economic Characteristics of Emigrants and Emigrant Households: A Case Study of Two Villages in Kerala', *Economic and Political Weekly*, 13(28): 1978, pp. 1141-53.

Mohan, Man, 'Child Beggars in Saudi Arabia: Operators Earning Rs. 20 Crore a year', *The Hindustan Times*, New Delhi, 20 March 1997.

Nair, P.R. Gopinathan, 'India', in Godfrey Gunatilleke (ed.), *Migration of Asian Workers to the Arab World*, Tokyo: The United Nations University, 1986, pp. 66-109.

———, 'Incidence, Impact and Implications of Migration to the Middle East from Kerala (India)', in Rashid Amjad (ed.), *To the Gulf and Back: Studies on the Economic Impact of Asian Labour Migration*, New Delhi: ILO-ARTEP, 1989, pp. 95-142.

Nayyar, Deepak, *Migration, Remittances and Capital Flows: The Indian Experience*, New Delhi: Oxford University Press, 1994.

Omran, Abdel R. and Farzaneh Roudi, 'The Middle East Population Puzzle', *Population Bulletin*, 48(1): 1993, pp. 1-38.

Parekh, Bhikhu, 'Some Reflections on the Indian Diaspora', Second *Global Convention of People of Indian Origin*, 27-31, December 1993, New Delhi (Mimeo).

Prakash, B.A., 'Impact of Foreign Remittances: A Case Study of Chavakkad Village in Kerala', *Economic and Political Weekly*, 13(27): 1978, pp. 1107-11.

———, 'Gulf Migration and its Economic Impact: The Kerala Experience', *Economic and Political Weekly*, 33(50), 1998, pp. 3209-13.

Rahman, Anisur, *Indian Labour Migration to the Gulf Countries*, New Delhi: Rajat Publications, 2001.

Russell, Sharon Stanton, 'Migration and Political Integration in the Arab World', in Giacomo Luciani and Ghassam Salame (eds.), *The Politics of Arab Integration*, London: Croom Helm, 1988, pp. 183-210.

Serageldin, Ismail et al., *Manpower and International Migraition in the Middle East and North Africa*, Washington, D.C.: The World Bank, 1981.

Singh, Anil, 'The Silence of the Lambs', *The Sunday Times of India*, New Delhi, 30 January 2000.

Tinker, Hugh, *The Banyan Tree: Overseas Emigrant from India, Pakistan and Bangladesh*, Oxford: Oxford University Press, 1977.

Tellis, Olga, 'Dawood versus Dawood', *The Sunday Observer*, New Delhi, 18-24 August 1991.

Weiner, Myron, 'International Migration and Development: Indians in the Persian Gulf', *Population and Development Review*, 8(1): 1982, pp. 1-36.

——, 'Labour Migrations as Incipient Diasporas', in Gabriel Sheffer (ed.), *Modern Diasporas in International Politics*, London: Croom Helm, 1986.

Zachariah, K.C. et al., *Kerala's Gulf Connection: CDS Studies on International Labour Migration from Kerala State in India*, Thiruvananthapuram: Centre for Development Studies, 2002.

CHAPTER 9

Aspects of Indian Labour Diaspora in the United Arab Emirates

K.C. ZACHARIAH, B.A. PRAKASH AND
S. IRUDAYA RAJAN

A large number of Indian workers have been migrating to the Gulf countries since the mid-1970s. During the past three decades or so the major destinations of Indian contract workers have been Saudi Arabia, the United Arab Emirates (UAE), Oman, Kuwait, Bahrain and Qatar, in that order. Thanks to the sustained though fluctuating migration outflow over the years, presently there are over 4 million Indian expatriates in the above mentioned Gulf countries. With 1.5 million Indian immigrants, Saudi Arabia has the largest expatriate Indian community followed by UAE (1.0 million), Oman (400,000), Kuwait (350,000), Bahrain (170,000), and Qatar (160,000). A noteworthy feature of the Indian expatriate community in the Gulf has been the numerical predominance of the Malayalis (often referred to as Keralites) – ranging from 40 per cent to 60 per cent in different countries. Against this background this paper focuses on the Indian, i.e. Keralite labour diaspora in the UAE. Based on a survey among the Indian workers in the UAE it examines aspects of employment, wages, and working conditions and future prospects of Indian immigrant workers in the UAE.

Although a number of studies have been done on Indian migration, return migration and their impact on Kerala and other regions of the country, this is perhaps the first ever systematic study of contract Indian labour in any Gulf country. A review of the literature on emigration to West Asia shows that most of the studies dealt mainly with the profiles and socio-economic backgrounds of emigrants, processes of emigration, economic and social impacts of remittances and issues and problems of return migrants. The studies conducted during the late 1970s and the early 1980s were mainly micro level studies examining the profiles of migrants, their socio-economic background, causes of migration and the impact of remittances based on village surveys (e.g. Prakash, 1978; Mathew and Gopinathan Nair, 1978; Kurien, 1979; Radhakrishnan and Ibrahim, 1981; Agro Economic Research Centre, 1982). Impact of Gulf Migration on society, especially the impact of male emigration on women and family is another topic in which a few studies were conducted by sociologists (Gulati, 1983; 1987; 1993; Sekhar, 1997). The economic impact of Gulf Migration on Kerala is a topic which attracted considerable attention from economists and demographers (Gopinathan Nair, 1989; Thomas Isaac, 1993; Prakash, 1998a; 1998b; Zachariah, Mathew and Irudaya Rajan, 2001). A hypothesis put forward in one of the studies is that 'since the mid 1970s, the factor which had the greatest impact on Kerala's economy especially on labour market, consumption, savings, investment, poverty, income distribution and economic growth has been the Gulf migration and migrant remittances' (Prakash, 1998). A similar conclusion was arrived by another study based on a statewide survey (Zachariah, Mathew and Irudaya Rajan, 2001). Issues connected with return emigration such as the causes of return, socio-economic background of the returnees, the current activity status of the returnees and the problems faced by them is another area where a number of studies are available (Gopinathan Nair, 1986; Nambiar, 1995; Prakash, 2000; Zachariah, Gopinathan Nair and Irudaya Rajan, 2001). Among the studies conducted so far on Kerala emigration, the study of Zachariah et al. provides a detailed taluk-wise, district-wise estimation of migrants and return migrants and detailed economic and demographic analysis. The study was based on a sample survey of 10,000 households covering all taluks of Kerala (Zachariah, Mathew and Irudaya Rajan, 1999). Apart from these studies, one by Deepak Nayyar (1994) provides a profile of international labour migration from India and analyses the macroeconomic impact of labour force and the associated financial flows on the national economy and examines the issues or problems that arise in a wider macroeconomic context with reference to the Indian experience.

Though these studies provide rich information about the issues of emigration from Kerala to the Gulf countries based on primary information collected from migrant households, we do not have much information about the labour market situation and the employment, wages and working conditions of emigrants in the Gulf countries. Hence this study.

SOURCES OF DATA

The data for the study are collected from primary and secondary sources in the UAE. In order to study details of employment, wages, working conditions of Indian emigrants, their living conditions, the facilities and perquisites that they enjoyed, the migration prospects, the study team conducted a field survey in the UAE covering a sample of 361 Keralite emigrants. The data were collected in 2001 in Abu Dhabi, Dubai, and Sharjah using a structured interview schedule. The samples were selected from all major categories of emigrant workers who live in cities in rental accommodation as well as those who live in worker camps. In order to know about current migration issues and problems detailed discussion were held with ten major Indian socio-cultural associations in the UAE, particularly in Abu Dhabi, Dubai and Sharjah.

CONCEPTUAL FRAMEWORK

The International Labour Organization (ILO) has classified international migration for employment into two major categories, viz. settlement migration and contract migration (ILO, 1989). Settlement migration is a traditional type of migration in which people migrate from one country to another to secure jobs and settle there. People having high skills and professional qualifications from developing economies used to migrate to developed countries to secure better jobs, opportunities, living conditions and to settle there. This type of migration is often associated with the concept of 'brain drain'. The volume of movements of this type of migrants from developing to developed countries declined during the 1970s (ILO, 1989).

International contract migration occurs when a worker is officially granted permission to enter another country and take up employment in a given job and where a contract is entered into on his behalf or between him and the employer or enterprise for which he is to work. Contract itself takes several forms like individual contract and collective contract. In collective contract a number or a group of foreign workers are being admitted for the purpose of employment under a single authorization or on behalf of a single employer. It has variously been referred to as block visa migration, collective contract migration or project-tied migration. Project-tied migration conjures up a picture of foreigners admitted to a migrant-receiving country for a period of time on the basis of a work contract with an enterprise or employer to carry out in that country specific projects that by their nature are limited in time. Migrant workers are persons admitted by a country other than their own for the explicit purpose of carrying out an economic activity. The category of migrant workers includes seasonal migrant workers, project-tied migrant workers, contract migrant workers, temporary migrant workers, established migrant workers and highly skilled migrant workers.

A number of scholars have reviewed the existing models of international migration (Heisel, 1982; Schoorl, 1998; Massey et al., 1993). From these studies it is evident that there exists no integrated theory of the process of international migration but only a set of partial theories and models developed from different disciplinary viewpoints. While the earlier theoretical models exclusively concentrate on the process of labour migration, the recent ones try to explain why migration continues once it has started. Though several theoretical approaches are followed to discuss settlement migration, none discusses issues connected with contract migration and return migration. In the context of contract migration to West Asian countries, the labour market factors have a crucial role in determining the nature, category and flow of migration as well as of return migration. Wages and working conditions in the labour-importing countries are also determined by labour market factors.

EXPATRIATE LABOUR MARKET IN UAE

Structure of Employment

The UAE was established on 2 December 1971 comprising the seven emirates of Abu Dhabi, Dubai, Sharjah, Ras al-Khaimah, Ajman,

Umm al-Qaiwain and Fujairah. Over a relatively short time span of three decades, the UAE has been transformed from a subsistence economy to a highly prosperous modern economy. This transformation was made possible by the utilization of its huge export earnings from petroleum products into infrastructure building and promotion of economic activities. Country's proven resources of oil are estimated at around 98.1 billion barrel representing 10 per cent of the world's oil reserves. Abu Dhabi is the biggest oil producer in the UAE accounting for more than 85 per cent of its oil output and 90 per cent of its crude reserves. The sudden rise in oil prices in the 1970s and the 1980s had resulted in the accumulation of large volumes of foreign exchange. The oil earnings were used largely for large-scale investment in physical and social infrastructure resulting in rapid transformation of the economy. In 1971, the UAE had a population of 180,000 in an area of 83,600 square kilometres. There were substantial differences between the individual emirates in terms of size of population and the level of economic development. By 1997, the total population of the UAE was estimated at 2,624,000 including expatriates (Table 9.1). Of the seven emirates, Abu Dhabi accounts for 39 per cent, Dubai 29 per cent and Sharjah 17 per cent and the other emirates account for only 15 per cent of the total population of the UAE.

Though the UAE achieved rapid economic growth during the early 1990s, the economy had experienced a severe recession in the

TABLE 9.1: POPULATION OF UAE, 1997

	Total Population (in thousand)			*Per cent*		
Emirates	*Male*	*Female*	*Total*	*Male*	*Female*	*Total*
Abu Dhabi	705	312	1017	40.17	35.90	38.76
Dubai	528	229	757	30.09	26.35	28.85
Sharjah	278	161	439	15.84	18.53	16.73
Ajman	82	55	137	4.67	6.33	5.22
Ummal-qaiwan	23	16	39	1.31	1.84	1.49
Ras al-khaimah	89	63	152	5.07	7.25	5.79
Fujairah	50	33	83	2.85	3.80	3.16
Total	1,755	869	2624	100.00	100.00	100.00

Source: UAE Year Book, 1998.

late 1990s. In 1997 the growth rate was only 1.2 per cent compared to 11 per cent during 1996. This recession was the basic reason for the large-scale decline in employment and the consequent return of large number of expatriates. The sectors which registered a negative growth rate were crude oil production, construction, real estate and business services. There was also a decline in construction, real estate activities and a slump in trade and commerce.

The structure of employment in the UAE is characterized by an extremely large sector of tertiary activities such as trade, restaurants and hotels, transport and communications, finance, real estate business, personal services and government services. The tertiary sector accounted for 58 per cent of the total employment in 1998 (Table 9.2).

The secondary sector comprising manufacturing, water supply, electricity and construction accounted for another 33 per cent. The primary sector comprising agriculture, livestock, forestry, fishing and mining, employed only 9 per cent of the work force. In the UAE the activities which provide the largest employment are construction,

Table 9.2: STRUCTURE OF EMPLOYMENT IN UAE

Category		*1998 (Number)*	*Per cent*
Agriculture, livestock and fishing		101,800	7.38
Mining and quarrying	A. crude oil	21,900	1.59
	B. others	3,700	0.27
I. Sub Total: Primary		127,400	9.24
Manufacturing		173,800	12.61
Water and electricity		23,935	1.74
Construction		255,800	18.56
II. Sub Total: Secondary		453,535	32.91
Wholesale/retail trade, maintenance service		234,700	17.02
Restaurants and hotels		52,850	3.83
Transport, storage and communications		98,710	7.16
Financial institutions and insurance		20,866	1.51
Real estate and other business services		35,440	2.57
Social and personal services		63,450	4.60
Government services		153,659	11.15
Domestic services of households		137,880	10.00
III. Sub Total: Tertiary		797,555	57.84
Total		1,378,490	100.00

Source: UAE Year Book, 1998.

followed by trade and government services. Almost all unskilled construction workers and those working as household workers are expatriates. It is estimated that of the total workers, the UAE nationals accounted for only 9.2 per cent in 1995.

Expatriate Population in UAE

Accurate data are not available about the total number of foreigners in the UAE. According to a census conducted in 1968 by the British, the UAE had a population of about 180,000 of which 63.5 per cent were enumerated as nationals belonging to the seven emirates. It was estimated by the UAE government that the percentage of nationals had declined to 25 per cent by 1995 (Table 9.3). The expatriates include the workers and their dependants which account for a sizeable proportion. The total number of expatriates was estimated as 1,777,000 constituting 75 per cent of the total population of U.A.E. Of them the total expatriate workers is estimated at 1,391,000 in 1995 (Table 9.4).

TABLE 9.3: POPULATION OF UAE NATIONALS AND EXPATRIATES, SELECTED YEARS

Year	*UAE Nationals (per cent)*	*Expatriates (per cent)*
1968	63.5	36.5
1975	30.0	70.0
1995	25.1	74.9
1997	25.0	75.0

Source: UAE Year Book, 1998.

TABLE 9.4: TOTAL POPULATION OF UAE IN 1995

	Number (in thousand)			*Per cent*		
	Male	*Female*	*Total*	*Male*	*Female*	*Total*
1. Nationals	303	293	596	19.20	36.86	25.12
2. Expatriates	1,082	309	1,391	68.57	38.87	58.62
3. Dependent expatriates	193	193	386	12.23	24.28	16.27
4. Total expatriates (2+3)	1,275	502	1,777	80.80	63.14	74.88
5. Total population	1,578	795	2,373	100.00	100.00	100.00

Source: Estimates based on work/residence permits issued to expatriates by UAE Ministry of Interior.

TABLE 9.5: EMIGRANT WORKERS IN UAE IN 1995

	Number (in thousand)			*Per cent*		
	Male	*Female*	*Total*	*Male*	*Female*	*Total*
1. Asian countries	923	263	1,186	85.30	85.11	85.26
2. Arab countries	136	39	175	12.57	12.62	12.58
3. European countries	16	5	21	1.48	1.62	1.51
4. American countries	4	1	5	0.37	0.32	0.36
5. African countries	2	1	3	0.18	0.32	0.21
6. Others	1	--	1	0.09	–	0.07
Total	1,082	309	1,391	100.00	100.00	100.00

Source: UAE Year Book.

The country-wise data of expatriate workers suggest that Asian countries accounted for the largest share of emigrant workers in 1995. The total number of workers from the Asian countries was estimated as 1,186,000 accounting for 85 per cent of the total emigrant workers of the UAE (Table 9.5). The total number of workers from other Arab countries was estimated as 175,000 or about 13 per cent. The shares of European, American and African workers were quite small. The emigrants from the Arab region belonged to Egypt, Syria, Jordan, Palestine, Lebanon, Sudan, Yemen and Somalia. Among the Arab countries Egypt accounted for the largest share of emigrant workers in the UAE followed by Syria, Jordan, Lebanon and Sudan.

The migrants from the Asian countries are mainly from India, Pakistan, Bangladesh, Sri Lanka, Philippines and Iran. The total number of Indian emigrant workers is estimated as 585,000 accounting for 42 per cent of the total emigrant workers in the UAE (Table 9.6). Of the Indian workers 122,000 are female workers. Emigrant workers of Pakistan came to 293,000 constituting 21 per cent of the total emigrant workers in the UAE. Sri Lanka, Philippines and Iran are the other Asian nations having sizeable number of emigrants in the UAE. The Indian emigrant population in the UAE consists of workers and their dependants. The total Indian population is estimated as 729,000 in 1995 (Table 9.7). The dependant population comprising wives, children and parents was estimated as 144,000. The dependants account for 20 per cent of the total number of Indian emigrants.

TABLE 9.6: ASIAN EMIGRANT WORKERS IN UAE, 1995

	Number (in thousand)			Per cent		
	Male	Female	Total	Male	Female	Total
1. India	463	122	585	42.79	39.48	42.05
2. Pakistan	232	61	293	21.44	19.74	21.06
3. Bangladesh	83	22	105	7.67	7.12	7.55
4. Sri Lanka	64	23	87	5.91	7.44	6.25
5. Philippines	45	25	70	4.16	8.09	5.03
6. Iran	28	7	35	2.59	2.26	2.52
7. Other Asian countries	8	3	11	0.74	0.97	0.79
Total	923	263	1186	85.30	85.11	85.26

Source: UAE Year Book.

TABLE 9.7: INDIAN EMIGRANTS IN UAE, 1995

	Number (in thousand)			Per cent		
	Male	Female	Total	Male	Female	Total
Workers	463	122	585	86.54	62.89	80.25
Dependants	72	72	144	13.45	37.11	19.75
Total	535	194	729	100.00	100.00	100.00

Source: UAE Year Book.

Total Population of Keralites in UAE in 2001

The information that we collected from the Indian Embassy in Abu Dhabi and some of the Indian associations in Abu Dhabi, Dubai and Sharjah, suggests that the total population of Indian emigrants in UAE during 2001 was about 1 million persons. The Indian Embassy and Indian emigrants associations are of the opinion that the share of Keralities in the total population of Indians was about 50 per cent. Thus the total number of Keralities in UAE was about 500,000 in 2001.

IMMIGRATION POLICY OF THE UAE

Demographic Imbalance

In the UAE the central criterion on which the entire immigration, labour and economic policies are formulated is based on the demographic imbalance theory. The UAE government, the Federal National Council (FNC) and the UAE nationals feel that owing to the large and increasing proportion of expatriate workers, the role and importance of the UAE nationals are getting marginalized in the economy and society; creating a very dangerous situation. A report presented in FNC in June 2001 pointed out that the Indian expatriates account for 33.5 per cent of the total population of UAE. Around 50 per cent of the population comprises people from one single geographical region, the Indian subcontinent comprising India, Pakistan and Bangladesh. It is reported that foreigners account for about 60 per cent of the public sector workforce in UAE. A recent study on workforce found that construction and services employ the majority of workers. Of them two-thirds do not have secondary education. Eighty per cent of the applications for work permits received in the Ministry of Labour and Social Affairs were for unskilled and cheap manpower. The influx of foreign labour was obliterating the Arab character of the region; in fact some areas in the UAE resembled parts of India or Pakistan. The general feeling is that the UAE is in danger of losing its identity because most of the important activities are in the hands of foreigners. The core of the immigration policy has, therefore, been to set right the demographic imbalance through appropriate policy measures. The Ministry of Labour and Social Affairs of the UAE has prepared a document called *Labour 2000 Report* containing the immigration policy approach. The report specifies three major problems: demographic imbalance, increasing number of foreign workers, and dependants of unskilled workers, mainly Asians. The policy suggestions put forward were, reduction of the demographic imbalance, controlling of the inflow of unskilled labourers, imparting of training to the existing workforce to cope with developments of modern technology and coercing the private establishments to invest in modern technology. The Ministry also intended to introduce several measures to make the recruitment of unskilled expatriate manpower costlier. It envisages a work environment that depends on skilled manpower and advancing technology, an environment free of marginal and menial workers. It is also decided to fix the minimum qualification even for unskilled workers, as high school certificate. The major policy measures implemented in recent years to curtail immigration are the following.

Ban on Visas for Unskilled Workers

The Ministry of Labour of the UAE government stopped accepting applications for visas for unskilled workers with effect from 18 July 1999. It was pointed out that the move to stop accepting visa applications from Asian countries for unskilled jobs was in line with the Ministry's efforts to rectify the demographic imbalance in the labour force. The UAE government has not lifted the ban imposed on unskilled Indian workers till now. Besides, strict action was initiated against illegal and unskilled expatriates already in the UAE. Owing to this measure thousands of illegal immigrants were sent back home.

Move to Make Unskilled Labour Expensive

In order to curtail the number of unskilled labourers, the UAE government has introduced several measures to make recruitment of unskilled labour costly. The objective is to force private establishments to invest in modern technology. It is pointed out that as long as unskilled manpower was available at low wages, the private sector would not go for modern technology. Therefore, the policy is to make the private sector experience a scarcity of unskilled labour so that it would be forced to invest in labour-saving and productivity-augmenting modern technology.

Emiratization

The objective of Emiratization is to give priority to the natives of the UAE in job placements and to reduce unemployment among UAE nationals. With this objective, the UAE government has already started measures to replace foreign labour with nationals in the public sector. Some of the important public sector undertakings have already taken measures to emiratize their workforce. The Emirates Telecommunication Corporation (ETISLALAT) has undertaken a policy of emiratizing half its workforce by the end of 2000. Programmes have been designed to encourage nationals to take-up top administrative and technical jobs. As part of this effort, students are being sent to European countries for higher studies. The Ministry of Labour has also intensified its efforts to convince the private sector the need for giving preference to nationals in job placements. The UAE nationals working in private sector companies are ensured of the same social security benefits as are available to workers in the government sector companies. The new National Pension and Social Security Scheme provides for retirement benefits, disability benefits and compensation for death for the nationals working in the public sector. Currently the UAE government is considering a proposal for stopping issuance of employment visas for professional places that could be filled by UAE nationals. In line with the emiratization drive the Ministry of Labour and Social Affairs would pursue the policy of gradual replacement of foreign workforce with nationals.

60-Year Age Ceiling for Renewal of Labour Card

The UAE government has decided not to renew the labour cards of private sector employees above the age of 60 with effect from 30 May 1999. However certain categories of professionals are exempted from the ban. They include doctors, engineers, consultants, legal advisers, economists, financial experts, teachers at all levels, auditors and accountants, translators, computer workers, laboratory technicians, delicate equipment maintenance technicians, sportsmen and professional coaches, and some other kinds of specialists.

Other Factors

We may also examine the other factors which contribute to changes in the demand for migrant labour in the UAE. The important factors are the following:

(i) The major infrastructure projects requiring large numbers of unskilled, semi-skilled and skilled construction workers have been almost completed. In another two years almost the entire infrastructure work will be over. There is, therefore, a possibility for large scale decline in the demand for unskilled, semi-skilled and skilled categories of construction workers.

(ii) The UAE has been witnessing a decline in business, trade and other economic activities during the past three years. A liquidity crisis is also experienced by the UAE, the government departments finding it difficult to honour payment obligations relating to major infrastructure and housing projects. Large numbers of business collapses are reported. There is less demand for buildings, flats and commercial complexes due to the ongoing economic recession.

(iii) Dubai, the biggest commercial city in the UAE lost its importance as an intermediary station for re-export of many commodities. Now Dubai is given importance more as a place of exhibitions and conferences and as a tourism destination.

(iv) The UAE is vigorously following a policy of privatization of public utilities such as water, electricity and other public goods. This has resulted in a shift of the concerned units from the public to the private sector. Workers who used to receive wage and non-wage benefits at par with the workers in government departments now get much lower wage and non-wage benefits.

(v) The Ministry of Labour has introduced a new measure by which each employer seeking a new visa for work will have to deposit 3,000 Dirham in the Ministry. The intention is to make it possible for the Ministry to pay salary and other dues in case the employers concerned fail to make the payments. This measure has acted as a disincentive to the issue of fresh visas. From the preceding analysis we may make the following observations. The UAE economy has been witnessing a rapid structural change; large employment opportunities are generated in tertiary sector activities such as trade and commerce, transport and communications, government services and social and personal services. Owing to the immigration policy of rectifying demographic imbalance, controlling the inflow of unskilled labourers and training of the existing workforce to cope with modern technology, the future requirement of manpower will be confined to skilled categories. Policies such as emiratization, banning of visas for unskilled Asian workers and making employment of unskilled labour expensive, are likely to result in the decline of demand for workers of unskilled and semi skilled categories. The completion of major infrastructure projects, recession in business and trade, privatization policies and other restrictions imposed on visa issues would also reduce the demand for such categories. In future, the manpower demand in the UAE would be for categories such as doctors, pharmacists, nurses, engineers, consultants, legal advisers, economists, financial experts, teachers at all levels, auditors and accountants, translators, computer workers, laboratory technicians, delicate equipment maintenance technicians, sportsmen and professional coaches, and rare specialists of all other categories.

EMPLOYMENT, WAGES AND WORKING CONDITIONS: RESULTS OF A FIELD-SURVEY IN THE UAE

Profile of Emigrants

The distribution of the 361 sample emigrants on the basis of place of birth revealed that they came from all the districts of Kerala. The emigrants belonging to Malappuram district constituted the largest share. The emigrants from the districts of Thiruvananthapuram, Kollam, Alappuzha, Thrissur, Malappuram and Kannur together accounted for 70 per cent of the total sample.

Nearly two-fifths had passed the secondary school and about 30 per cent were graduates. The percentage of non-educated, i.e. those who have an educational level below secondary is 30 per cent. The proportion which had education of less than the secondary level formed another 30 per cent.

Around four-fifths of the sample reported that they were in a foreign land for work for the first time in their lives. For another 16 per cent, it was the second time; they had worked once earlier in the UAE itself or in another Gulf country. There were a few emigrants (less than 3 per cent) who had two earlier emigration experiences. In order to understand the trends in emigration, we collected information about the year of arrival of the sample emigrants in the UAE. It was found that 23 per cent arrived during the 1980s and another 20 per cent during the first half of the 1990s. A recent trend in emigration observed is the continuous decline in the numbers since 1999. The sharp fall experienced during 1999, 2000 and the first half of 2001 could be attributed to the ban on issuance of visa imposed for unskilled and low skilled categories of Indian workers. The categories of workers who emigrated during the second half of the 1990s were technicians, accountants, auditors, executives, managers, salesmen, shop assistants, house keepers, electrical workers, plumbers, welders, sheet metal workers, construction workers and transport equipment operators.

Employment

We have classified the employment status of the sample emigrants using the National Classification of Occupations. It was found that nearly one-fifth were employed in professional and technical categories; about 6 per cent were in administrative, executive and managerial categories; 15 per cent were clerical and related workers, 13 per cent were sales workers, less than one-tenth were service workers and more than one-third were production related workers, transport equipment operators and related workers. The category of production related workers in the sample included electricians, electronic equipment operators, plumbers, welders, sheet metal workers, metal workers and construction workers (Table 9.8).

The sample emigrants are classified into four categories: regular, long term employees with monthly salary/wage; regular employees with daily or piece wages; casual workers; and the self-employed. It is found that more than three-fourths of the sample workers were employed with monthly salary/wage. Another 15 per cent worked were regular employees, but were paid wages on a daily basis or under the piece wage system. On the other hand, the share of casual workers on piece wages and self-employed persons were quite small. In the case of professional, technical, administrative, executive and managerial workers, more than 92 per cent were employed as regular long-term employees on a monthly salary basis (Table 9.9). In other categories such as clerical and related workers, sales workers, service workers, production workers, transport equipment operators and

TABLE 9.8: OCCUPATIONAL DISTRIBUTION OF SAMPLE EMIGRANTS

Category	*Per cent*
Professional/Technical and Related Workers	20.78
Administrative, Executive and Managerial Workers	5.72
Clerical and Related Workers	14.76
Sales	13.25
Service	9.04
Farmers, Fishermen and Related Workers	0.60
Production and Related Workers, Transport Equipment Operators and Related Workers	35.84
Total	100.00

Source: Field Survey conducted at United Arab Emirates, 2001.

TABLE 9.9: OCCUPATIONAL DISTRIBUTION OF SAMPLE EMIGRANTS BY NATURE OF JOB

(*in percentage*)

Category	*Regular long term employee with monthly wage*	*Regular with a daily or piece wage*	*Self-employed*	*Others*	*Total*
Professional, Technical and Related Workers	91.8	–	3.3	4.9	100.0
Administrative, Executive and Managerial Workers	94.4	–	–	5.6	100.0
Clerical and Related Workers	85.0	2.5	2.5	10.0	100.0
Sales Workers	76.3	10.5	10.5	2.6	100.0
Service Workers	80.77	11.54	3.85	3.85	100.0
Farmers, Fishermen, Hunters and Related Workers	100.0	–	–	–	100.0
Production and Related Workers, Transport Equipment Operators and Related Workers	63.06	32.43	–	4.5	100.0
Total	77.36	14.86	2.70	5.07	100.0

Source: Field Survey conducted at United Arab Emirates, 2001.

related workers, more than three-fourths were also employed as regular, long term salaried employees with a monthly wage. The proportions of workers in regular employment but paid daily or piece wages were small and belonged mostly to the categories of production and related workers, transport equipment operators and construction workers.

It is found that one-fifth of the workers are employed in government or public sector institutions (Table 9.10). Another one-fifth each are employed in establishments owned by non-UAE employers and UAE nationals. A significant finding is that 29 per cent of the sample emigrants were employed in establishments owned by Keralite or Indian entrepreneurs. These establishments provided employment mainly to professional and technical workers, sales workers, production and related workers and transport equipment operators and related workers.

TABLE 9.10: OCCUPATIONAL DISTRIBUTION OF SAMPLE EMIGRANTS BY CATEGORY OF EMPLOYER

Occupation	*Category of Employer*					
	Government/ Public sector	*Private Non-UAE Employer*	*Private UAE Employer*	*Private Keralite/ Indian Employer*	*Others*	*Total*
Professional/Technical and Related Workers	27.94	20.59	26.47	23.53	1.47	100.0
Administrative, Executive and Managerial Workers	10.53	42.10	21.05	21.05	5.26	100.0
Clerical and Related Workers	38.78	20.41	14.29	14.29	12.24	100.0
Sales Workers	9.30	9.30	23.26	37.21	20.93	100.0
Service Workers	13.33	26.67	26.67	20.0	13.33	100.0
Farmers, Fishermen, Hunters and Related Workers	50.0	–	50.0	–	–	100.0
Production and Related Workers, Transport Equipment Operators and Related Workers	14.29	22.69	19.33	40.34	3.36	100.0
Total	20.0	21.51	21.51	29.39	7.58	100.0

Source: Field Survey conducted at United Arab Emirates, 2001.

The places of work of the sample emigrants included offices, shops, houses, factories, workshops, construction sites, and open fields. It was found that of the total sample, about two-fifths were employed in office-related jobs. Another 17 per cent worked in construction sites. About 14 per cent were employed in workshops and factories mostly as production workers, transport equipment operators and related workers. Less than one-tenth were engaged in shops and commercial establishments. Workers who had to toil in open spaces were those related to construction and transportation activities; this category accounted for 4 per cent. Our sample had only less than 2 per cent in the category of domestic (household) servants (Table 9.11).

TABLE 9.11: OCCUPATIONAL DISTRIBUTION OF SAMPLE EMIGRANTS BY NATURE OF WORKPLACE

(in percentage)

Occupation	*Place of Work*								*Total*
	Office	*Shop*	*House*	*Factory*	*Work-shop*	*Constr-uction site*	*Open-space*	*Others*	
Professional/Technical and Related Workers	63.77	1.45	–	1.45	–	11.59	2.90	18.84	100.0
Administrative, Executive and Managerial Workers	73.68	5.26	–	–	–	5.26	10.53	5.26	100.0
Clerical and Related Workers	73.47	4.08	–	–	–	2.04	2.04	18.37	100.0
Sales Workers	32.56	32.56	–	2.33	2.33	2.33	9.30	18.60	100.0
Service Workers	43.33	26.67	6.67	–	–	3.33	–	20.0	100.0
Farmers, Fishermen, Hunters and Related Workers	50.0	–	–	–	–	–	–	50.0	100.0
Production and Related Workers, Transport Equipment Operators and Related Workers	5.93	2.54	2.54	2.54	33.05	38.14	4.24	11.02	100.0
Total	39.09	8.79	1.52	1.52	12.12	17.27	4.24	15.45	100.0

Source: Field Survey conducted at United Arab Emirates, 2001.

Education and Employment

Table 9.12 reveals the occupational classification of the sample emigrants by educational level. Persons with educational levels of less than secondary school are found to be working in construction, production, transport and related activities and in other service sector occupations. On the other hand those who have passed secondary school and/or possess higher educational qualifications are found to be employed in professional, technical, administrative, executive, clerical and sales-related work. It may be noted that only a small proportion of the persons having degrees worked as production-related workers, or as transport equipment operators.

Persons who had passed the secondary school or acquired higher educational qualifications were found to be in better employment

TABLE 9.12: OCCUPATIONAL DISTRIBUTION OF SAMPLE EMIGRANTS BY LEVELS OF EDUCATION

(in percentage)

Occupation	*Below Primary*	*Below Secondary*	*Secondary and Post Graduate*	*Degree*	*Total*
Professional/Technical and Related Workers	–	2.86	24.29	72.86	100.0
Administrative, Executive and Managerial Workers	–	11.76	52.94	35.29	100.0
Clerical and Related Workers	4.08	14.29	30.61	51.02	100.0
Sales Workers	11.11	20.0	35.56	33.33	100.0
Service Workers	24.14	37.93	27.59	10.34	100.0
Farmers, Fishermen, Hunters and Related Workers	–	100.0	–	–	100.0
Production and Related Workers, Transport Equipment Operators and Related Workers	10.34	31.03	56.03	2.59	100.0
Total	7.93	21.04	36.93	31.40	100.0

Source: Field Survey conducted at United Arab Emirates, 2001.

and drawing monthly salaries (Table 9.13). Only very few graduates were found working as daily wage or piece wage earners. Thus we observe a positive correlation between levels of education and quality of jobs.

It is found that persons with secondary and higher levels of education were employed in government, other public sector institutions, enterprises run by non-UAE investors, and firms owned by UAE nationals, and Indians (including Keralites) to a larger extent than persons with lower educational qualifications (Table 9.14). It is revealed that only a small proportion of workers having education below secondary school, work in government, other public sector units and establishments owned by non-UAE entrepreneurs from the West as well as India (including Kerala).

WAGES

Almost all enterprises and public offices work six days per week. Friday is the official holiday for all establishments in UAE. It is found that the average working day for our sample emigrants ranged from 8 to 14 hours. About half of the respondents worked, on an average, 8 hours per day. Two-fifths worked 8 to 11 hours. There were more than one-tenth who worked, on an average, between 10 to 13 hours.

TABLE 9.13: DISTRIBUTION OF SAMPLE EMIGRANTS BY NATURE OF JOB ACCORDING TO EDUCATIONAL LEVEL

(in percentage)

Nature of Job	*Below Primary*	*Below Secondary*	*Secondary*	*Degree above*	*Total*
Regular long term employee with monthly salary/wage	7.95	21.34	36.40	34.31	100.0
Regular employee with a daily wage/piece-wage	6.38	10.64	76.60	6.38	100.0
Casual worker under Piece Wage	–	33.33	33.33	33.33	100.0
Self-employed	12.50	37.50	–	50.0	100.0
Others	18.75	31.25	18.75	31.25	100.0
Total	8.31	20.77	40.58	30.35	100.0

Source: Field Survey conducted at United Arab Emirates, 2001.

TABLE 9.14: DISTRIBUTION OF SAMPLE EMIGRANTS BY EDUCATIONAL LEVEL ACCORDING TO CATEGORY OF EMPLOYER

(in percentage)

Category	*Below Primary*	*Below Secondary*	*Secondary*	*Degree*	*Total*
Government/Public Sector	10.00	17.14	42.43	31.43	100.00
Foreign Establishment	10.67	26.67	36.00	26.67	100.00
UAE National	1.33	28.00	36.00	34.67	100.00
Establishment of Keralite or Indian	5.88	16.67	50.00	27.45	100.00
Others	25.00	4.17	29.17	41.67	100.00
Total	8.09	20.52	40.75	30.64	100.00

Source: Field Survey conducted at United Arab Emirates, 2001.

In the case of sales, production related works, transport equipment operating and related items of work, especially in construction related activities, the majority work more than 8 hours. On the other hand, persons employed in professional, technical, administrative, executive and managerial and clerical jobs work only 8 hours per day (Table 9.15).

The monthly earnings of workers ranged from less than 500 Dirhams to more than 5,000 Dirhams. Of the total sample, 48 per cent received monthly remuneration of less than 1,500 Dirhams. A notable finding is that 9 per cent of the emigrants are getting a monthly wage of more than 5,000 Dirhams. Those who are getting more than 5,000 Dirhams are persons belonging to professional, technical, administrative, executive, clerical and sales categories. On the other hand, those who are getting a wage rate below 1,000 Dirhams are engaged in sales, service and activities connected with production, construction and transport. A detailed break up of the monthly wage earned in Dirhams and its equivalent Indian rupee is given in Table 9.16.

Discussions with the sample emigrants suggest that payment of salaries in the UAE is not, in general, prompt and regular, particularly in the non-public sector units. It is reported by 22 per cent of the sample emigrants there are delays in payment of salaries/wages. The categories of workers who reported delay are sales persons, and other service sector workers and those engaged in production, construction

TABLE 9.15: OCCUPATIONAL DISTRIBUTION OF SAMPLE EMIGRANTS BY WORKING HOURS PER DAY

(in percentage)

Occupation	*Average Working Hours Per Day*				
	8	*8-10*	*10-12*	*13+*	*Total*
Professional/Technical and Related Workers	67.65	27.94	4.41	–	100.0
Administrative, Executive and Managerial Workers	61.11	38.89	–	–	100.0
Clerical and Related Workers	63.27	28.57	6.12	2.04	100.0
Sales Workers	34.09	38.64	18.18	9.09	100.0
Service Workers	44.83	20.69	20.69	13.79	100.0
Farmers, Fishermen, Hunters and Related Workers	50.00	50.00	–	–	100.0
Production and Related Workers, Transport Equipment Operators and Related Workers	39.50	52.94	5.04	2.52	100.0
Total	49.85	38.86	7.90	3.65	100.0

Source: Field Survey conducted at United Arab Emirates, 2001.

TABLE 9.16: DISTRIBUTION OF SAMPLE EMIGRANTS BY MONTHLY SALARY/WAGE LEVELS

Salary in UAE Dirhams	*Indian Rupees*	*Per cent*
251- 500	3,012- 6,000	2.63
501- 750	6,012- 9,000	8.50
751-1,000	9,012-12,000	14.07
1,001-1,500	12,012-18,000	23.75
1,501-2,000	18,012-24,000	15.54
2,001-2,500	24,012-30,000	3.51
2,501-3,000	30,012-36,000	5.27
3,001-3,500	36,012-42.000	6.45
3,501-4,000	42,012-48,000	4.98
4,001-4,500	48,012-54,000	2.93
4,501-5,000	54,012-60,000	3.22
5000+	60,012 +	9.01

Source: Field Survey conducted at United Arab Emirates, 2001.

and transport and related activities. The period of delay reported ranged from less than one month to more than six months. Of the sample emigrants who reported delay in payment of salaries, the delay in the case of more than four-fifths, was two to three months. Another 6 per cent reported four to five months' delay. In the case of another 5 per cent the delay was six months or more. Delay in the payment of salaries and wages is one of the basic problems faced by emigrant workers in UAE. It is pointed out that due to economic recession, payments are increasingly getting delayed for workers in the construction sector.

One of the major reasons for the return of emigrants from the Gulf countries is reported to be abandonment of jobs by the emigrants caused by non-receipt of salaries. It was found that 7 per cent of the sample emigrants were forced to quit their earlier jobs due to non-payment of their salaries. The major category of workers who were forced to quit jobs on this account was workers connected with construction, production and transport. However, salary and wage rates did not show any signs of decline during the period since 1997 when recession set in. The available information suggests that wage rates and the inflow of expatriate workers from foreign countries remained stable in the UAE during the period.

Visa, Work Contract and Non-wage Benefits

In contract migration, all conditions relating to employment, hours of work, wages, non-wage benefits, accommodation, air-ticket for return, etc., are stipulated in the terms of contract. According to the UAE immigration rules, it is the responsibility of employers to meet all costs connected with recruitment and the onward and return journeys of the worker. The worker is entitled to free air ticket for return home after the expiry of the contract period. No fees are to be levied for visas either. The only cost the emigrant is expected to bear is expense for medical check up. Though these rules are in force, the employers and the recruiting agents try to exploit workers in several ways. Most of the problems the workers face in the UAE for living and working and for return home pertain to the terms of contract and their implementation. Usually workers who have proper visas and work contracts specifying the working conditions, do not face serious problems. On the other hand, workers who migrate without proper visas for work and work contracts face severe problems.

In our sample 83 per cent of the emigrants came to the UAE with proper visas for work. Another 17 per cent came here with tourist visa or other categories of visa. Visas were obtained through a variety of sources: licensed recruiting agents, unlicensed recruiting agents, relatives and friends. It is reported that 60 per cent got their visas through relatives and friends already in the UAE. Many who came to the UAE with the help of relatives, friends and recruiting agents had not been excessively concerned about the conditions laid down in their work contracts. In their anxiety to migrate to the Gulf, many of them had been willing to work on whatever terms and conditions the foreign employers prescribed. In many cases work contracts signed prior to departure from Kerala were cancelled on arrival in the UAE; they were forced to sign new contracts before job placement. A disturbing development is that the employers in the UAE try to impose contracts on the workers, which violate rules in vogue regarding the non-wage benefits. It is reported that the practices of negation or cutting down of non-wage benefits, denial of accommodation and refusal of air fare for return home, are widespread.

It was reported by more than one-fifths of the sample emigrants that they did not receive the same job, the same wages and the same non-wage benefits laid down in their work contracts. The categories who have not received the wages and other benefits as per the contract are workers connected with construction, production and transport. According to UAE immigration rules, the employer will have to meet the airfare for onward and return journey of the contract worker. But the employers and recruiting agents are forcing the emigrants to bear all travel costs. An enquiry about the year in which they returned last to their native place revealed that 26 per cent returned in 2001, 57 per cent in 2000, 12 per cent in 1999 and 3 per cent in 1998. It was found that 52 per cent of them spent money from their own pocket for purchasing air ticket to return home. On the other hand, in the case of 48 per cent, their employer had given free air ticket to return home. The persons who paid for the return journey belonged to all categories of workers.

A serious problem faced by the emigrants in the UAE is the custody of passports. The usual practice followed by the employers in the UAE is to collect the passports of the emigrants at the time of their reporting for work. By this practice the employer gains absolute control over all movements of the emigrants in his employ. In many cases, the employer refuses to release the passport to the emigrant workers on the ground of minor labour problems or disputes regarding payment of wages. In our study we found that 11 per cent of the employers refused to release passport when the emigrant wanted to return. The categories that were denied return of their passports belong to all the sectors of economic activity: construction, production, transport and services, causing considerable hardship to the emigrants.

It was found that 26 per cent of the emigrants lived in flats and another 27 per cent in portions of flats in the cities of Abu Dhabi, Dubai and Sharjah. Another 15 per cent lived in rented rooms in cities. The rest (about one-third) lived in worker camps. The majority of the emigrants in cities lived in flats, in portions of flats or rented rooms and paid rent from own earnings. It is reported that two-thirds belonged to this category. Only in the case of the rest, employers paid the rent of their workers.

Worker Camps

In the UAE almost 70 per cent of the contract workers are provided with accommodation in worker camps constructed mainly for housing single male workers. These worker camps located away from the cities have construction workers, production-related workers, sales workers and service workers housed in them. Most of the low-wage categories are housed in worker camps. In Abu Dhabi, the camps are located at Mussafah. In Dubai the worker camps are located at Sonapur, about 15 km away from the city. The other places where work camps are located are the Al Quaz and the Jebel Ali Free Trade Zone. These camps are maintained by employers. The workers are transported daily to the construction sites, factories, production units and other establishments in which they are employed. In the case of 75 per cent of the camps, water, electricity, air-conditioning and cooking facilities are available. About one-third of the sample emigrants are found to be living in worker camps. The number of persons per room ranges from one to eight. It is reported that in one-third of the rooms the average number of persons living is 4. In another 28 per cent the average number of persons per room is as high as 8. Thus we find that 88 per cent of the total emigrants living in worker camps are living in rooms having an average number of persons ranging between 4 and 8. The employers meet the rent for the accommodation of workers in worker camps.

Savings

Based on the sample survey we have estimated the monthly savings of the sample emigrants. Savings are estimated based on the earnings and the expenditure incurred in the UAE. From their savings, emigrants spend money for their return journey and meet expenditure for education of their children in India or abroad as well as for repayment of debts.

As the majority of the emigrants have to meet the cost of their air tickets for return journey home for themselves and for the members of their families, it is likely that a good part of the savings would be spent for travel. It is found that 36 per cent of the emigrants had monthly savings of less than 500 Dirhams and another

TABLE 9.17: DISTRIBUTION OF SAMPLE EMIGRANTS BY MONTHLY SAVINGS GROUPS

Earnings in UAE (Dirham)	*Savings (Indian Rs)*	*Per cent*
Less than 250	3,000	3.7
251- 500	3,012-6,000	32.5
501- 750	6,012-9,000	11.6
751-1,000	9,012-12,000	22.6
1,001-1,500	12,012-18,000	7.5
1,501-2,000	18,012-24,000	7.1
2,001-2,500	24,012-30,000	4.4
2,501-3,000	30,012-36,000	2.7
3,001-3,500	36,012-42,000	1.7
3,501-4,000	42,012-48,000	1.7
4,001-4,500	48,012-54,000	0.3
4,501-5,000	54,012-60,000	0.3
Above 5,000	Above 60,000	1.3
Total		100.0

Source: Field Survey conducted at United Arab Emirates, 2001.

34 per cent a saving ranging from 501 to 1,000 Dirhams (Table 9.17). Thus nearly 70 per cent had monthly savings of less than 1,000 Dirhams. It is seen that only less than 6 per cent had a monthly savings of more than 3,000 Dirhams. The categories of workers getting higher monthly savings are professional, technical, administrative, executive, clerical and sales workers.

Demand Prospects

Judged in terms of the changes in the labour market and also the changes in the composition of employment, we find that the following categories are likely to be demanded in the future. Under professional, technical and related workers the categories which would be in demand are engineers, physicians and surgeons, nurses and other paramedical staff, health technicians, accountants and auditors and all category of teachers. Executives and management experts would be another category, which would be in demand in the coming years. Salesmen, shop assistants and sales representatives are still another category, which has bright prospects. Under service workers, the categories which are likely to be in demand are caterers, restauranteurs, housekeepers, stewards, cooks, waiters and other service workers. The technicians and skilled workers who would be in demand include miners, metal processors, chemical processors, machinists, fitters, precision instrument makers, electricians, workers, plumbers, welders and sheet metal workers. Skilled construction workers, heavy equipment operators, and transport equipment operators also may be in high demand in the UAE in the immediate future.

CONCLUSION

The paper concludes that changes in the immigration policy of the UAE Government, completion of major infrastructure projects and economic recession in the region have reduced substantially the demand for unskilled and semi-skilled labourers in the UAE. The new policies are related to demographic balancing, emiratization, banning visa for unskilled Asian workers, large-scale mechanization to make unskilled labour very expensive, etc. The UAE government has also stopped accepting applications for visas for unskilled workers from India, Pakistan and Bangladesh with effect from 18 July 1999. Future demand will be for categories of skilled workers, technicians, computer workers, heavy equipment operators, electrical workers and professional categories such as doctors, nurses, engineers, teachers and accountants. The future emigrants from Kerala should be equipped to meet the changing demand for migrant labour in UAE.

Our survey in UAE among the Kerala emigrants revealed that the largest proportion (36 per cent) of workers was engaged in unskilled, semi-skilled and skilled categories in construction, production and transport activities. Nearly one-fifth were in professional and technical work. The other major categories in which Kerala emigrants were employed were clerical, sales and service activities; more than three-fourths of them were employed in regular employment drawing monthly salaries.

The majority of the Kerala emigrants work for more than 8 hours per day; and more than one tenth work for about 10 to 14 hours per day. The major problems faced by several Kerala emigrants in the UAE are non-payment of salaries, denial of wages and non-wage benefits stipulated in their work contracts, refusal to release passport and non-payment of air-ticket fare for return to Kerala. Nearly one-third of the Kerala emigrants live in worker camps and in the majority of cases, the number of persons per room range from four to six. The survey found that 36 per cent of the emigrants had a monthly savings of less than 500 Dirhams (Rs 6,000) and another 37 per cent a monthly savings of 500 to 1,000 Dirhams (Rs 6,000 to Rs 12,000).

Taking into consideration the changes taking place and envisaged to take place in the labour market conditions and also the changes in the structure of employment, we find that the following categories would be in demand in the future. Under professional, technical and related workers the categories which would be in demand are engineers; medical and para-medical staff such as physicians and surgeons, nurses and laboratory technicians; production executives, managers and supervisors; accountants and auditors; and teachers of all categories. Salesmen, shop assistants and sales representatives would also be in large demand. Under other service categories, the demand would be for hotel workers, housekeepers, stewards, cooks and waiters. Skilled workers demanded would be miners, metal processors, chemical processors, machinists, fitters, precision instrument makers, electricians, plumbers, welders and sheet metal workers, and skilled construction workers, heavy equipment operators and transport equipment operators.

REFERENCES

Agro-Economic Research Centre, 'Impact of Foreign Remittances on the Economy of a Rural Area in Kerala', *Agricultural Situation in India*, vol. 37, no. 7, October 1982.

Bilsborrow, R.E., Graeme Hugo, A .S. Oberai and Hania Zlotnik, *International Migration Statistics*, International Labour Office, Geneva, 1997.

Bohning, W.R., *Employing Foreign Workers*, International Labour Office, Geneva, 1996.

Department of Economics and Statistics (DES), *Survey on Housing and Employment*, DES, Thiruvananthapuram, 1982.

———, *Report of the Survey on the Utilisation of Gulf Remittances* in Kerala, DES, Thiruvananthapuram, 1987.

Heisel Donald, F., 'Theories of International Migration', in *International Migration in the Arab World*, vol. II, United Nations Economic Commission for Western Asia, 1982.

Gopinathan Nair, P.R., *Asian Migration to the Arab World: Migration from Kerala (India)*, Mimeographed, Thiruvananthapuram, Centre for Development Studies, 1996.

———, '*Incidence, Impact and Implications of Migration to the Middle East from Kerala*', in Rashid Amjad (ed.) *To the Gulf and Back*, New Delhi: ILO-ARTEP, 1989.

International Labour Organization (ILO) *Social and Labour Issues Concerning Migrant Workers in the Construction Industry*, International Labour Office, Geneva, 1995.

———, *International Migration Statistics*, International Labour Office, Geneva, 1997.

———, *World Labour Report* (1989), International Labour Office, Geneva, 1989.

Gulati, Leela, '*Male Migration to the Middle East and its Impact on the Family: Some Evidence from Kerala*', *Economic and Political Weekly*, vol. 18, nos. 52-3, 24-31 December 1983.

———, 'Coping with Male Migration', *Economic and Political Weekly*, vol. 22, no. 44, 31 October 1987.

———, *In the Absence of their Men: The Impact of Male Migration on Women*, Sage Publications, New Delhi, 1993.

Massey, D.J., et al., 'Theories of International Migration: A Review and Appraisal', *Population and Development Review* (New York), vol. 19, no. 3.

Mathew, E.T. and P.R. Gopinathan Nair, 'Socio-economic Characteristics of Emigrant's Households: A Case Study of Two Villages in Kerala', *Economic and Political Weekly* 13 (28), 1978.

Ministry of Labour, *Annual Report, 1994-95*, Government of India, New Delhi, 1996.

———, *Annual Report, Ministry of Labour*, Government of India, New Delhi, 2000.

Ministry of Information and Culture, UAE, *United Arab Emirates Year Book*, 1998.

Nayyar, Deepak, *Migration, Remittances and Capital Flows: The Indian Experience*, Oxford University Press, New Delhi, 1994.

Nambiar, A.C.K., *The Socio-Economic Conditions of Gulf Migrants*, Commonwealth Publishers, New Delhi, 1995.

Prakash, B.A., 'Impact of Foreign Remittances: A Case Study of Chavakkad Village in Kerala', *Economic and Political Weekly*, vol. 13 (27), 8 July 1978.

———, 'Gulf Migration and its Economic Impacts: The Kerala Experience', *Economic and Political Weekly*, vol. 33 (50), 12 December 1998.

Prakash, B.A. (ed.), *Indian Migration to the Middle East: Trends, Patterns and Socio-Economic Impacts*, Spellbound Publications, Rohtak, 1998a.

———, 'Exodus of Gulf Emigrants-Return Emigrants of Varkala Town in Kerala', *Economic and Political Weekly*, vol. 35 (51), 16 December 2000.

Radhakrishnan, C. and P. Ibrahim, 'Emigration, Inward Remittances and Economic Development', *The Manpower Journal*, vol. 16, no. 4, January-March, 1981.

Raju, Kurian, 'Patterns of Emigration from Kerala', *Social Scientist*, vol. 37, no. 6, January 1979.

Rashid, Amjed (ed.), *To the Gulf and Back: Studies on the Economic Impact of Asian Labour Migration*, ILO-ARTEP, New Delhi, 1989.

Sekhar, T.V., *Migration and Social Change*, Rawat Publications, Jaipur, 1997.

Stalker, Peter, *The Work of Strangers: A Survey of International Labour Migration*, International Labour Office, Geneva, 1994.

State Planning Board, *Economic Review*, 1999, SPB, Thiruvananthapuram, 2000.

Isaac, T.M. Thomas, 'Economic Consequences of Gulf Crisis: A Study of India with Special Reference to Kerala', in Wickramasekhara Priyasinin (ed.), *The Gulf Crisis and South Asia*, New Delhi: UNDP-ARTEP, 1993.

World Bank, *Global Development Finance*, World Bank, Washington, 1999.

Zachariah, K.C., E.T. Mathew and S. Irudaya Rajan, *Migration in Kerala*

State, India: Dimensions, Determinants and Consequences, Working Paper, no. I, Centre for Development Studies, Thiruvananthapuram, 1999.

———, *Migration in Kerala State, India: Dimensions, Determinants and Consequences*, Working Paper II, Centre For Development Studies, Thiruvananthapuram, 2000.

———, 'Impact of Migration on Kerala's Economy and Society', *International Migration*, vol. 39, no. 1, 2001a, pp. 63-88 (first published as a CDS Working Paper, no. 297).

———, 'Social, Economic and Demographic Consequences of Migration on Kerala', *International Migration*, vol. 39, no. 2, 2001b, pp. 43-71 (first published as a CDS Working Paper, no. 303).

Zachariah, K.C. and S. Irudaya Rajan, 'Gender Dimensions of Migration in Kerala: Macro and Micro Evidence', *Asia Pacific Population Journal*, vol. 16, no. 3, 2001a, pp. 47-70.

———, 'Migration Mosaic in Kerala: Trends and Determinants', *Demography India*, vol. 30, no. 1, 2001b, pp. 137-65.

Zachariah, K.C., P.R. Gopinathan Nair and S. Irudaya Rajan, 'Return Emigrants in Kerala: Rehabilitation Problems and Development Potential', Centre for Development Studies, Working Paper, no. 319, 2001.

Zachariah, K.C., B.A. Prakash and S. Irudaya Rajan, 'Gulf Migration Study: Employment, Wages and Working Conditions of Kerala Emigrants in the United Arab Emirates', Centre for Development Studies, Working Paper no. 326, 2002.

Zachariah, K.C., E.T. Mathew and S. Irudaya Rajan, *Dynamics of Migration in Kerala: Dimensions, Determinants and Consequences*, Orient Longman Pvt. Limited, New Delhi, 2002.

CHAPTER 10

South Asians in the Gulf: Aspects of Ethnic Encounter

AKBAR S. AHMED

Social scientists believe that ethnicity – language, food, folk art, dress, custom, the rubric which we may define as local culture – is created within and by society during the passage of time; it is therefore particular to that society. Religion, it is argued on the other hand, is something introduced into – or superimposed upon – society from outside. This is especially true of the world's great universalistic religions. Whereas a society creates its own ethnicity, it is a passive recipient of religion. In certain specified situations a contradiction may develop between a strong particularistic local ethnic tradition and a universalistic religion exhorting the removal of barriers such as ethnicity. Islam, born in a highly developed tribal society, confronted this problem from the beginning. The Holy Prophet of Islam – himself a member of the Quraysh tribe – was aware of the fissiparous dangers of ethnicity. In the context of the social structure and organization of Arabia he equated ethnicity with tribalism. In a *hadith*, a saying he warned '*la badawi fil Islam*' – 'there is no Bedouinism in Islam'. His was a universal message transcending race and tribe. All Muslims belonged to the *Ummah*, the community. But in spite of the Prophet's warning, ethnicity remained to identify – and separate – groups within Islam.

When two ethnic groups with developed cultural traditions interact in an unequal relationship within the frame of one religion the problem becomes more interesting. The United Arab Emirates provide us with a contemporary situation in which Muslim ethnic groups interact intimately and unequally with each other. Although there are many non-Arab Muslim groups in the UAE, we will concern ourselves here with the Pakistanis. Arabs, speaking the Arabic language, proud of Arab history, conscious of their Arab genealogies and their local origins define themselves as *watani* (or natives). In contrast their employees, the Pakistanis (mostly) spreak Urdu, the national language and are conscious of their South Asian origin and belong to diverse cultural and ethnic backgrounds, Punjabi, Baluch and Pukhtun. Added to this is the fact that sudden wealth, a great deal of it for the Arabs and a relative increase for Pakistanis, has shaken the cultural kaleidoscope out of the pattern of the past for both groups.

As Islam is not the issue – both groups being Muslims of the same sect, Sunni – ethnicity becomes important in definitions within and between the groups. This is further exacerbated by the employer – employee nature of the relationship.

The mechanism whereby boundaries are defined and maintained between groups has interested anthropologists recently (Ahmed, 1980; Barth, 1970). Anthropologists have concerned themselves with tribal boundaries and maintenance of ethnicity, usually involving neighbouring tribes or ethnic groups. Important issues have been raised as to how ethnicity is maintained. In this paper I examine two major Asian ethnic groups interacting intimately with and learning to adjust to each other.

I wish to point out in a speculative manner the interesting and complex questions that arise: What is the nature of the encounter – is it to be seen in political or social or economic terms? What mechanisms are evolved by society to resolve the problems? What is the visible impact on both groups of the encounter? Does ethnicity revive at the cost of religious unity? Is it possible to determine the stronger ethnicity through culture and, if so, how? More concretely, how do the Pakistanis, who are at the receiving end in an economic sense, exhibit and cope with the stress?

These interesting and important questions are missing or barely touched upon in the contemporary flourishing literature on the UAE (Abdullah 1978; Blandford 1978; Hawley 1971; Hay 1959; Heard-Bey 1982; Kelly 1968, 1980; Mann 1962; Marlow 1962; Moore 1977; Raban 1970; UAE n.d.).

THE UAE AND PAKISTAN

The saying *Dubai Chalo* – 'let us go to Dubai' – which is the equivalent of the expression 'Westward ho' in Western tradition – has become part of Pakistani culture (popular Pakistani films around this theme are *Dubai Chalo* in Urdu and *Visa Dubai da* – 'visa for Dubai' in Punjabi). It signifies the possibility of gathering relatively quick, legitimate, and a great deal of wealth in the Arab states. Dubai therefore has come to mean in Pakistan a modern-day El Dorado or Shangri-La. For many Pakistanis *Dubai Chalo* has indeed been a fortunate slogan.

There are estimated to be over two million Pakistanis in the Arab Gulf States sending home about three billion dollars annually. The figure is almost half of the country's entire foreign exchange earnings. Indeed, Pakistan's economy from the 1970s has come to depend heavily on this source of foreign exchange. The government of Pakistan has a full-fledged Overseas Employment and Manpower Division to deal with migrant labour. The Pakistan International Airlines manager in Dubai informed me that the highest number of operations in landing and taking off and the second highest revenues (after Jeddah) for the airline were in Dubai. However, there has been a price to pay.

Doctors, especially psychologists, in Pakistan talk of a 'Dubai syndrome' afflicting Pakistanis working in the UAE, which we shall discuss below. Recently journalists in Pakistan have been concerned with the problems that will inevitably arise when the Gulf workers return (see, for instance, cover story 'Return of the Petroworker', *Herald*, November 1983). Perhaps matters are made worse for the Pakistanis by the sharply different worlds the two countries represent.

The contrast between the UAE and Pakistan is striking. The UAE is sparsely populated with 1½ million while Pakistan's population is about 85 million. The per capita income of the former is in the highest bracket in the world (34,000 dollars) and Pakistan's among the lower ones (about 350). However, Pakistan has a basic infrastructure of education, civil and defence services which is one of the best in the region and which the UAE lacked (but is fast acquiring). The people of the UAE speak Arabic and are culturally part of the Arab world; Pakistanis speak Urdu, a language of South

Asia (although with a significant percentage of borrowed Arabic and Persian vocabulary) and are part of South Asia. The UAE has remained on the periphery of Arab history and culture. Pakistan – or its putative ancestors – have been in the main stream of South Asian politics and culture. Its culture includes the poetry of Mirza Ghalib – probably the greatest Urdu poet – its architecture the wonder of the Taj Mahal, the monument built by Shah Jahan, the Mughal emperor. Complex bureauracy, irrigation networks and revenue systems were – and are – its features.

The UAE is in large part a tribal society. Pakistani society is a mixture of tribesmen, agricultural peasants and city-dwellers. Since Independence the UAE has been ruled by traditional chiefs, wearing traditional clothes, living traditional lives and speaking Arabic. Pakistan, in contrast, was the creation of a barrister educated in London and has been ruled for the most part by Sandhurst trained generals or Oxford and Cambridge educated politicians, speaking English. The official language in the UAE is Arabic, while in the official files of Pakistan it is still English. (In the UAE Foreign Office – where an instant corps diplomatic has come into being – the bright young officers wearing immaculate Arab dress, clean white robes and smelling faintly of expensive perfumes, conduct office procedure in Arabic.)

Justice in the UAE is retributive and swift (people are lashed for crimes daily, according to the *Gulf News*). In Pakistan justice is ponderous and conducted in courts organized by, and in language moulded by, Lord Macaulay in the last century. The favourite sport of the rulers of the UAE is traditional falconry; in Pakistan it is golf, imported recently from the West. The national emblems and flags reveal something of the history and ideology of the two countries. The UAE emblem displays an eagle with a dhow beneath it. The bird is a symbol of power and flight while the dhow connects the land with the outside world. The Pakistan flag displays a star and a crescent against a green background; all symbolic of Islam. The historical contrast between the two is dramatic and in the context of our paper, poignant. At the turn of the century, India represented the Jewel in the crown of the British Empire. It was ruled by a bureaucracy of Governors, Deputy Commissioners and Political Agents headed by the Viceroy. The Gulf states were tiny dots on the periphery of British India. In these, which included Dubai and Abu Dhabi, the Government of India was represented by one Political Agent.

Once upon a time, not so long ago, there were only two buildings in Abu Dhabi: the Sheikh's modest palace (now the Documentation Centre) and the Political Agent's bungalow. But in British India there were Political Agents and Political Agents. In terms of importance the Political Agents of the North-West Frontier Province in charge of the Khyber Pass and Waziristan were front line officials. The Political Agent South Waziristan Agency, for instance, had at the turn of the century direct access to the Viceroy and was in constant touch with and was visited by key figures such as Lord Kitchener, the Commander-in-Chief of the British Indian Army. The Mahsuds of the Agency, probably the fiercest tribe in South Asia, were giving the Empire trouble (Ahmed 1983a). Lord Curzon visited the Gulf, too, (and the symbolic, rather delightful, photograph of him being carried ashore on the back of an attendant survives). But this trip was to the backwaters of his charge. Today, because of the difference in wealth the two countries have developed differently.

The UAE appears clean, neat, tidy, and its few people well cared for and well organized. On the other hand Pakistan, only 36 years old, gives the appearance of age. Its cities are over-crowded, its streets filthy, its traffic anachic. In the UAE a newly graduated Arab – *a watani* – will land up with a high executive job while a Pakistani in the UAE, far more qualified and senior, will have to be content with a subordinate position. In any case, no foreigner may own land, property or an independent business in the Gulf.

Bu in spite of the vast difference in incomes Pakistan has always held a special place in the UAE. Both are self-consciously Islamic in their political and social stances. Pakistan was the first to acknowledge the independence of the UAE by establishing its Embassy there in 1971. It provides a wide-range of services to the UAE, from top advisers to the rulers to humble construction workers. When the Pakistani community wished to open their own cultural centre in Abu Dhabi the Sheikh donated 1.5 million dollars. The grateful Pakistanis called their school after the Sheikh's son. Many citizens of the UAE own property in Pakistan. Karachi, in particular, attracts wealthy UAE Arabs. In turn, many of the wealthy business families (the Haroons from Karachi and the Saigols from Lahore, for instance) have invested in the UAE. Conscious of the need to expand into the Gulf are Pakistanis like the editors of the *Pakistan Economist*, who changed their title to *The Pakistan and Gulf Economist*. According to certain Pakistani writers these editors are not alone in having an eye to Gulf dollars. Organizations such as the United Bank of Pakistan have been accused of providing armies of prostitutes – 10,000 – to satisfy Arab appetites (Ali 1983: 125, for my criticism of Ali see Ahmed 1983e).

Let us look briefly at the United Arab Emirates, in which are located the main emirates and towns, Abu Dhabi and Dubai.

THE UAE

The fact which makes the UAE important in the region and in contemporary affairs is its oil (*Economist*, 1982). Its successes and its failures both stem from its oil revenues. In 1982 the Federal budget for the UAE was 6.1 billion dollars. Abu Dhabi, which is the dominant partner in the UAE, showed an income of 8.3 billion dollars. UAE 'allowables' were fixed at 750,000 barrels per day compared to 1,195,000 in 1981. As a consequence, the income per capita of the UAE is probably the highest in the world at 34,000 dollars (oil prices quadrupled in ten years). Of the total population of about one and a half million eighty five per cent are expatriates. Abu Dhabi is the largest emirate, about 26,000 square miles, and forms eighty per cent of the UAE. Dubai, once a dependency of Abu Dhabi, has an area of 100 square miles and a population of about 60,000 living mainly in Dubai.

With such vast revenues and sparse population the rulers of the UAE can afford to build lavishly and dream ambitiously. Abu Dhabi is building a sports complex costing 225 million dollars. It will house a future world Olympics and will possess a football stadium with a seating capacity of 100,000. The airport, patterned after the Charles de Gaulle airport in Paris, is costing 200 million dollars. The BCCI headquarters boast the most sophisticated banking technology in the world. But in spite of this enormous wealth Abu Dhabi has not lost its head. It is the cultural and political capital of the UAE. And it is rather self-consciously dignified and sober.

Dubai, in contrast, is the commercial and fun capital of the area; a place for 'buccaneers', Blandford called it (Blandford 1978: 268). The turquoise waters and excellent beaches of the Gulf attract women in bikinis (no apparent problem with Islamic revivalism here). Not to be outdone by the capital, Dubai is building a sports complex, complete with an ice rink, for 130 million dollars. It is also engaged in constructing one of the biggest and best dock complexes in the world for the biggest possible tankers. Another dock complex is under construction at Jabal Ali.

The main roads of Dubai and Abu Dhabi, with green neat islands in between are models of symmetry and engineering. Only the best roads in North America or West Europe could compare with these. Along these roads I noticed the neon lights after dark, in flower designs with four tubes each on every electric pole, on all night each bulb glowing. It was the comfortable warm glow of opulence, steady and bright. In contrast I thought of the erratic electricity of Pakistan, of the constant 'load-shedding' there, especially in the hot summer months. Abu Dhabi is unlike the great capitals of Islam, Karachi or Cairo, where the lights and voltage fluctuate and telephones are out of order for much of the time.

The Hyatt hotel in Dubai is surely the centre of the UAE wonderland. Situated by the shore it overlooks the clear waters of the Gulf. The hotel's luxury rooms and swimming pool on the 30th floor, cater for every jet-set need. Its ice rink is a wonder. The Arabs who come to skate, many in their traditional robes, to the latest pop music on the loud-speakers, are a long way from the Arabs of T.E. Lawrence.

Luxury is on display. And the world's entrepreneurs compete to outdo one another in promoting their goods. A new French perfume was introduced to the world by gushing forth from water fountains and into pools in a Dubai hotel. Marie Antoinette in Dubai, where drinking water is scarce, would have approved an injunction to 'give them perfume'.

In any case drinking water, like almost every thing else, is imported (from Italy). Water for Abu Dhabi – some nine million gallons daily – is extracted from recently installed foreign plants. Entire plays with their casts are flown in from New York and London for a few days performance. During my stay the *Gulf News* announced the imminent arrival of Lulu. Like the French perfume, sometimes new plays are first introduced to the world in the UAE.

Ice skating, Kentucky Fried Chicken, Olympics stadium, cartoon strips including Andy Capp, Blondie and Garfield (in the *Gulf News*) – it is all happening in the Gulf. Little wonder that Dubai has caught the imagination of the world and not only of the Pakistanis who are, after all, simply poor neighbours.

R. Moore, the author of *The French Connection*, has recently published a new novel called *Dubai*. The cover sports a dashing Western hero with a machine gun in his hand. Alongside him is pictured a halfnaked, dusky 'oriental' female. In the background is a minaret. The three parts of the book, called respectively, gold, oil and insurgency, reflect the three ingredients which to the West constitute the modern Arab State.

Westerners who have to deal with the UAE betray their sense of indignation at the humiliation of having to accept jobs and favours on the terms of the latter by being over-critical of the Arabs. Perhaps they are also revealing envy of Arab wealth. To them the UAE is an 'instant' civilization, built on sand, which will suddenly vanish. They see it creating paranoia and neurosis in its inhabitants and also in those who come in touch with it. The UAE diplomats abroad, Blandford claimed, all possessed Ph.Ds., the letters according to her, standing for prostitution, hashish and drugs. Her chapter on the UAE was titled 'Nutty present, dotty past' (Blandford 1978: 153). Lurid Stories and lewd doings are hinted at in such tracts. In a more serious work Raban noted that 'Plato's ideal city-state had its base on a slave class and so did Abu Dhabi' (Raban 1979: 158). The Pakistanis, or Raban constitute the latter class.

Arab intellectuals dismiss most of these charges as inspired by racial or religious prejudice. Those with Jewish backgrounds like Blandford and Raban, they claim, can make especially harsh judgements. But this is a simplistic rejection of a complex phenomenon.

Certain writers still talk of the Western inheritance 'east of Suez' and argue for the need to control the Gulf directly and militarily (Kelly 1980). They argue that, left to themselves, the Arabs will destroy each other in tribal fashion thereby inviting in the Soviets. The Sheikhs are not to be trusted to stand and fight in the region, they argue, as they have insured themselves by buying property in the West and will therefore fly out when political problems become severe.

Islam came early to this region. The Sheikh of Abu Dhabi is said to have in his possession a letter written by the Holy Prophet inviting the leaders of the region to accept Islam. Traditional tribal structure and organization adapted themselves to Islam and therefore survived. Today both are clearly visible in the social and political life of the area. The mosque, the symbol and focal point of Muslim society, is every where. There are estimated to be 1,400 mosques in the UAE.

The rulers of the Emirates are tribal chiefs leading their tribe on the basis of loyalty and past history. Abu Dhabi itself was founded by the grandson of Nahayyan, the direct ancestor of the present ruler, Sheikh Zayd Nahayyan, in 1761. Nahayyan claimed descent from the Holy Prophet, and origin from Najd in Saudi Arabia. The tribe Nahayyan historically dominated the area and, on the basis of this domination, has a monopoly of power and therefore access to the new wealth. Its sixty seven tribal sections and sub-sections form the core of government. Non-tribesmen, settlers, expatriates, overseas employees, all remain outsiders in the most profound sense. For instance, the name Galadari is displayed in neon on many shops and buildings but the owners, because they are of Iranian decent, remain outsiders.

Women, too, in traditional tribal fashion play a prominent role in political affairs especially in dynastic matters, although this role is contrary to the popular image of tribal Muslim women. When Sheikh Zayd deposed his brother Sheikh Shakhbut and became ruler he honoured his promise to his mother, Sheikha Salma. She had made her sons swear never to kill each other. Today, Sheikh Zayd's wife, Sheikha Fatima, plays a leading role in business enterprises and women's development schemes. Her influence at court is considered formidable.

Life in the UAE is not all jet-set frivolity and material values. The United Arab Emirate University at Al-Ain is a good example. The university, the first and major institution of its kind, was begun in 1977. The Faculty has a staff of over 400, which includes Egyptians and Pakistanis. Art, Science, Agriculture and Sharia, Islamic Law, are taught. The language of instruction is Arabic, but English is used in Science. By 1981 some 400 students had graduated. This year there are about 4,000 students, of whom almost half are women. Women are educated on a separate campus and are taught up to B.A. level. The Pakistani Professor of English informed me that his female students were more hard-working and brighter than the males. But the question he raised of their future is an important one. Will their talents be allowed to expand so that they will contribute to the development of the nation or will these students be married off and locked in homes to supervise domestic chores?

In an interview with Professor Ezzedin Ibrahim, an eminent Egyptian scholar and the President of the University, I was informed of the aim to make the University one of the best in the region (reported in the *Gulf News*, 17 September 1982). Professor Ibrahim is also an adviser to the Sheikh, and both are keen to develop links within the Muslim world – especially with Pakistan. The Sheikh has already donated money for three Islamic centres in Pakistan. Both Sheikh and Professor were in close touch with Pakistanis concerned with education. They were following closely the attempts in Pakistan to 'Islamize'.

It is at this level that the power and significance of Islamic brother-hood – the concept of the *Ummah* – is most notable. There is mutual understanding and respect between Muslim academics regardless of ethnic backgrounds. These men are striving to set and reach Islamic ideals. They are no longer Egyptians or Arabs or Pakistanis but Muslims tied together by the bonds of Islam.

In some sense the UAE rulers are brave men. They are courageously rushing their countries in the span of one life-time through historical sequences which often take three to four lifetimes. Fortunately they are also mostly wise men, ruling as concerned chiefs, caring for their kind and ensuring distribution of wealth. The vast wealth, tight tribal organization and small population allow the system to function smoothly. However, there are structural flaws in it.

Perhaps the major structural weakness in society is its dependency on foreign labour. Expatriate labour – some 200,000 Pakistanis and about 250,000 Indians – make the wheels of the UAE go round. They contribute on all levels of life. At the bottom of the social ladder South Asians sweep UAE streets, clean UAE houses and man UAE taxis. At the middle level are medical doctors, bankers, engineers and lawyers. And at the highest level South Asia also provides key men. The Director of the Al-Ain Museum is a Pakistani. So is the Commander-in-Chief of the UAE airforce. The personal pilot and doctor of Sheikh Zayd are also Pakistanis. The Sheikh is quoted as saying that although the Egyptians and Palestinians provide the brains for the UAE – the academics, government advisers – the Pakistanis are its heart, with their uncomplaining stance and identification with Islam. The entire UAE show would collapse if the expatriates were to be abruptly withdrawn. Let us briefly examine the consequence of this sudden wealth in encounters between Arabs and Pakistanis in the UAE.

CLOSE ENCOUNTERS

Pakistanis in the UAE may be divided clearly into two categories: the highly trained professionals (who include the whole range of bankers, doctors, lawyers) and the manual labourers (construction workers, drivers, domestic servants). Both categories have contributed to the development of the UAE.

Culturally, the language of Pakistan, Urdu, has been established as the strongest language after Arabic. In parts of Dubai it is the *lingua franca* and Arabs, familiar with it through Indian films (which are in Hindi, akin to Urdu) speak it easily. Language thus acts as the main distinguishing feature in the maintenance of ethnic boundaries.

Both categories of Pakistanis have done well in economic terms. The first, reflecting some of the original opulence of their employers, wear western clothes, use expensive perfumes and live in air-conditioned rooms. They may be seen strutting about in the lobbies of the UAE hotels with the arrogance of those who have made money quickly and sometimes shadily. They participate in the *dolce vita* of the Arabs, if not as partners at least as junior colleagues. For them their entire family unit lives in and shares the UAE dream.

This group is culturally malleable and socially docile, clinging to the money they make and determined to make the most of it. Highly placed Pakistani executives can earn up to 20,000 dirhams monthly (ten times more than they would at home). But their sudden wealth makes them insecure. Blandford found these Pakistanis 'scared stiff' (1978: 260). They will not rock the boat at any cost. But among members of this group are a few who are out to make quick money and therefore cut corners.

In attempting to cut corners and make illegal money some Pakistanis were caught up in the rigid code of the Arab tribesman. One such incident involve Pakistanis who were on the personal staff of Sheikh Zayd (*Newsweek*, 7 March 1983). They were discovered to have been quietly siphoning off the Sheikh's money to their own accounts abroad while operating a multi-million dollar company based in London and registered in Panama. The authorities acted in tribal manner when the code is involved and loyalties betrayed. The accused were swiftly put under arrest and their associates came under a cloud; their assets and their lives were frozen.

The other category, on which the *dolce vita* rests, lead harsh lives. These are the hardy Baluch and Pukhtun tribesmen, noted working on the roads by foreigners (Blandford 1978; Raban 1979): 'These were the people who were keeping the opera afloat' (Raban 1979: 158). The working conditions for this category, in the open sun constructing roads or buildings, are difficult. Equally difficult is their job security which depends on ruthless agents and bosses. They risk deportation at the slightest provocation, which in local terms could include requesting their rights. Stories of shattered lives abound, men put on boats and sent back across the Gulf, agents disappearing, local employer profiteering at the cost of illiterate villagers. Their families are in Pakistan. They come from the villages of the Frontier, Baluchistan and Punjab. Tribal and rural life – and their codes sustain this category. They are lonely men working desperately to live up to the *Dubai Chalo* myth. They are expected to return home rich with money, laden with radios and watches annually. They live in rooms knocked together from tin and bits of wood. Their living conditions are appalling.

Jarnia Fur, a makeshift shanty-town outside Abu Dhabi, expresses and symbolises the lives of the labourers in the UAE. It is inhabited by a mixture of South Asian Muslims, Egyptians and Sudanese. Jarnia Fur is not the make-believe world of the Dubai Hyatt; it is reality and an Afro-Asian reality. And here reality festers.

In the Jarnia Fur camp there are pools of stagnant water covered in green slime. The lanes are filthy with drainage water; old boots, tyres and garbage lie about in them. The 'homes' are little more than pieces of wood hammered hastily together. Rents, nonetheless, are exorbitant. A group of men usually hire a room, often as small as 40 square feet, for 600-700 Dirhams per month. In the midst of this filth and squalor are the symbols of affluence which make the enterprise worthwhile for the labourer: the odd air-conditioner jutting out of a room, or a Mercedes taxi parked outside one.

Corrupt local officials and rapacious agents on both sides, and a sense of alienation haunt the labourer. Horror stories of ethnic discrimination are told in hushed voices ('the authorities have sharp ears and swift methods', I was told). The Pukhtuns were the boldest in recounting injustices and making comparisons: 'were better Muslims than these people'. A story was related of an Arab who raped an Indian woman in the camp and got away with it. There are two laws in the land: one for *watani* and the other for the foreigners. Nonetheless, the spirits of the South Asians are high as they stand rooted in their own ancient cultures and civilization. They refer to the Arabs as *bidu* – from Bedouin – with contempt. 'The "bidu" has no culture, only sudden money', they observe.

For all the sullen defiance in the camp it is an established fact that Indians, Egyptians and Sudanese are well-behaved and docile. They are in a Muslim country, within their Muslim *Ummah*, Community, in pursuit of legitimate earnings. Whatever the reality of ethnic divisions in society they are prepared to turn a blind eye. They are good labour. So, too, are the Pakistanis. But Pakistani society is not uniform.

Pakistani society consists of broadly three categories: agriculturalists, city-people and tribesmen. The first two are abroad to make money and go about their business diligently and quietly. But the Pukhtun tribes-man from the North-West Frontier Province is himself too much of a tribesman to make allowances for the sudden wealth and its attendant complexities that afflict the UAE tribesman. His life revolves around the concept of Pukhtunwali or the code of the Pukhtun (Ahmed 1980; Barth 1970, 1972). At all costs he will not compromise his own sense of personal honour as case studies testify (Ahmed 1980). He wears his Pukhtunness like a badge (knowledge of Pukhtu, the language of the Pukhtuns, will ensure a free ride in a taxi driven by a Pukhtun). He retains his traditions in language, in dress, in behaviour and in the rites of passage (for birth, marriage and death the Pukhtun goes home). Their unity in the face of non-Pukhtun opposition has become proverbial; a story widely circulated was that of a Pukhtun teacher in the Pakistan school who was reinstated due to their united pressure in spite of opposition by the local authorities. Ethnicity, clearly, can be ignored in the argument so far and no more.

Two well-known recent episodes further illustrate the point. A young Pukhtun driver was driving his truck along one of the main highways when a Mercedes, driven by an Arab, attempted to overtake him. The truck was heavy and the sand along the road made it difficult to clear the road immediately. So the truck-driver did not give way. The driver of the car made desperate but futile passes to overtake the truck. By now the passengers in the car were yelling and the driver honking furiously. All to no avail. Then an opening allowed the car to speed forward. Accelerating to gain distance the car stopped, blocking the road for the truck.

The truck-driver was asked by the passengers in the car to step down. Hot words followed between them. The truck-driver was slapped. He immediately hit back. A revolver was pulled out and he was shot dead. The driver of the car sped away. He little realized the complex laws of honour, which rest on revenge, that he had invoked among the Pukhtun community. That he was a prince of the land would simply add to, not detract from, the problem.

The Pukhtuns reacted in their traditional manner, swiftly and boldly. Members of the family of the deceased were outraged. The news spread rapidly and infuriated Pukhtuns were soon demanding revenge. They demanded that the culprit be handed over to them for execution or that his family be prepared for his assassination. If he was not available, they conceded, any adult male member of his family would be acceptable as a substitute. Elaborate plans for ambush were made and rumours circulated of shots fired in the night.

The authorities were as horrified as they were helpless in this case. Their own justice is retributive; it is also swift, sure and condign. Being tribesman themselves they understood the code of tribesmen, especially the part relating to revenge. They offered up to three million dirhams, it is said, if the truck-driver's family would forget the matter, and were refused. They had no idea how to cope with the situation. To treat it with the usual stern administrative measures such as banishment of the victim's family would widen the conflict and scandal. Ignoring it would not work, as the Pukhtuns were mounting an increasingly vociferous campaign. In the end a complex and tortuous negotiation succeeded. It involved tribal leaders from both parties, promises, financial deals and substantial concessions to the family of the deceased. The unity of the *Ummah* was invoked as was the special relationship between Pakistan and the UAE. Finally, the strategy of employing both tribal and official channels succeeded. Blood money was paid and accepted and honour thus satisfied.

There was another incident involving Pukhtuns and the administration. This one involved the Mahsud tribe, among the fiercest fighting men in South Asia with a formidable history of unity in battle (Ahmed 1983a). The Mahsuds were working as labourers in Al-Ain and lived in a makeshift shanty town just outside it. The hills and terrain resemble that of South Waziristan Agency, the home of the Mahsuds. On being repeatedly provoked by their employers on what they interpreted as unjust grounds the entire tribe gave the battle cry and prepared for a showdown. They clambered up the hills around Al-Ain with guns, the possession of which is illegal, and took up positions at vantage points. The authorities had no idea how to cope. A shoot-out would have been costly and also scandalous. It would have made international headlines. Finally members of the Pakistani Embassy were rushed from Abu Dhabi to act as mediators. The situation was defused and the Mahsuds were persuaded to come down. No retribution would follow, the authorities promised. The Pukhtuns saw this incident as vindicating their position and their honour.

It is for such reasons that employers often prefer the more docile Indians. Especially popular, particularly as domestic servants, are Muslims from Kerala in South India. Their films and posters testify to their numbers. The Kerala Muslims, like the Pukhtuns but for opposite reasons, have made distinctive marks in UAE society.

Only members of the second category of Pakistanis, the labourers, can afford to rock the boat; their illiteracy allows them to maintain some integrity. Nonetheless both groups pay a price.

The price for working in the UAE has been termed as the 'Dubai syndrome' by Pakistani psychologists. The syndrome is defined as a sense of disorientation resulting from the harsh working conditions, social isolation, culture shock and sudden acquisition of (relative) wealth in the UAE, which together produce psychosomatic disorders. Dr. Malik Mubashir, Head of the Department of Psychological Diseases at the Rawalpindi General Hospital, talks of the 'Dubai syndrome' which consists of the pre-Dubai and post-Dubai stage. The victim feels isolated and guilty for leaving his family and overcompensates with gifts on his return. He 'tries to justify himself by earning more and more money' *(The Muslim*, 4 May 1983).

Dr. Malik calculates that about one quarter of the entire population of Pakistan—those working in the UAE and their relatives – is affected by the Dubai syndrome. Its effects will be felt over the coming years in Pakistani society. Pakistanis are concerned about the syndrome. *The Muslim* carried an editorial called 'The Dubai Syndrome' on 7 May 1983 (promptly picked up by the *Times of India* under the banner 'Dubai syndrome creates problems for Pakistan' on 10 May).

My own preliminary findings among those who worked in the Gulf confirmed the impact of this experience on local social structure and life (Ahmed 1980, 1981, 1983a). For one thing, morality, which is directly linked to Pukhtunwali, was affected, as husbands were often away for a period of one to two years.

My own observations confirm that Pakistanis working in the UAE do so under considerable socio-psychological stress. They may ignore it or in some cases convert it to the *dolce vita life style* (though cursing the place in private) as happens among the affluent category. Alternatively, they may re-assert their ethnicity through outward symbols such as dress. For instance, the Pukhtuns, the most aggressive Pakistani group in the UAE, are distinctive in their traditional dress, the *salwar kameez*. By contrast many others in this group, including Baluch, have taken to wearing the Arab shirt. The boundaries are blurred between them and the Arabs. Pukhtuns are adamant that their dead be buried back in their native land. The Baluch too, perhaps learning from the Pukhtun have now begun to send their dead back to Baluchistan. Pukhtu films like *Tofani Shabi* are exhibited. The two popular Pukhtu stars, Badar Munir and Yasmin Khan, are seen in Pukhtu films regularly.

Islam offers an ideological framework within which the two communities meet and interact. Islam is the belief, and its rituals the set of social actions which identify Muslims. Pakistanis in particular identify vigorously with Islamic value and symbols. However, we have noted that in a situation of economic inequality which confirms an employer-employee relationship both groups may experience a revival of ethnicity. This revival serves both. It provides the dominant group with a justification for its superior position and the dominated group with a rallying point.

The interesting and complex question is what happens to nationalism as ethnicity revivse. The edges of nationalism are blunted or, alternatively, are sharpened as social groups redefine themselves in the new environment. In the UAE a Mari Baluch or a Mahsud Pukhtun is more likely to be known and recognized as a Pakistani than as a Baluch or Mahsud. These groups in the UAE may thus re-discover their own sense of nationalism, which overrides their disparate cultural and ethnic backgrounds. Pakistanis may express their disenchantment with the encounter by emphasising their Muslimness and the wayward ways of some of their employers. For them UAE wealth is not totally 'foreign'. It belongs to members of the Muslim community, theoretically, spiritual brethren. They are working for legitimate income in a Muslim society. We are thus examining not only ethnicity but, more broadly, nationality, and within the frame of the same religion.

The phenomenon of economic growth in the UAE may also have something serious to say to those planning for, and thinking of, development issues. Third World economists, largely following material models developed in the west, emphasise statistical units – roads, buildings, etc. – in development. Almost nowhere do they acknowledge the relationship of these to culture or to the ideological frame of the country. Development takes the former not the latter road for them. This leads to what may be called disproportionate social development: that is, the creation of a modern, even instantaneous, infrastructure with no ideological or cultural pegs to hang it on to. Prefabricated frames of development are imported and imposed on traditional society. In the UAE the only infrastructure so far provided is by imported labour, such as Pakistanis, which, as we saw, creates its own problems.

The essential lesson is that in development both economy and society must be considered side by side, otherwise serious problems may result. The sociologist and anthropologist have a great deal to tell us about society (two recent and exhaustive studies on migrant labour in the UAE, one by the Pakistan Institute for Development Economics and the other by its Bangladesh counterpart, and both supported by the World Bank, remain flawed as no sociologist or anthropologist was associated with the ventures). But, important in itself, this has not been our immediate problem in this paper.

CONCLUSION

There is considerable contemporary interest in Muslim society. The Muslim response to problems over the Muslim world varies as indeed the problems vary. In Egypt and Pakistan large aggressive Muslim populations confront choices between religious revivalism, socialism and forms of capitalism (Ahmed 1982, 1983a); in India they have to come to terms with an overwhelmingly larger population which they once dominated (Ahmed 1983b and c). The Muslims of the USSR are learning to adjust to a socialist system (Ahmed 1983d). the interest in Muslims has resulted in high-quality work among Muslim groups all over the world.

However, the particular set of theoretical and methodological problems created by sudden wealth in the UAE and the influx of Pakistanis there has not been satisfactory examined. Not only politicians and administrators but also the *ulema* – the traditional religious scholars who are increasingly involved in decision-making in government – would benefit from the answers.

The analysis in this paper reveals ethnic rifts within UAE society between local and non-local groups. The concept of *watani* negates that of the *Ummah*. But equally clearly it is apparent that Islam helps to bridge the ethnic and cultural alienation between the groups and allows a sense of familiarity – through mutually accepted mythologies, rites, customs – to be fostered in spite of difficult conditions. There is always the common ideological frame with the concept of the *Ummah* at its centre to provide a focus for all Muslims. Therefore social scientists may usefully turn the question of ethnic rifts in society around the other way. That is, not how rifts in society are created by ethnicity but how Islam helps to bring groups together in spite of cleavages based on ethnicity and unequal economic relations. We therefore learn to heed religious and cultural factors apart from economic ones when studying issues in developing societies.

More information is needed on the complex issues and questions raised in this paper. Rapid economic change as a result of development strategy and the resultant social stresses create problems in understanding contemporary attitudes to religion, ethnicity, migrant labour and traditional codes of behaviour. A long-term study which would include UAE and Pakistani social scientists is clearly required.

Author's Note

Acknowledged with warmth is the hospitality I received in the UAE from Shagufta and Azmat Hasan and Gillo and Ali Afridi in September 1982. In particular, Azmat, in spite of his numerous and important duties as acting Ambassador, Pakistan Embassy, took time off to humour my demands, accompanying me on my visits and arranging interviews. The paper attempts to raise questions rather than provide answers and also suggests further avenues of research.

REFERENCES

Books

Abdullah, M.M., *The United Arab Emirates: A Modern History*, Croom Helm, London, 1978.

Ahmed, A.S., *Pukhtun Economy and Society: Traditional Structure and Economic Development in a Tribal Society*, Routledge, London, 1980.

———, 'The Arab Connection: Emergent Models of Social Organization among Pakistani Tribesmen', in *Asian Affairs*, vol. XII, pt. II, London, June 1981, pp. 167-72.

———, 'Under Cairo's Calm', in *The Christian Science Monitor*, op-ed page, 19 October 1982.

———, *Region and Politics in Muslim Society: Order and Conflict in Pakistan*, Cambridge University Press, New York, 1983(a).

———, 'A Muslim in India', in *The Times of India*, 4 September 1983(b).

———, 'A Pakistani come to Delhi', in *The Times of India*, 11 September 1983(c).

———, 'Deep Structures in Russian Society: The Soviet Position on Afghanistn', talk given to the *Institute of Strategic Studies*, Islamabad, 13 October, 1983(d).

———, 'Review of Ali, 1983', in *Journal of Asian Studies* (forthcoming) and longer version in *The Muslim*, 16 December 1983(e).

Ali, T., *Can Pakistan Survive? The Death of a State*, Penguin Books, 1983.

Barth, F., (ed), *Ethnic Groups and Boundaries: The Social Organization of Culture Difference*, George Allen and Unwin, London, 1970.

———, *Political Leadership among Swat Pathans*, Athlone Press, London, 1972.

Blandford, L., *Oil Sheikhs*, Allen and Unwin, 1978.

Hawley, D., *The Trucial States*, G. Allen and Unwin, London, 1971.

Hay, R. *The Persian Gulf States*, Washington, 1959.

Heard-Bey, F., *From Trucial State to United Arab Emirates: A Society in Transition*, Longman, N.Y. and London, 1987.

Kelly, J.B., *Britain and the Persian Gulf*, London, 1968.

______, *Arabia, the Gulf and the West*, Weidenfeld and Nicolson, London, 1986.

Mann, C., *Abu Dhabi: Birth of an Oil Sheikhdom, Beirut*, London, 1962.

Marlow, J. *The Persian Gulf in the Twentieth Century*, London, 1962.

Moore, R., *Dubai*, Corgi Books, London, 1977.

Raban, J., *Arabia: A Journey through the Labyrinth*, Simon and Schuster, N.Y., 1979.

United Arab Emirates A *Record of Achievement 1979-1981*, Ministry of Information and Culture, Abu Dhabi (n.d.).

Journals, Newspapers

Economist (1982) Quarterly Economic Review – UAE – 2nd Quarter – The *Economist Intelligence Unit* (London).

Gulf News (Dubai and Abu Dhabi).

Herald (Karachi), November 1983.

Muslim (Islamabad).

Newsweek (1983), 7 March.

Pakistan and Gulf Economist (Karachi).

CHAPTER 11

The Orphaned Non-Resident Indian

RAM BUXANI

Breathes there a man with soul so dead who never to himself has said: 'This is my own, my native land.'

When I left India, I was an Indian. Later, I was given an appendage, a new name – Non-Resident Indian (NRI). When I'm being introduced in India as a NRI, I feel quite odd – like a stranger, a foreigner, in my own country.

Who are these NRIs?

They mean different things to different people. For the government, they're a good source of money. For the customs, they're potential smugglers. For the relations, they're source of envy. But, in the end, they don't belong anywhere.

I think there's a great misunderstanding about people who migrate from India to settle permanently elsewhere and people who leave in search of job. It's true that in both cases people leave in search of greener pastures. But in the latter's case, once they finish their contract, they are bound to return – today, tomorrow or the day after. Their savings are ploughed back into India and that forms a substantial part of the nation's income from abroad. I think there's a need to look at the two streams of migration from two different viewpoints.

In recent history the migration of Indians began during the British Raj. They sent indentured labourers to the plantations in Ceylon (Sri Lanka), Burma (Myanmar), Malaya (Malaysia), South Africa, East Africa, the Caribbean Islands and other places under the British influence. Later, there was migration of traders, mostly to South Asia, South East Asia, the Far East, Africa, West Asia and western countries. Then there was a wave of migration of professionals, mostly to Western countries.

The descendents of this group of migrants are now naturalised citizens of their adopted country. However, many of them still have an emotional attachment to India and some of them still continue to have an active relationship with their home country. This group of people of Indian origin is 17-million strong.

The second group of Indians migrated abroad because of the attraction of lucrative labour markets. They left India in search of jobs but with no intention of permanent settlement. Anyway, in many places, local laws did not give them the right of permanent settlement. The Gulf and some of the Middle East countries threw open their labour markets from the late 1950s and labour migration peaked at the time of the oil boom in the mid-1970s. Today there are about 3.5 million Indians in this region.

During the last century, when two world wars compelled a movement of labour from the colonies according to the crumbling empire's financial needs, the Indian diaspora made its first tentative spread into the world. While indentured labour had moved as far as the plantations of the West Indies and all the way down to the southern coast of Africa; the trade winds from the Malabar coast to the Gulf countries, and the staging post they had become for the British Empire, also attracted the business community. Between labour and commerce the Indian entity began to establish itself around the world.

Later, well into the twentieth century, these people would become the largest congregation of settlers in the world, arguably beating even China in the number of countries its people had moved to and established themselves as a creative and positive force.

In England itself, the mother country of the Empire, Indians were way ahead of anyone else. But the epithet of NRI was not yet stuck upon them. On the contrary, there was little prejudice at that early stage and the Indian adventurer was fêted.

Through history the Indian approach to *yatra* or *safar* has been markedly ambivalent. It was either to dredge out a living, in response to the crossing of a significant family milestone, as in the dutiful presence at a birth, marriage or death, or to answer the dictate of religion.

There was little pleasure in what was looked upon as an arduous journey and there was minimal greatness to the Indian traveller for whom the parting and the goodbye was tantamount to a little death. All too often, the journey was one-way. And while seafarers and the more enterprising business communities created a global diaspora of the sort never seen before – and unlikely to be seen again – it was less a sense of adventure and more an obligation borne of a Hindi word for which there is no equivalent in the English language.

The affection for a status quo of nativity manifests itself even today. Travel has been traditionally bleak and fraught with danger. India's folklore abounds with tales of highwaymen, dacoits, thugs and other such human flotsam laying ambush for even the wary traveller.

The association in the Indian psyche is largely an unhappy one, as if going abroad was an exile and indicative of some shameful failure. Not for us the swashbuckling conqueror reaching foreign shores in a splash of glory. Not many Marco Polos in the making. Instead, the one sacrificed to the foreign monster was in some ways despoilt and corrupted, no longer pure of body and soul.

Despite the natural reluctance of Indians to be travellers, India has made its presence felt.

The irony is that the traditional suspicion to the outsider continues to flourish at home and foreign-based Indians still pay a price for their intransigence. NRI's reputation is a bit like the curate's egg: good and bad in parts.

It has been made so through a growing chasm of understanding between his needs as a foreign-based Indian and his country's priorities *vis-à-vis* the domestic situation and response to his frequently updated charter of demands and requests.

To a great extent the media has succeeded at caricaturing the NRI into a selfish, loud and unpatriotic carpetbagger interested in satisfying his economic greed rather than contributing to the mother country.

These NRIs for all practical purposes are treated in India as foreigners. Most of the Indian universities and colleges treat the children of NRIs as a different category and charge higher fees than the children of resident Indians. In some technical institutions and professional colleges, the fees for the children of NRIs are as high as the fees in some universities in the West. Even hostel fees are charged at a higher level. In America the universities charge higher fees from non-nationals. That's understandable, but I don't think they charge higher fees from any American student just because his or her parents happen to work outside America.

The Indian universities have a mistaken notion that NRIs are rich and therefore can afford to pay higher fees. The fact is that the vast-majority of Indians working in the Gulf are people who struggle to make both ends meet. The labour markets are highly competitive and the NRIs have to compete with people from other labour-exporting countries – people who are willing to work for much lower salary. Therefore, there's no justification in generalising the purchasing power of NRIs back home and treating all of them as moneyed class.

The apathy of the Indian authorities, partly because of a lack of understanding about the potential of NRIs, and partly because of a misunderstanding that they are better off than their counterparts in India, have created untold miseries.

The 'envy syndrome' has conspired with the snarls of red tape to create an unpleasant canvas on which NRI shrillness and occasional arrogance have vied with indigenous hostility and deliberate foot dragging to replace policy at centre stage.

The blame, if one sees it as that, is not solely on the resident at home. NRIs, as an entity, have not been able to get their act together and project any sort of cohesive image to the authorities in the mother country.

On the contrary, they've allowed the belief to exist, through default and a lack of collective purpose, that they come home to India merely to collect pickles, papadams, spice and spouses, not necessarily in that order. Retaining their values, often being criticised for not joining the mainstream of their adopted lands but continuing their customs and traditions, they undeniably spelt success.

Even as the brain drain of the 1960s and 1970s hit India, and a robust middle class was formed, second- and third-generation Indians holding passports of the mother country discovered that the protectionism offered Indian industry under the Nehru-Gandhi dynasty was making them unwelcome.

The feeling of hostility was populist and engineered. Gradually, not overnight, the insidiousness of being labeled manifested itself. In all fairness, the foreign-based Indian took it in his stride, losing neither love nor reverence for his country. Indian patriotic fervour rises high above political machinations. But the bruising continued and slowly the prejudice steeped into the relationship. The 'Not-Required Indians' twist had a cruel truth to it and created a chasm of misunderstanding.

On both sides there were people of good sense who railed against the divide and wanted it bridged. Regrettably, their voices were drowned as even the media picked up the call and indicted Indians for living abroad. The system kicked in and suddenly it was like some great betrayal had taken place. Protectionist Indian commerce and industry certainly came into an unwritten contract with politicians and bureaucrats to make the NRI sticker a messy business. At the same time schemes such as 'Sons of the Soil' and 'Be Indian buy Indian' further alienated the main populace and coming home became more of a trial and a tribulation.

Indeed, NRIs as we had uncomfortably come to be known, were now completely befuddled and bemused if not entirely hurt by the whole attitude. Investment efforts were thwarted. Paperwork and red tape further choked the relationship. Things went downhill so swiftly that NRIs helplessly fell for the guilt trip and turned into apologists.

The approach did not change during the 1970s. Right through the decade delegation after delegation went to India only to find resistance. If you were an NRI you were not only an object of derision you were not even eligible to stand in the queue.

History will record this 30-year period between the 1960s and the 1990s as a period that defied explanation. 'Bring us your dollars but don't expect gratitude. You're not welcome, you're a different breed. We do not need you.' Hurtful sentiments made worse by the lip service paid to Indians abroad by leaders who meant not a word of what they said.

They received Non-Resident-Indian delegations and, besides the mandatory photograph, did little else of tangible worth. Very slowly, almost imperceptibly, the NRI began to feel the hurt. What was this all about? From criticism by the nuclear family, to criticism by friends, to criticism by the bureaucracy, to criticism by the politicians, it was almost as if he had committed a crime by leaving his shores.

More than 2,000 NRI enterprises were applied for in this period and stalled in what came to be known as a pillar-to-post runaround for licences and no-objection certificates. Between 1980 and 2000, more than 46 seminars were held under the auspices of the government and its elected representatives, to underscore an affection for the foreign-based Indians, but each and every one of them was insincere and some were downright scams.

'We're Indians, we demand the respect,' shouted the 23-million global contingent.

'No, you are not,' shouted New Delhi, 'you're NRIs, you don't totally belong.'

At which point, in their efforts to right the balance, NRIs also did themselves a disservice when they fed the fires of hostility by demanding concessions as if they were a breed apart. Self-important and self-propelled NRI leaders self-elected themselves and became pseudo-representatives, travelling to India and misusing their press contacts to distort the true picture.

The shrillness of their demands became fodder for a nation that half believed Indians living outside the country were spoilt, rich and undeserving of any empathy. These demands for concessions and special favours were naturally wrongly misconstrued by the authorities and the public and much damage was done. In fact, at one stage in the early 1990s, I can go as far as to say that the situation deteriorated into open war. NRIs were not only unwanted, their motives were suspect.

What comes to my mind is the Draconian law prevalent until mid-1980s with regard to estate duty. Overseas Indians, mainly from Dubai, can take the credit for its total abolition although this tax exists even in developed countries such as the UK and USA.

I was one of the delegates in the group, along with Russi Patel, G.V. Eswar, Praful Patel, Hasmukh Shah and Nishit Desai, who met successive finance ministers such as Pranab Kumar Mukherji and V.P. Singh and emphasised why this corruption-generating legislature needed to be abolished.

When a person died, the state levied a duty of up to 95 per cent on the personal property left behind by the deceased. The duty was calculated on the basis of market value. If a person inherited a property worth Rs 2 lakhs and the market value of the property at the time of his death was Rs 20 lakhs, the estate duty was calculated on the basis of the market value. The state where the deceased was a domicile would be the beneficiary of the duty.

In India, to escape the estate duty, people manipulated accounts to conceal the real value of a property or evaded tax by greasing the palm of bureaucrats. It was estimated that Government of India was collecting about Rs 200 million in estate duty every year. But the overheads for collecting such a paltry amount was much more.

Overseas Indians were accustomed to simple and transparent tax laws. They would keep their money in Indian banks and when they died the drama would start. In the case of NRIs the Indian missions would not authenticate certificates and documents before the estate duty was paid and proof was submitted.

There was also a very intriguing question with regard to the collection of estate duty from Indians who died abroad. Estate duty should go to the government of which the deceased was a domicile. But the money collected as estate duty from Indians died abroad went to the federal coffers, to which account nobody knew. Thank God, wisdom prevailed and estate duty does not exist any more. A rich Indian can die peacefully without having to share anything with the exchequer.

In 1987, to bridge the communication gap between the Indian government and overseas Indians, Madhukar Gupta, head of the Indian Investment Centre in Abu Dhabi, an Indian government undertaking, mooted the idea of Overseas Indian Economic Forum – UAE and I became founder chairman, while the then ambassador of India to the UAE, Inderjit Singh Rathore, became patron. The Indian consul general in Dubai, Arun Kumar, was one of the observers. Arun Kumar, Russi Patel and G. Bhandari played an important role in the formation of the organisation.

John Mathew, president of Indian Association, Sharjah, became vice-chairman of the forum, Mahendra Asher, secretary and S.R. Krishna Moorthy, treasurer. Bharatbhai Shah, Mahabir Singhal, Lachu Bhatia and the late T.M. Nair and Khimchand Khiara (Chacha) were among the members of the committee.

In 1985, I proposed to the Government of India that the Andaman and Nicobar Islands should be converted into a free port along the lines of Hong Kong, which functioned as window for China. The idea was well received by the people and the government. Subsequently, a committee under the late Raunaq Singh was formed by the Ministry of Commerce, when Subramaniam Swamy was minister. Besides me, the members of the committee were K.

Ravindran, K.R. Motilal, V.S. Vankataraman, Dr Jayanta Roy, Gary N. Harilela, Gian T. Vachani, John Mathew, M.J. Pherwani, Syamal Gupta and J.S. Gill. After much work and travel it was found that the islands would not justify the purpose, being too far from the mainland. There were many other contenders including Kutch (Gujarat), Pondicherry, Goa and Tuticorin (Tamil Nadu), but the committee finally recommended Goa followed by Tuticorin.

Goa, which had remained in Portuguese hands even after India obtained independence, was a perfect site. It has all the attractions a tourist would look for. And the people there are every visitor-friendly. There is sufficient land to encourage international industrial houses to establish themselves and export their products worldwide as happened in Malaysia. It would also provide excellent job opportunities for the people of neighboring states, such as Maharashtra and Karnataka, and would earn valuable foreign exchange. The free port within India could serve as a logistical hub to multinationals and could also be a shopping paradise within India for Indians – leaving the margins within the country. The recommendation submitted by Raunaq Singh's committee was discussed – and appreciated – by the cabinet but, with change of governments, all the effort seems to have gone down the drain.

Overseas Indians are obviously concerned about the education of their children. Ironically, India while liberalising various avenues, has short-changed education. As a chairman of the Overseas Indian Economic Forum – UAE and otherwise – several representations have been made by me to liberalise and make education an industry so that people are encouraged to invest in this area to cope with domestic as well as overseas demands.

Billions of dollars are spent by Indian students in the USA on their studies. The faculty there is also Indian. The money, students and the faculty all are Indian – only the soil is foreign. Why India cannot provide the soil to save billions of dollars is beyond anybody's understanding.

Some years ago, when a delegation of NRIs from the Gulf visited India to meet the then prime minister, Narasimha Rao, it was anticipated that NRIs would at last get some representation and the so-called NRI cell that uselessly served the NRI cause would be upgraded to something more tangible than mere window dressing.

A case could even be made to have a fully-fledged ministry responding to the call of 20-million Indians living abroad. People whose sense of affiliation with the mother country is most tangibly impressed by the foreign exchange they funnel home each year: a figure upward of $50 billion.

NRIs, as a group, still have no representation in India's parliament. Although there are nominated members to represent and protect the interests of minority groups, numbering much less than the Indian contingent abroad and arguably producing much less by way of financial contribution, this prejudice continues to manifest itself. It's been said that unless NRIs are given the right to franchise, something guaranteed by the constitution, there's no vote bank and, therefore, no political interest in this huge entity. That may well be true and the few stabs made in that direction have never really been effective.

With the information highway now wending its eight-lane track through the Indian psyche, the argument that gathering votes from foreign-based nationals would be difficult doesn't ring true. Voting by Internet with sufficient safeguards would resolve that aspect very easily. The fact is that the will is not there. Over the years there has been little push from NRIs to validate their right to vote on the grounds that they hold Indian passports and respond to Indian laws and regulations through the conduit of the embassies and the consulates.

Another defence frequently thrown up by India's successive governments refers to the difficulty inherent in choosing two representatives for the Indian diaspora, what with it being so dramatically splintered in its spread. Though few studies have been done on this issue there seems to be little cause for despair. The world could be divided into various enclaves with each Indian enclave voting one individual to an NRI electoral college. The college would then meet for a convention every five years and elect two people to the Lok Sabha (parliament) to represent global NRI problems and create that much-needed political bridge. These two elected individuals would then be nominated to the house so that there's no constitutional irregularity.

There's much merit in the idea because the NRI image is at present held to ransom by a motley squad of so-called NRI organisations that hold conventions and conferences in various venues and style themselves as representatives in a self-serving manner. They print certificates of merit, hammer out various trophies and awards and bring along some defunct politician to address the gatherings. These are largely money-making exercises with those winning awards usually paying the bill for the dubious honour being bestowed upon them.

Over the years these tawdry events have meshed together to create an erroneous and often sleazy view of what the NRI is all about. In contrast, there have been few really serious and upgraded conferences called by governments in the centre or at the state level to create a platform for better understanding.

If there's a genuine flaw in the relationship between the NRI and the authorities in the home country, it lies in the meek manner in which the frontline Indians abroad have surrendered their prerogatives for representation. The high profile and powerful have found it more lucrative to go it alone and 'compete' for favours rather than provide a consolidated forum of opinion. Very often, NRIs, in their bid to win these favours, let each other down and are divided and uncertain over exactly what the texture of their relationship should be.

By that very token, the Indian image of the NRI, stoked by media and globs of misplaced envy and scorn, is seen as that of a traitor who has left home for greed and should be isolated rather than espoused. This ridiculous image of what is a national asset endures and, even today, colours the relationship.

The Vajpayee government hasn't made significant moves in closing the breach. Although the BJP-led alliance has often spoken of the need to protect and preserve the bonds between Indians abroad and the mother country, nothing really changes. The need to have a fully matured infrastructure to attract Indian investment in much larger measure is now mandatory. But this will not happen unless the suspicion is removed and there's a genuine understanding and acceptance that NRIs are part of the national fabric.

At the turn of the century the voice in the wilderness was heard in New Delhi. After years of petitioning successive governments and requesting them to be practical, the Vajpayee administration has seen the sense of granting dual citizenship. Now, obtaining a passport from another country doesn't mean you have to be less Indian or surrender the right to being a citizen.

In its present form this proposed facility was meant only to allow NRIs a greater sense of identity. It fails to confer any political rights on them. Those who opt to be citizens of the country of their domicile as well as India cannot contest in elections in India and neither can they vote in them.

Dual citizenship was extended right away to those settled in the US, UK, Canada, European mainland, Australia, New Zealand and Singapore. This is because these countries permit dual citizenship and so the system there is already accustomed to the working of this concept. Indians settled in other countries such as Sri Lanka, Mauritius and Malaysia will have to make do with 'person of Indian origin' (PIO) certificates.

The five-member committee set up in September 2000 by the Ministry of External Affairs said that dual citizenship could be introduced merely by amending the Citizenship Act 1955. The status of dual citizenship would surely encourage Non-Resident Indians to relate to India in economic terms and invest.

Another spin-off effect of dual citizenship is the 'emotional satisfaction' Indians settled abroad would have for entering into 'an abiding relationship with India's rich heritage'. This move, though encouraging, had no direct impact on the 3.5-million NRIs living in the Middle East and the Gulf, where dual citizenship is largely irrelevant.

After the ushering in of the Rao-Singh duo in the 1990s, the rhetorical promises for change and the tiresome bleatings of visiting Indian leaders assuring NRIs of tender, loving care were given some credence. The sudden lifting of Draconian rules and outdated protectionism in India has put to rest most of the fears of the NRI community. But whether it has compelled the non-resident to increase his investment is a moot question.

Until recently, the guilt of diverting monies to better havens than home was easily assuaged by pointing flinty fingers of accusation at New Delhi for its choking whorls of red tape and dusty bureaucracy. So, a good portion of NRI savings never went to India and it's ironical that India continued borrowing money from Western lending agencies.

With huge foreign-exchange cash reserves, opening markets and a lifting of its protectionist policy, India has given the NRI a certain sense of belonging. But, after the BJP took over power, priorities have changed rapidly. The government has attempted to address this flaw and, since the impossible takes a little time, at least the miracles have begun. The point now is whether the NRIs, not in singles but as a community, can rise above the call of pure commerce and respond in a tangible measure.

The element of philanthropy seems to be eminently absent. Whereas Indian settlers around the world were forerunners in financing schools, hospitals, orphanages, charitable institutions and even religious centres, NRIs buy land, make houses, spoil the rate structure and make insufferable neighbours. What's needed is some basic acceptances on both 'sides'.

A ministry at the state level for NRI affairs is now validated. It is interesting that while the national attitude has been slow, progressive states such as Gujarat, Andhra and Maharashtra, have set aside their anti-NRI attitudes and gone in for major ventures, which is the way it should be.

The representation of 23-million passport holders as a 'vote bank' has to be taken seriously. Logic demands that there be at least two nominated MPs in the Houses of Parliament. The level of meetings between genuine NRI front-liners and the top government and industrial captains should be expedited. The media must be harnessed for positive imaging, something that has not been done up till now.

This is not just the coverage of a clutch of NRIs with high profiles but a long-term exercise to create 23-million individuals in more than 120 countries into an entity that is viable and identifiable as a contributing and valid element in the Indian mosaic.

Patriotism and business make poor bedfellows and arm-twisting NRIs to surrender one for the other is unfair. If the Government of India can create the ambiance that is globally competitive, the fears of too many false starts created by a bumpy past can be exorcised by a consistency of policy and a cutting down of the endless paper chase or, what is known as 'the NOC knot'. The word that gives the game away is 'woo'. India's representatives use it extensively to underscore NRI reluctance to invest.

What we forget is that NRIs are sentimental people. They take nothing for granted and are often more Indian than the Indians at home. In this rapidly changing world we need to be close to our country and our heritage. It's vital that our children know their roots. The yearning to be at home as we make a living abroad is a given. We may live a million miles away but the world is no longer a huge globe. It shrinks by the hour and the closeness is now heartfelt. It would be a shame to undervalue the association. Instead, it makes common sense to generate togetherness and see NRIs as an asset to the nation.

When all else is forgotten, always remember that when India cries, we cry too.

CHAPTER 12

Ethnicity and Marginality: A Study of Indian Jewish Immigrants in Israel

MARGARET ABRAHAM

There have been Jews settled in India from ancient times though the exact date of their arrival in India and their origins are full of historical uncertainties. At their peak, in the mid-twentieth century, the total Indian Jewish population was approximately 30,000. Today there are about 5,300 Jews left in India, the majority having migrated to Israel.[1]

Although there are a fair number of studies on the Indian Jews in india and a few on their situation in Israel, scant attention has been paid to the problem of their social integration in Israel.[2] For example, Shalva Weil's excellent study of the persistence of ethnic identity among the Bene Israel in Israel does not go into the important problem of the linkages between ethnic identity and marginality among Indian Jews in Israel, nor does it incorporate the Cochin Jews into the study.

This paper examines the social structure, the maintenance of social boundaries and the cultural dynamics of the Indian Jewish communities in Israel. The foci of this study are the Cochin Jews of Kerala and the Bene Israel of Maharashtra who emigrated from India to Israel. The social area here is the interplay between the process of articulation of 'community identification' and a set of existing sociocultural forces which have resulted in the marginalization of these communities. This study examines: (1) how the ethnic identity of the Indian Jewish immigrants gets defined in Israel and (2) the implications of these ethnic identity patterns on the integration of Indian Jewish immigrants into Israeli society. The aim of this paper is to explicate the factors that result in 'marginal statuses' for Indian Jews in Israel. It demonstrates the complexity of such processes and indicates their impact on a group's position in the social stratification system.

Fieldwork for this study was conducted in India and Israel between January 1987 and August 1988. The fieldwork was done in three phases – the first two in India and the third in Israel. During the entire course of the fieldwork, 157 informants were interviewed; 117 were Indian Jews who still resided in India, and the other 40 were Indian Jews who emigrated to Israel and included 21 Bene Israel and 19 Cochin Jews. In this paper the former are called 'non-immigrant informants' and the latter are called 'immigrant informants' for purposes of differentiation though admittedly the terms are somewhat confusing. The selection of these informants evolved during the course of fieldwork and was based on 'selective sampling'. The informant selection was conducted through a series of links starting from key informants in each community who identified other members of the community who in turn identified other members. Only one informant from the multiple subjects that each informant was interviewed and informants were selected from multiple sites. This was done to reduce bias stemming from the identification of informants included in the sample. The aim was to attain quality in-depth interviews, rather than provide an overview giving an illusion of numbers.

I begin by briefly stating the general background of the Cochin Jews and the Bene Israel. I then explain the nature of the setting into which the Indian Jews immigrated and the processes of ethnicization that have occurred.

BACKGROUND

The Indian Jews are unusual in that they are among the few Jewish communities in the world who had not experienced anti-Semitism in their host country. The many centuries of settlement in India, the influence of the Hindu caste system, and the simultaneous attempts at preserving their Judaic faith, resulted in these Jewish communities forming and articulating identity patterns which have had major consequences for their integration in both India and in Israel.

Among the Jewish communities of India, the Cochin Jews are the better known. Situated in the Malabar coast of South India, they claim descent from the 'ten lost tribes'. Though their origin and period of arrival in India are clouded in ambiguity, there is evidence that they had begun living in India as early as the eleventh century. Historically, the Cochin Jewish communities have been divided into three groups – the Malabar or Black Jews, the Pardesi or White Jews and the manumitted or Brown Jews. The Malabar Jews are the earliest settlers among the three groups. Their dark complexion and the similarity of their physical features to the native population of the Malabar is presumed to be a consequence of intermarriage with the non-Jewish inhabitants of the Malabar. The Pardesi Jews are later arrivals in India. Fair complexioned and relatively small in number compared to the Malabar Jews, this group has maintained its separate Jewish identity and played an important role in Cochin's economic history. The manumitted Jews are the offspring of slaves of the Pardesi Jews (who had been given their freedom from slavery and had converted to the Judaic faith) or of unions between Pardesi Jews and native women. During their stay in India all three of these Malabar Jewish communities adopted some of the customs and traditions of the local Hindu population. Yet they have always been strict in the observance of their Jewish faith and thus differentiated themselves from the non-Jewish local inhabitants.[3]

The Bene Israel comprise the largest Jewish population in India. Situated in Maharashtra, this community too traces its origin to the 'ten lost tribes'. But their historical background differs from that of the Cochin Jews. Unlike the Cochin Jews who have always been aware of their Jewish identity and been able to maintain contacts with world Jewry, the Bene Israel were isolated from other Jews for many centuries. This period of isolation resulted in prolonged lapses in their religious observances and resulted in their partial assimilation into the Hindu caste structure. They only retained some basic Judaic practices such as the usage of the *Shema*, the confession of the Judaic faith, the observance of the Sabbath, circumcision and some dietary laws.[4] These Jewish practices were indicative of their non-Hindu status and eventually became the basis for the discovery of their Jewish identity by the Cochin Jews. With this discovery of their Jewish identity the Bene Israel were able to re-enter the fold of

Judaism. However, due to their prolonged lapses in religious observance and their inability to substantiate their legend of origin with historical facts, this community has experienced considerable problems with reference to the authenticity of their claim to a Jewish identity in both India and Israel.[5]

Compared to the Cochin Jews and the Bene Israel Jews, the Baghdadi Jews are relatively recent settlers in India. Originally from Baghdad, Aleppo, Yemen and Basra, these Jews settled in Calcutta and Bombay in the early nineteenth century, when British rule was already established in India. Dominated by a few extremely wealthy Jewish families, the Baghdadi Jewish community maintained strict boundaries between themselves and the local non-Jewish inhabitants. Since they entered India during the British rule their socio-historical circumstances were different from those of the other Indian Jewish communities. Rather than adopt Indian cultural practices in food and clothing, they turned to the British as their social reference group and adopted their customs and traditions.[6]

All of these Indian Jewish communities have in common their claim to a Jewish identity. However their varying historical circumstances resulted in differing positions within the systems of social stratification. In pre-independence India, the Jewish minority, especially the Bene Israel and the Baghdadi Jews, occupied a privileged position under the patronage of the British. In keeping with their policy of divide and rule, the British had favored minorities who where numerically too small to pose a political threat to British supremacy. As Gussin states in his study of the Bene Israel:

> They were favored by the politics of insignificant numbers. Precisely because the community was so small and, therefore, presented no threat to the British overlords, it was disproportionately rewarded (Gussin 1972: 74).

While there had always been a certain degree of boundary maintenance between the Indian Jews and the other communities, it was a harmonious coexistence.. The boundaries were a function of the caste structure. The principles governing the caste structure had been internalized by all the communities, including the Indian Jews, thereby allowing for a relatively smooth flow of social interaction. The nature of this interaction was changed by the British.

Through their quota system for the minorities and patronage on the basis of minority status, they had stimulated among the Indian Jews a sense of distinctiveness *vis-à-vis* the Hindu and the Muslim populations.

Under the British, the Indian Jews were encouraged to manifest and articulate an ethnic identity which could not be defined within the caste framework. Religious differences became the focal point in defining ethnic identity and the marker for cognition and behavior in social interaction. Economic opportunities provided by the British and their access to education under the missionaries had placed the Indian Jews in an advantageous position. The attainment of this position was also a visible marker of the ethnically defined differences between the Indian Jews and the rest of the population. In return for the patronage they received from the British the Indian Jews remained loyal to the British. Even the Cochin Jews were indirectly aligned to the British, since the Maharaja of Cochin had signed a treaty with the British in 1809 whereby Cochin would enjoy peace and protection under British suzerainty. Thus the departure of the British was perceived by the majority of Indian Jews as the end of a golden era and era in which patronage had improved their socio-economic status.

The early part of the twentieth century witnessed an increased momentum in India's nationalist movement. It also witnessed the establishment of the Zionist movement in India.[7] These two movements played a pivotal role in determining the Indian Jews' perception of their ethnic identity and how they perceived themselves as being defined by 'others'. It resulted in a heightened awareness of their Jewish identity as well as an awareness among them that the dominant majority was mainly protecting their own interests.

The ethnicization of their Jewish identity and its reinforcement through the Zionist movement in India deflected Indian Jews from active participation in the Indian nationalist movement. Having been the recipients of a privileged status under the British, the Indian Jews were also reluctant to oppose them by joining the nationalist movement. Under the influence of Zionism and as a reaction to Indian nationalism, the Indian Jewish communities saw themselves as a distinct religious and national minority living, as they had no nation of their own, in a specific host country.[8] Having identified themselves on the basis of their Jewish identity the Indian Jews saw Israel as the symbol of their Jewishness.

The formation of various Zionist organizations in India from 1905 onwards provided the necessary means to shift to a Jewish referent *vis-à-vis* an Indian one. The means and goals for the majority population and the Jewish minority were not defined in any common terms. The identification with Zionism and simultaneous lack of active participation in India's struggle for freedom, at a time when it was the central issue for the dominant population, were to have indirect political and economic ramifications in post-independence India. The privileged minority position of Indian Jewry under the British, their total identification with the Zionist movement and the articulation by the dominant Indian population for an independent India provided the initial setting for the emigration which followed the establishment of independent India in 1947 and the creation of the state of Israel in 1948.

CAUSAL FACTORS FOR MIGRATION

From 1948 onwards Indian Jews started emigrating to Israel in relatively large numbers. Between 1948 and 1987, 25,214 Indian Jews emigrated to Israel. Though the number has declined in the last ten years, the process still continues.[9] Unlike the majority of Jews from other parts of the world who emigrated to Israel as alternative to anti-Semitism experienced in the countries where they previously resided, what were the causal factors for the emigration of Indian Jews? The responses given by my informants can be categorized into six broad factors. These are:

(1) *Economic Factors:* The lack of job opportunities, low income, housing problems, inflation and low economic status in India were the main economic push factors while better economic opportunities, greater amenities, low cost housing, loans for immigrants and a comparatively higher standard of living in terms of material possessions in Israel were some of the pull factors.

(2) *Social Factors:* The decline in social and cultural activities among the Jewish community in India and a hope for a better social life and social status in Israel.

(3) *Political Factors:* The indirect consequences of communal tensions between the Hindu and Muslim population, lack of political viability in India as a minority community, political hegemony of the dominant Hindu groups, especially in Maharashtra.
(4) *Religious Factors*: Religious fervor to return to the promised land, a desire to live in an environment where Judaism is the way of life, i.e. where Sabbath and holy days are holidays and where they can easily obtain Kosher food.
(5) *Family Factors:* The need to maintain the unity of the family, where the emigration of one member of the family results in other members emigrating, and for reasons of matrimony among the unmarried younger generation.
(6) *Age Factor*: The informant's perception of the advantages or disadvantages of his/ her age as a causal factor for emigration.

An analysis of the data indicate that informants, both immigrant and non-immigrant, perceived economic factors as important in influencing emigration. Economic and family factors were stated by a little more than half of the immigrant sample (55 per cent and 52.5 per cent respectively). However, when asked, there was a difference between the informants' perception of the factors which influenced their own emigration compared to their perception of the factors influencing the emigration of others in the Indian Jewish community. In my study, 80 per cent of the immigrant sample expressed their own emigration as having been influenced primarily by religious factors. On the other hand, the immigrant informants did not place much emphasis on religious factors when stating their perception of the factors influencing emigration among other in the Indian Jewish community. Rather, they stressed economic (67.5 per cent) and political factors (70 per cent). How do we explain this difference in perception between the informant's own explanation for emigration and their perception of the factors influencing the majority of the Indian Jewish community? The explanation of this paradox can be understood in terms of the normative and factual.[10]

Normative

All societies are governed by norms and values. A high value is placed on subscribing to the norms and deviation by the individual can lead to reproach or even exclusion of the individual by the members of the society. Central to Judaism are two tenets: (1) that Jews are the chosen people of God and (2) residing in the land of Israel is a commandment. For Jews who live outside the holy land, ideally the goal is to return to the promised land. Among the Jews then, the normative is to have religious attachment to Israel.

For the Indian Jews who defined their ethnic identity primarily in terms of a Jewish identity it is important to state the importance of the normative. This was achieved by defining the informants' own factors for emigration as linked to religious sentiment. To attribute one's own emigration or desire to emigrate as mainly a product of economic and political factors would be to deviate from the norm by replacing the sacred with the mundane. Thus, religious fervor and love of Zion were given as the most important factors influencing personal decisions to emigrate. Contrary to this emphasis on personal religious impulses, the informants stated economic and political issues most frequently as factors influencing other members of the Indian Jewish community. The informants clearly did not feel the necessity to explain the motives of others in normative terms. Defining one's own motives in normative terms may have also been to avoid being stigmatized in the eyes of the dominant populations in both India and Israel.

Factual

Despite post-independence India being constitutionally a secular nation, religious affiliation played an important role in the new socio-economic system. The struggle for independence and the post-independence communal tensions between Hindus and Muslims had imbued the Hindu majority with a sense of solidarity. There was a heightened awareness of the need for social cohesion among the majority population seeking to establish Hindu hegemony. This feeling of 'we-ness' also permeated the economic structure. Being the dominant majority, Hindus had greater access to economic opportunities. Although there was no obvious discrimination against the Indian Jews, some of my informants did tell me about their community members having difficulty in obtaining satisfactory jobs.

Lack of economic opportunities among the Bene Israel were attributed to the large number of Hindu applicants and the partial tendency of many employers to lean towards hiring those who were qualified and had the advantage of being Hindus. However this partiality was not obviously visible in government organizations as it was against the law. In addition, the introduction of new land ownership laws by the Maharashtra state government had far-reaching implications for the Bene Israel. Though large numbers of Bene Israel had moved from the rural to urban areas, there were still among them some who owned land in the rural areas. The new land laws were a major blow for those Bene Israel for whom land ownership was the main source of income. Among my Bene Israel informants, a few mentioned the effects of this law on their family or their community members. The economic impact of this can however be best described in the following lines from Weil's study on the Bene Israel.[11]

> In 1949, the Government of Maharashtra passed the Bombay Tallugdari Tenure Abolition Act by which tenants were to be given full occupancy rights in the land held by landlords if they paid a limited fee. In 1955, the Bombay Act No. 1 abolished the rights of landlords altogether. Bene Israel landowners sold their land where they could and joined the ranks of the urban migrants. Unable to make a good living in Bombay, emigration to Israel seemed the better alternative. There, so reports went, immigrants were provided with housing jobs, free blankets, a cash loan and other benefits. (Weil, 1977: 62)

During my research in India, members of the Bene Israel community in India frequently mentioned how many members of their community had emigrated in the hope of attaining better economic chances. Life in Bombay was getting 'tougher and tougher'. Housing was (and still is) a major problem. Most of my non-immigrant informants lived outside the limits of the city and commuted to work each day. The high cost of living and lack of availability of jobs were described as major push factors. Starting with the 1960s, the economic conditions worsened in the 1970s and 1980s. Occupational mobility was minimal. With the incomes they earned the majority of the Bene Israel found it difficult to make ends meet and this was exacerbated by the attitude of dominant Hindu majority in Maharashtra. Over crowding, inflation, lack of economic alternatives had made the economic situation of the Bene Israel in India virtually impossible, except for those who were highly qualified or very affluent. The Bene

Israel sought the resolution of this economic situation through emigration to Israel. The situation could be best summed up as a choice between two alternatives: continue living in India with the above mentioned problems or emigrate to Israel, on the basis of their Jewish identity, and hope for better economic prospects. The large numbers who emigrated in the 1960s and 1970s and the informants' perception of the factors influencing the emigration of members of the community, are both indicative of importance of economic factors in the emigration of the Bene Israel.

There were new political tensions as well. In 1947 the communal tensions between the Hindus and Muslims exploded. Prior to independence, the nationalist movement had been increasingly attaining Hindu undertones. Though the Hindus had always been tolerant of the Indian Jews and the latter had not faced anti-Semitism in India, this communal violence between the dominant majority and a significant minority was perceived by other minorities as symbolic of the situation that they could be in, if they in any way threatened the power of the dominant majority. The post-independence political environment had sensitized ethnic minorities of their change in political status from privileged minorities under the British. Communal tensions had more of an impact in North India than in the South since communal violence occurred predominantly in the former region.

While the political and economic instability of post-independence India influenced the early Bene Israel immigrants in the 1950s, the increasing trend for communal and caste affiliations to dominate political processes in the 1960s and 1970s resulted in further emigration. This has been discussed by Gussin in his analysis of the political conditions which rendered the Bene Israel politically powerless:

> . . . increasingly there has been a swing back to vernacular speaking politicians, very much influenced by the traditional, communalistic political ethic. These communal/traditional politicians have accepted the parliamentary system but are utilizing it primarily as a vehicle to raise their own [status] and their caste status. (Gussin, 1972:77)

The ideology and actions of political parties such as the Shiv Sena in Maharashtra took on a strong militant dimension. It emphasized the supremacy of the Hindus and directed most of its antagonism toward the Muslim minority. In the late 1960s, the Shiv Sena articulated their communal sentiments through the slogan 'Maharashtra for Maharashtrians', where Maharashtrian was equated with Hindu. Although there was no direct antagonism towards the Jewish community, for the Bene Israel who had a non-Hindu identity and who lived in primarily Muslim-dominated areas, this situation symbolically proved their exclusion as a minority from the political and economic structure. From a position of inclusion in the lower ranks of the administrative and political structure of pre-independence India, the Bene Israel had shifted to an externally imposed marginal position in post-Independence India.

The rate of emigration among the Bene Israel was the highest in the late 1960s and 1970s, according to a source in the Jewish Agency branch in Bombay. It is important to understand that the rate of emigration among the Bene Israel corresponded to changes in their status both in India and in Israel. From the beginning of the 1950s to 1964, the Bene Israel were involved in a struggle to resolve the controversy in Israel over their Jewish status.[12] It was only after the political resolution of this conflict that a larger number of Bene Israel started emigrating to Israel and this emigration was indirectly exacerbated by the attitude of political organizations like the Shiv Sena.

The economic situation of the Cochin Jews also influenced emigration. While all the sections of the Cochin Jewish community were orthodox Jews, their economic situation varied. The relatively less affluent sections of the Cochin Jews were the first to emigrate. These less affluent Cochin Jews were mainly small shopkeepers and traders who saw no chances of improving their economic situation in Kerala and hence emigrated in large numbers. Evidence of the low economic status of this section of the Cochin community even in British India is evident from the letter written to the President of the English Zionist Federation by the 'elders of Kadavumbhagom and Thekkumbhagom Synagogue'.[13] The creation of Israel was an opportunity for upward economic mobility. However, while Cochin Jewish informants did identify economic motives, they were the only group to emphasize the religious dimension too when discussing the emigration of other members of the community.

During my interviews with non-immigrant Cochin Jews, informants often discussed the economic situation of the less affluent members within the Cochin and Bene Israel community. Like the Bene Israel in Maharashtra in the 1960s many of the Cochin Jews who owned land suffered economic losses resulting from changes in the land ownership laws established by the state government of Kerala. The 1970s and 1980s witnessed increasing inflation. Good job opportunities for the few remaining Jewish youth in India were relatively scarce. While the informants did mention exceptional cases where an individual emigrated solely for religious reasons, most were inclined to perceive the economic situation in India and the hope for better economic prospects in Israel as a causal factor for emigration of the majority of the Jewish population.

In the political arena, this Jewish community also experienced changes in the post-independence era. After 1947, the Cochin Jewish minority could not expect the kind of prospects and rewards they had received under the British or the local Maharajas. The introduction of an electoral system based on adult suffrage meant that numerically insignificant minorities would be rendered ineffective as political entities. The process of democratization necessarily implied the will of the majority, making minuscule minorities powerless.

While communal tensions were never a major problem in Kerala for it to have influenced the Cochin Jews, there were some political incidents which may have contributed to their awareness of political changes detrimental to their interests. For some Cochin Jews, this situation was symbolic of the changing political relations between the Cochin Jewish community and the new political powers. While they were still perceived as having a high social status (especially the Pardesi Cochin Jews) they had been marginalized in the political system. Emigration to Israel provided possibilities unattainable in India.

For the Baghdadi Jews economic factors were important in influencing emigration but with a difference. For the majority of the Baghdadi Jews, who had manifested their ethnic identity as Jews throughout their stay in India, excluded themselves from the mainstream native population and were visibly pro-British, living in independent India was unthinkable. What started as self initiated exclusion form the Hindu majority became an externally imposed exclusion on ethnic grounds in independent India. The power structure had changed, shifting into the hands of those with whom they had minimal social interaction. They perceived remaining in India as in no way economically or politically beneficial to them. The economic and political conditions of the 1940s and 1950s were also seen by the wealthier Baghdadis as detrimental to their business interests. Hence they decided to emigrate — not to Israel, but to the United Kingdom. The choice of the United kingdom had as much to do with economic rationale as the desire of the Baghdadi elite to continue their social interaction with the British. For most of the remaining Baghdadis, especially the large numbers who worked in the companies and firms of the Baghdadi elite, the departure of the more affluent spelt uncertainty and they too followed, emigrating to Canada, Australia and United States in addition to Britain.

There were, and are, other reasons for emigration besides the economic and political. During my interviews, some informants spoke of the lack of cultural and social activities in the Jewish community, especially among the Cochin and Baghdadi Jews. This problem was most frequently attributed to their dwindling numbers and was stated as an important factor influencing the desire to emigrate among some of the non-immigrant Jews. Among the Indian Jews, a lot of the social life had revolved around religious events such as circumcision, bar mitzvahs, marriages and holy days. The gradual reduction in these occasions due to the departure of the first few batches of immigrants influenced others to emigrate. However, an even more important factor reported by immigrant informants was their desire to keep the family together. Given the normative value placed on the family staying together in both Indian and Jewish society, several informants emphasized the role of family factors in influencing their own emigration (52.5 per cent). Emigrant informants often spoke of having emigrated because of 'my brother being here' or 'my husband wanted to come to Israel' or 'for the future of my children' or 'because our children had come here and we wanted to be close to them'.

Of all the factors influencing emigration, age was the least important. But a small percentage of informants attributed the age of an individual as influencing their emigration. For some of the Baghdadis emigration was linked to old age and the lack of any support system such as social welfare in India. For Cochin Jews and the Bene Israel, young adults perceived their age as an asset and they hoped to maximize their economic, social and political opportunities after emigration.

It then appears that emigration for the Indian Jews was a function of: Increasing Jewish identification and the influence of Zionism; and the effects of Indian nationalism and structural economic and political conditions in post-independence India.

THE SETTING IN ISRAEL: THEORY AND PRACTICE

With the establishment of the modern state of Israel, world Jewry could express religious identification in terms of territoriality. By the 'Law of Return' of 1950 all Jews had equal rights to citizenship of Israel. Citizenship was based on an open policy of membership for all Jews irrespective of their countries of origin. Israel was to be an egalitarian state, the symbol of Jewish solidarity, where *mizug hagaluyot* (fusion of exiles) would occur.

With the creation of the modern state of Israel, the Zionist movement had achieved its goal of a national frame of reference for the resettlement of Jews. The background for the emergence of political Zionism was the crisis faced by Jewish communities in Eastern Europe during the nineteenth and twentieth centuries. Drawing on the development of nationalism in Europe, Zionism sought the creation of a Jewish state as a solution to the problem of *galut* (exile). Through political movement the Zionists hoped to achieve the resettlement of Jews of the diaspora into one unified nation. The pioneers of the political movement were the European Jewry. Many of these early nationalist pioneers settled in Palestine prior to 1948 and began developing 'a national and secularized framework of cultural reference for all'.[14] To provide a unified framework, which would maintain Jewish solidarity within Israeli ideology and culture it was perceived as imperative by the pioneers to minimize, within Israel, the cultural specificities of the returning groups. Theoretically, the concept of *mizug hagaluyot* implied a fusion of exiles and a melting of cultures to produce one enriched common Jewish national culture. That is, ethnic identities based on cultural particularism were to be replaced by a national Jewish identity. However, since the founding immigrant communities of Israel were predominantly European, the national cultural framework for Israel was shaped by them.

Underlying this process were the biases of the founding European immigrant communities to mold the structure keeping their own values and practices as the predominant basis for the shaping of Israeli society. This was accompanied by a desire to avoid incorporating the cultural specificities of Asian, North African and Middle Eastern countries as they were perceived to be less developed than the European societies. Thus the avoidance of incorporating these cultures in the main Israeli cultural framework stemmed from the ethnocentrism of the dominant communities. On the basis of their veteran immigrant status, sections of the European Jews, i.e. the Ashkenazim, were able to acquire prestige in Israel in its early years. They shared this prestige with their succeeding generations who attained it due to their links to the veteran immigrant communities. Thus theoretically, while all Jews were equal on the basis of their Jewish membership in Israel, in practice an asymmetrical structure developed with the Ashkenazim forming the dominant communities (core culture) and the Asian, North African and Middle Eastern communities, i.e. predominantly the Sephardim, forming the subordinate communities (peripheral cultures).

CONTACT OF INDIAN JEWRY WITH THE ISRAELI SETTING

Believing in the Zionist principle of *galut hagaluyot* in Israel and having identified themselves as a part of world Jewry, the Indian Jews sought membership of Israel. By the Law of Return (1950), the Indian Jews had a right to return to Israel. They perceived membership in Israel as a means to strengthen Jewish solidarity and as the resolution of their problems of economic and political marginalization in independent India. It was to be a shift from a minority status in India to equal status in Israel. From 1948 onwards Indian Jews started migrating to Israel with the assistance of the Jewish Agency, which was responsible for assisting Jews from all countries to immigrate to Israel. Upon immigration, however, their experience contradicted the principle of an egalitarian society. They realized that equal rights to membership was not a sufficient condition for equal social status. During the early years instead of fusion of cultures to produce a common Jewish national cultural framework, ethnicization occurred (the process whereby ethnic identities are formulated). The first level of differentiation was the dichotomization of Israeli society into Ashkenazi and Sephardic. Further differentiations were based on countries of origin.

Despite the Indian Jewish immigrants having identified themselves as Jews, they were distinguished from the mainstream Jewry in the same setting on the basis of their primordial and cultural specificities. The dark complexion of the majority of the Indian Jewish immigrants *vis-à-vis* the fair complexion of the European communities became a visible marker of difference. In addition, their use of Indian languages, customs, food habits and clothing were seen as nonconformist to the dominant culture and defined in terms of 'non-Jewishness'.

Since the setting was shaped by the culture as defined by the dominant group, the cultural particularism of the other communities were distinguished by the usage of ethnic labeling. The Indian Jewish immigrants were labeled 'Hodim' (Indians); the Moroccans, 'Moroccim', etc. The use of such an ethnic labeling process was perceived by those labeled as a marker of externally imposed ethnicization. The Indian Jewish immigrants perceived their being labeled as 'Hodim' as an emphasis on their 'Indian-ness' rather than their 'Jewishness' and as stemming from the negative attitude of the dominant communities to the primordial and cultural particularism of the Indian Jews. The immigrants were made conscious of being set apart from the mainstream culture.

ELEMENTS OF ETHNICIZATION AND MARGINALIZATION

Spatial Structure

While the social differences between the dominant communities and the 'others' have decreased in recent years, the Indian Jewish immigrants are still marginalized in terms of their geographic location. Although there was a small percentage of Indian Jewish immigrants living in large urban centers or big cities when the fieldwork for this study was conducted, the majority then resided in *moshavim* (smallholder cooperative farming settlements in the rural areas) or in development towns (established after 1948 by the state in specific areas to disperse the population and develop the region). This was in contrast to the Ashkenazi communities who formed the vast majority of settlers in the big cities such as Tel Aviv and Haifa. Thus geographically the Indian Jewish immigrants are located in what can be defined as 'peripheral areas' as compared to the dominant population who live in what can be defined as 'core areas'. The development of this structural pattern can be traced to the structural organization of the absorption of immigrants during the early years of resettlement. Until 1968, the Jewish Agency was not only responsible for assisting in immigration of Jews to Israel but also for the resettlement of these immigrants. The Jewish Agency provided housing, other amenities and social services. From 1969 the responsibility for resettlement was taken over by the Ministry of Absorption.

To cope with the large influx of Jewish immigrants (from Europe, Asia, Africa, and the Americas) in the early years after the establishment of Israel, two types of accommodation schemes were developed. The first scheme was the placement of immigrants in *Ma-abarot* (transit camps) and the other was the direct placement of immigration into *moshavim* or *kibbutzim* (collective farming settlements). The second scheme was referred to as 'from ship to village'.[15] That is, the immigrants were directly taken to these supposedly permanent settlements in the rural areas.

Between 1948 and 1959 the total number of *moshavim* increased from 104 to 366 and the population of these settlements rose from 30,000 to 1,240,000.[16] In addition, in the 1950s the government established 'development towns'. The government funded planned towns to divert the concentration of population from the big cities of Israel. The aim was to disperse the population and develop the under-developed areas through the distribution of industries in these regions. These development towns were also economic and administrative centers for the rural areas. The very nature of the 'absorption of immigrants' was such that Indian Jewish immigrants, like the majority of immigrants from Asia and Africa, were directly settled in the *moshavim*, or development towns. The Western immigrants, on the other hand, were offered a chance to live in the bigger cities.

In 1949, a *moshav* was created for Indian immigrants and predominantly settled by the Cochin Malabar Jews. Though today the community has made its *moshav* a relatively successful one economically, it has taken them many years of hard manual labor to achieve it. At the time it was allocated to them, this area was barren land with little potential for growth. Among the early Bene Israel immigrants some chose to live in *kibbutzim* rather the *moshavim.*

In the 1960s and early 1970s when large percentage of the Bene Israel emigrated they were considered unsuited to farming. They were channeled into settling in development towns despite the fact that some of them were professionals. The population in these development towns was comprised mainly of Asians and Africans as the Westerners lived in the cities. Contrary to the approach adopted towards Asian and African immigrants, the Jewish Agency and the Ministry of Absorption provided Western immigrants, especially professionals, with the opportunity of temporary accommodation in what were known as 'absorption centers' in the cities. This acted as a springboard for their later obtaining appropriate accommodation in the cities or suburbs. Thus from the very beginning a spatial structure was established separating the dominant communities from the 'others', the latter being the category in which Indian Jewish immigrants were included.

Though theoretically the Indian Jewish immigrants had unrestricted geographic mobility, in practice it was extremely difficult to move. While today there are a few Indian immigrants residing in the big cities, even now the majority of them continue to reside in *moshavim* and development towns. The Indian Jewish immigrants had little option to leave these locations into which they were settled upon arrival, since they lacked the financial resources to afford independent housing in the big cities. The combination of their limited financial resources in India and the strict Indian government policy towards removal of assets from India thus placed them in this undesirable position in Israel.

In the *moshavim*, the Indian Jews were provided with subsidized housing and land for farming; those who went to the development towns were provided with subsidized housing. Limited financial resources compelled the Indian Jewish immigrants to accept these subsidized accommodation schemes. However, stipulations attached to these governmental housing schemes acted as further deterrents to geographic mobility outside of government-sponsored accommodation. Subletting of houses by immigrants was legally prohibited. If the immigrants wished to move they had either to give up their subsidized accmmodation or appeal to the government housing company to exchange their house for another one in a government scheme elsewhere. The first choice in most cases was not feasible due to their straitened circumstances and the second was dependent on the discretion of the government housing company and the availability of housing in the areas selected by the immigrants. In addition, the provision of long and easy mortgages for those living in these areas inhibited immigrants from moving elsewhere. This restriction of mobility was expressed in a number of my interviews with the immigrants informants, especially among the Bene Israel. As one interviewee noted:

> We would like to move out of this house and live in a better area but we are helpless, since we don't have the money to buy our own house. I have asked the Amidar for a change of house as this house is too small for my family but I am still waiting for something to be done about it. We are not lucky like the Ashkenazi who have a lot of influence and money to live in the cities.

For those living in the *moshavim* it was even harder to move since they had invested their labor in the land. Another interviewee pointed out:

> I cannot think of moving out of here, after all we [his family] have put in a lot of hard labor into this land. We had to pay off the loans we took from the government. When I first came here nothing grew on this land. It has taken us many years to achieve this much. Besides if I leave this what job will I get and houses in the city are too expensive for most of us as it can only be afforded by the rich Westerners.

The result is spatial marginalization for the majority of the Indian Jewish immigrants who have little option but to remain in the *moshavim* and developments towns. Over a period of time, many of these immigrants found it hard to uproot themselves from these areas as they had developed their communal network of friends and other activities. This resulted in increased ethnicization of the Indian Jewish immigrant community. The spatial structuring also restricted them from the opportunities available in big cities. Rather than being geographically integrated into the mainstream, marginalization through 'ethnic ghettoization' took place.

Social Structure

The social structure of Israel can be explained in terms of multiple dichotomies. At the most general level, there is the dichotomy between Jews (82.7 per cent of the population) and non-Jews (17.3 per cent). With reference to non-Jews, all Jews irrespective of their internal divisions define themselves as a unified whole. The non-Jews are perceived as 'outsiders' on the basis of their non-Jewish status and hence are not included in the social divisions which govern interaction between Jews.

While all Jews identify with the Israeli ideology of a single nation of Jews, there exists a basic social dichotomy which plays an extremely significant role in the overall social structure of Israeli society and more specifically in explaining the social status of the Indian Jews, especially in the early phase of migration. This is the two-fold hierarchical division of Jews into the Ashkenazim and Sephardim. Originally the term Ashkenaz referred to Jews of German descent and Sephard to those of Spanish or Portuguese descent. However, over a period of time these terms have been extended to incorporate other categories. The term Ashkenazim has been extended to refer to all Jews of European descent who observe the Ashkenazi religious patterns and the term the Sephardim includes all those who observe the Sephardi religious patterns. The latter category includes all the Asian and North African Jewish communities.

In Israeli society, especially in the early phase following the creation of the nation state of Israel. Ashkenazi Jews were attributed the highest social status by both Ashkenazi and Sephardi, the latter having internalized this hierarchical order as initially defined by the former. Within the two categories there were further subdivisions which were hierarchically ranked. The order of the hierarchy was not fixed and was relative to who defined the ordering. However there appeared to be a general overall pattern. Among the Ashkenazim the highest social status was attributed to the veteran immigrants from Russia, Poland, Rumania and Germany who came prior to the creation of Israel, between 1919 and 1947. These were followed by the North American and British Jews. The relatively high status of these groups can be attributed partially to Israel's social, economic and political relationship with these two nations. Finally there were the other European Jewish groups who had varying social status.

Among the Sephardim, those of European origin, such as the Bulgarians, were attributed a high social status. In the middle range of the hierarchy were those from the Middle Eastern countries such as Iraq, Persia, Syria, etc. and at the lower range of the hierarchy were the Indian and African Jews. However, the Moroccans had a higher status than the Indians and the Indians a higher status than the Ethiopian Jews. It is important to note that this was not a rigid hierarchy and could vary according to who was doing the ranking. The above hierarchical ranking is based on my discussion with Indian and non-Indian Jews as well as my own observations in Israel.[17]

In their social life, the Indian Jewish immigrants had minimal social interaction with other communities. Among both the Bene Israel and Cochin immigrant informants, over 70 per cent had minimal or no social interaction with other non-Indian Jewish communities and had as their closest friends members from within the Indian Jewish communities.

Perceptions of their community's status tended to be in the lower range especially among the Bene Israel. The lack of social interaction with mainstream Jewry was perceived by the Indian Jewish immigrants to be a consequence of their spatial marginalization and the negative image of the Indian Jews held by the dominant community, which had also been internalized by other ethnic communities. The low social status of Indian Jews and the nature of their interaction with other communities is thus based on the formation of a 'negative stereotype'. What are the factors which result in their low social status? These can be understood in terms of physical features, language, dress, food and drink, marriage and religion.

Before proceeding to analyze these factors, it is relevant to note that there are slight social status variations between the Indian Jewish communities. In Israel today the Cochinis, irrespective of whether they are Pardesi or Malabar, have a higher social status than the Bene Israel. This is related to the problems which the Bene Israel have faced in establishing their claim to a 'full Jewish' identity as well as the relative economic success of the Cochinis.

Physical Features

Socially, the Indian Jewish immigrants have been stigmatized on the basis of color, especially during the first ten years after the establishment of Israel. But according to some of my informants, stigmatization based on color still persists. As stated by many of my informants, it has shifted from 'visible discrimination' to 'invisible discrimination'. That is, people do differentiate on the basis of color but do not express it verbally as they previously did. To quote one informant:

When we first arrived, people would make all sorts of loud comments about us being dark. Children of other communities would not play with our children. Our color influenced how people treated us. It was as though being darker was bad or dirty. But this has changed quite a lot nowadays. It has not stopped altogether but at least they don't make rude comments in front of us. You understand? I mean it is more invisible discrimination—like how the people treat you at work or who they keep as friends.

Comments such as the above were frequently narrated by informants. Among the early Bene Israel immigrants, such stigmatization was perceived as serious enough for them to have demanded and achieved their repatriation to India between 1951 and 1952. Color differentiation became a visible marker for boundary formation and maintenance. It restricted the permeation of Indian Jewish immigrants into the social strata occupied by the dominant communities. The prejudice of the dominant communities towards dark skin involved their endowing these groups with negative attributes such as uncleanliness, primitiveness or lower levels of social development. To the Indian Jewish immigrants, labeling on the basis of color was a sensitive issue since in India too negative value is attached to dark skin and fair skin color usually corresponds with high status. The white Jews of Cochin are an exception to this experience of color discrimination as their fair complexion allows a certain degree of 'passing' into slightly higher status communities. As expressed by one such member:

In terms of color, I have experienced no discrimination. For that matter, they rarely take me for an Indian. They pass me off for a middle Easterner. Once I was even considered as Spanish! When I tell them I am Indian in my office they were surprised. However I don't think this is the case with the other dark Indian Jews.

However the majority of the Indian Jewish immigrants in Israel can be differentiated on the basis of skin color and it thus becomes a visible marker of their 'Indian-ness'.

Language, Dress and Food Habits

Though there has been an on-going process of transformation from the use of Indian languages, dress modes and food habits among the Indian Jewish immigrants to those identified with mainstream Israeli society, the former still persists to a certain degree. Among the Indian Jewish immigrant informants, 71 per cent of the Bene Israel and 37 per cent of the Cochin Jews spoke Marathi and Malayalam respectively as the main language at home. The persistence of these usages has contributed to the ethnicization and social marginalization of the Indian Jewish immigrant communities and is more visible among the Bene Israel compared to the Cochin Jews.

As stated earlier, in India, Jews adopted the language, dress and food habits of the indigenous people. They spoke the local dialects, wore the local attire and cooked their food in the local styles. During the British period a certain degree of anglicization occurred among some sections of the communities. However, in general they maintained the local patterns, Hebrew was used only for prayers. When these communities emigrated, they carried over these patterns to Israel having incorporated it into their Jewish culture, only to find that they were perceived 'undesirable' by the dominant communities of Israel. These usages became markers for labeling and social marginalization. The persistence of these usages should also be attributed to their being geographically concentrated in ethnic pockets. Being spatially isolated from the dominant communities and having as neighbors either members of their own community or other low social status ethnic communities, the Indian Jewish immigrants had no choice but to retain social patterns which they had adopted in India.

Despite the fact that a large number of Indian Jewish immigrants knew English, their opportunity to use it in social interaction was limited. Most of the immigrants from English-speaking countries had a relatively high social status and lived in the major cities. Those immigrants who lived near the Indian Jewish immigrant communities spoke primarily the languages of their countries of origin. Hence social interaction for most of these ethnic communities including the Indian Jews tended to be with their own members.

The Indian Jewish immigrants were also differentiated on the basis of their Indian attire. Women wearing saris or in the earlier days Cochin men wearing the 'pillbox hat' were set apart from mainstream Jewry and identified as Indian. With this Indian-ness came the lack of social interaction between the Indian Jewish immigrants and the other communities. Today most Indian Jews have adopted the Western mode of attire, although some of the older women among the Bene Israel still wear saris.

Similarly the food habits of the Indian Jewish immigrants were perceived by other communities as typically Indian and 'undesirable'. Indian Jewish immigrants explained how some other ethnic communities feel that the smell of Indian food is too overpowering. Among the Bene Israel immigrants, the persistence of the Hindu practice of avoiding beef is often seen as indicative of their Indian-ness and perceived as another marker of differentiation from mainstream Jewry.

Marriage

Marriage and the selection of partners is another dimension through which one can see the social marginalization of the Indian Jewish immigrants. All my informants in Israel stated that marriage between Indian Jewish immigrants and members of the dominant community was extremely rare. Recently among the children of the Indian Jewish immigrants there have been some intermarriages; informants were aware of Indian Jewish immigrants marrying Middle Eastern immigrants. But these are exceptions. In general, marriage occurs between members of one's own community. This is partially the result of the lack of access to members of other communities, especially to members of the dominant communities.

The crisis experienced by the Bene Israel immigrant community in the 1960s is also particularly relevant is this context for it affected their marriage patterns. From the time of their arrival in Israel, the Bene Israel had been the most stigmatized of the immigrant communities. Despite their claims to a Jewish identity they were perceived as Indians whose Jewish claims were suspect. The Bene Israel were informed that they were not 'full Jews' as they did not practice *halitzah* and, as such, marriage to Bene Israel was proscribed for other Jews as the former were suspected of being *mamzerim* (bastards).[18] For the Bene Israel this was a catastrophe since it threatened the very existence of their future as Jews in Israel. Considerable controversy revolved around their status and several responses were issued by different Rabbi, most of which showed the Bene Israel in a negative manner. These aspersions cast on their Jewish identity can be seen as an extension of the problems faced by the Bene Israel with the Baghdadi Jews in India who had also refused to acknowledge them as Jews.

The problem was taken to the Supreme Rabbinical Court in October 1961 which proclaimed that Bene Israel were Jewish but that for every marriage verification of their background would be necessary. To the Bene Israel, this was no solution as it still implied discrimination and they demanded that the rules of marriage applicable to others be the same for them. Having failed to receive a satisfactory solution, the issue was taken to Parliament in 1963 but the bill declaring Bene Israel as full Jews was defeated by the Mapai and National Religious parties. The issue reached major dimensions with the Bene Israel demonstrating in 1964 against their social discrimination. What started as a socio-religious issue soon became a major political issue. The Liberal Party convened a special session on the status of the Bene Israel in Parliament. On 9 August 1964, the ruling party defeated the National Religious Party and came out in favor of the Bene Israel and issued a resolution calling for the Chief Rabbinate to remove the directive concerning the Bene Israel. Though this was done, it left its mark on the Bene Israel and members of the community continued to perceive themselves as socially stigmatized. While this was specific to the Bene Israel community, the negative attitude of the dominant communities and other ethnic communities has resulted in social marginalization of the Indian Jewish immigrant communities as a whole.

Religion

Prior to their immigration to Israel, the Indian Jews had articulated their Jewish identity through the observance and practice of Judaic Law. The synagogues were the centers of community organization and the symbols of their Jewish identity. Upon immigration to Israel they assumed that they would be integrated into a religious organization which was common to all on the basis of their Jewish identity. However this was not the case. At the individual level most immigrant informants articulated their Jewishness through the observance of the Sabbath, the Jewish festivals, dietary prohibitions and synagogue attendance. These are common to all Jewry. Yet at the community level, religious organization appeared to be differentiated on an ethnic basis. Due to cultural pluralism in the rituals, Hebrew pronounciation, religious tunes and ceremonies among the different ethnic communities, most communities have built their own synagogues. Thus the Cochinis and the Bene Israel have their own synagogues like other ethnic groups. Approximately 75 per cent of my immigrant informants attended their own community synagogue. While this process of ethnicization was a self-initiated process, it has clearly stemmed from their inability to identify their Jewishness in the religious organization of the dominant communities and their perception of being defined as 'outsiders' in these socio-religious institutions. An immigrant informant noted:

> I go to my synagogue because there our traditions are kept. We feel comfortable. We know the prayers, tunes and customs and can participate. If you go to synagogues of other communities it feels odd. They have different customs and tunes. We cannot join in it. One feels like an outsider, especially in the Ashkenazi synagogue. They are totally different. . . . Every community has different religious styles . . . the Baghdadis, the Tunisians, the Moroccan. If we go to their Synagogues it feels different . . . that's why most of us go to our own synagogue if there is one close by.

Such sentiments were frequently articulated by my informants. Ironically, the synagogue which had been the symbol of their Jewish identity in India is redefined in the Israeli context and becomes a marker of their Indian identity. Those informants who attended Ashkenazi synagogues or other Sephardim synagogues did so because they did not have easy access to their own community synagogue. The formation of synagogues on ethnic lines has contributed to the maintenance of boundaries and social distance between the various communities. While providing a means to express the cultural particularism of each community, these synagogues have also become an obstacle to the integration of the marginal communities into the mainstream Jewish culture.

During the course of my field work I attended various functions hosted by Indian Jewish immigrants. In most cases, nearly all those invited were members of the same ethnic community. There were very few people from other communities and in some cases there were no 'outsiders'. These occasions substantiated the fact that there is minimal social interaction between the Indian Jewish immigrants and the other Jewish communities and that the Indian Jews are socially marginalized in Israeli society.

Economic Structure

When the Indian Jews immigrated to Israel, they had envisioned Israel as the source of their religious and economic fulfillment. They thought that not only would they be in the land of Jews but also in a land of economic opportunity where all Jews would have equal access to the economic resources. Eighty-eight per cent of my immigrant informants perceived they had raised their general standard of living by migrating to Israel. My informants defined the possession of goods such as refrigerators, ovens, televisions, video cassette recorders, good furniture and, in some cases, cars as evidence of their better standard of living. Services such as free medical facilities, low interest government loans, low-cost housing and social welfare were described as services provided in Israel which they could not have expected in India. Hence, compared to the standard of living in India, most Jewish immigrant informants perceived themselves and their communities as being in a better situation. However, within the Israeli economy, the economic position of the Indian, Jewish immigrants *vis-à-vis* the dominant communities can be defined as marginal.

In the overall economic structure of Israel, the Indian Jewish immigrants tend to be concentrated in certain occupations which are generally attached a low socio-economic status. The occupation among the majority of the Malabar Cochini was farming and among the Pardesi Cochinis it was clerical work. The Bene Israel were concentrated in clerical and skilled/unskilled labor occupations. Today, an increasing number of Indian Jewish immigrants are retired and thus without occupations. This has further lowered their standard of living and increased their feeling of economic marginalization. The majority of the Bene Israel immigrant informants had low status occupations or no occupation. The Cochin Jews tended to be occupationally concentrated in farming. Despite the fact that there were two earning members in many families, the general net annual household income was not very high. In terms of the informants, perception of their economic status one sees that neither the Bene Israel nor the Cochin Jews attribute a very high economic status to their situation.. The Cochin Jewish, informants perceived their economic status as 'somewhat high' while the Bene Israel defined theirs as 'somewhat low' or 'extremely low'. While both the Cochini and the Bene Israel immigrant communities had low prestige occupations, the variation in perception of economic status stemmed from the fact that the Cochin Jews in *moshavim* had succeeded in improving their economic situation and thereby perceived themselves as having gained some respect for this economic success from other communities. It is therefore important to discuss the economic situation of these two Indian Jewish communities separately.

The Cochin Jewish immigrants in Israel are predominantly comprised of the Malabar section; the Pardesi Jews and Manumitted Jews make up the other components of the total Cochin Jewish population. In the 1950s the Malabar section of the Cochin Jewish population emigrated en masse to Israel while the Pardesi and Manumitted sections emigrated in the late 1960s and 1970s. The latter took up clerical jobs in the urban areas since, with the exception of a fortunate few, most of them had no professional degrees. Most of these Cochin Jews had a low socio-economic status in India. A few were landowners in India, but the majority were poor landless people. On their arrival in Israel they were channeled by the authorities to take up farming as an occupation. They had a choice between living in *kibbutzim or moshavim* for the choice of living in cities was not available to them. Nearly all of them chose to go to the *moshavim* as they had heard that the kibbutzniks were not religious and also because in *moshavim* they could have their own piece of land. Despite the fact that they had no farming experience they were made to take up this occupation under the supervision of official instructors for the first four years. The work was extremely hard for these immigrants as the land was desert. Physically they were not very strong and lacked the necessary orientation toward such an occupation. The economic hardship faced by these immigrants, especially in the early years was described by one of my Cochin immigrant informants:

> In the village we came to in 1956, then we did not have electricity or water supply. We worked on road maintenance, foresting and all these jobs. It was all desert here. Later we tried to grow some vegetables like tomatoes and cucumbers. . . . It was not profitable. Then we moved to growing factory crops such as sugar beet, cotton, and then in 1965 or so we started growing flowers for export . . . that was the beginning of a big change in these areas . . . we solved our problem by hard work we worked very hard, sometimes around the clock.

After many years of struggle and remaining at the margins of the economic structure, today a substantial number of these immigrants have made their occupation an economic success.[19] All the immigrant informants from this section perceived themselves as having fared better economically in Israel than they would have in India. They have acquired various material possessions and now form the new upper stratum within the Indian Jewish immigrant communities. However, they are still not economically integrated with the dominant communities. Since farming involves manual labor, it is not allocated a high socio-economic status. Thus while in terms of income they have attained a certain amount of economic mobility, this mobility has not corresponded with total socio-economic integration. During my interviews, while informants were proud of their economic achievements, the low prestige attributed to such occupations and the arduous nature of the work resulted in their desire that their children should not continue in this occupation and should try to attain a better socio-economic status.

Access to education was another area in which the Cochin Jews felt that they were marginalized. The immigrants are increasingly conscious of the need to educate the younger generation. Some of my informants expressed their dissatisfaction with the present approach to education. They felt that the Sephardim, especially those in the lower social status communities, do not have the same access to facilities compared to the Ashkenazim. This is perceived as detrimental to the future of Sephardic youth and to the state as the Sephardic are numerically dominant. Inherent in such statements was the keen desire to achieve equal status with the dominant communities and be perceived as an integral part of the mainstream Israeli society.

For the Bene Israel immigrants there is an even deeper sense of economic marginalization. Throughout my interviews with Bene Israel informants this was brought up. Most of my informants spoke of having been part of a community in India which had risen from oil pressers to white collar workers during the British period, in their eyes a considerable achievement. However, in Israel, they were channeled into low status jobs. I quote two Bene Israel informants:

> I came here, left a good job in India. Here I was made to work in the factory. It was not a good job. Anybody could do it and the salary was not much. I had no choice. When I came here I signed saying that I would take up any job offered to me. Even then they tried to keep me as temporary. That way they can avoid some pension. This happened to a lot of Bene Israel. You can only succeed if you have *protectia* (influence) and we don't have that.

Another commented:

> I was a nurse in India but when I came here they told me that I was not qualified. So I did odd jobs. Because of this I don't have a pension. If I had not been a Bene Israel maybe I could have got a nursing job. I don't know. But we Bene Israel have not been able to do well economically and therefore have a lot of problems in our community.

The Bene Israel perceived themselves as unfairly treated by the mainstream society. Ethnic identification was extremely strong among the members of the community and was seen to be a result of the common situation in which the Bene Israel immigrants were placed. From the time of their arrival in Israel, they felt they had been given little opportunity for upward mobility compared to certain other groups. Though there are a few in middle range jobs and a significant number in clerical positions the majority are in extremely low status jobs such as skilled and unskilled labor. For the Bene Israel, who were economically privileged under the British in India this was defined as a case of downward economic mobility. Though the majority felt that they had a few more material possessions than they would have had in India, they saw the economic situation of other communities in Israel as the basis of comparison.

According to most Bene Israel informants, all the good positions were monopolized by the Ashkenazim and individuals from other ethnic communities who had *protectia* (influence). Some Bene Israel felt that their lack of economic opportunity had been a detriment to the education and economic success of their offspring. The sense of economic marginalization or lack of economic integration with mainstream Jewry was stronger among the Bene Israel than among the Cochin Jews. It would not be inappropriate to conclude that the Indian Jewish immigrant communities were relatively economically marginalized. I say 'relatively' since their economic marginality is far less than that experienced by African immigrant communities such as the Ethiopian Jews. Some sections of the Indian Jewish communities have been able to attain a degree of economic upward mobility, thereby experiencing a lessening of the sense of economic marginalization.

Political Structure

While in theory all individuals have the same political rights, the political structure of Israel has been characterized by various division on an ideological basis. Each of the parties representing these ideologies developed their specific tactics to gain the support of the ethnic groups. Often the tactics used were outside of any ideological framework. The parties recruited individuals from the ethnic communities to form organizations at the town or rural level which were aligned to central political bodies. However, these local political branches were perceived by many informants as being detrimental to the community's access or representation in the central political structure. During my research, informants complained that a number of these organizations were corrupt and wielded a lot of influence in the work sphere. In the words of an informant:

> Even in getting jobs there is politics. The political parties wield power in the work place. Sometimes your getting a job or a promotion will be closely connected to your voting for some particular party. Also those who have *protectia* with the political people, they get better jobs. Some Kibbutz are also formed with political connections. There is politics at all levels. For example, in the bank I work the Moroccim are very powerful because of

their party connections. On the other hand, our community has no political power.

Unlike the Moroccans who wielded some power, the Indian Jewish immigrant communities were characterized by a high level of powerlessness until quite recently. At the time that this research was conducted they were finally able to place one Bene Israel in the Knesset. However, in general, the members of the Indian Jewish immigrant communities perceived themselves as politically weak. This was attributed by some politically conscious informants as stemming to a large extent from the passivity and political apathy of the majority of the members. The lack of political participation among these communities further marginalized their position in Israeli society. The lack of unity between the Cochin Jews and the Bene Israel inhibited their ability to form a politically viable group and this has considerably reduced the chances of attaining political success as an ethnic community. A politically active informant noted:

> The problem is that all our people are not united. Since we are not a large community like many other communities it is important that we act as a joint group. Until now the Cochini and Bene Israel don't put up one common candidate. Bene Israel want Bene Israel, Cochini want Cochini. There is too much division. As it is many do not want to participate. That is they are not interested. Now we are trying to change this.

There were a few local organizations that tried to organize the Indian Jewish immigrants on an ethnic basis. But these were often not active and were further undermined by factionalism. While the organization known as the Indian Federation of Jews, established in 1968, was supposed to be the organization representing the interests of all sections of the Indian Jewish communities in Israel, it is not identified by many sections as being adequately representative. Excluding a few small groups, as a community, the Indian Jewish immigrants are distanced from the political arena. With the exception of the 1960 crisis when the Bene Israel created a formal organization, demonstrated against their status in Israel and forced the issue into Parliament, there has been no major articulation or participation or inclusion of the Indian Jewish immigrant communities in the political process of Israel.[20]

CONCLUSION

In conclusion we see that the Indian Jewish immigrants in Israel were ethnicized and marginalized in Israel. Though they immigrated to Israel on the basis of their Jewish identity and their desire to resolve their marginal situation in post-independence India, these people found themselves once again marginalized. The setting into which the Indian Jewish communities arrived in Israel was normatively defined as egalitarian but factually was based on an inegalitarian structure since the Ashkenazim, the European Jews formed the core and they determined the basis of absorption. Our findings based on the Cochin and Bene Israel immigrant communities indicate that despite claiming a Jewish identity, these communities were ethnicized in terms of their 'Indian-ness'. Since the Indian Jewish culture was perceived by the dominant group as incongruent with the core culture, there was boundary maintenance between the core and the Indian communities resulting in the latter's marginalization. The primordial and cultural characteristics of the Indian Jewish communities *vis-à-vis* the dominant community became visible markers of differentiation. Ultimately, their 'Indian-ness' became the basis for identification by the dominant communities. The immigrants were faced with the problem of dual identity and dual marginalization. In the longer term, most Indian Jewish immigrants hoped that their marginalization would decrease in the next ten years with the gradual breaking down of social boundaries and that changes in perception among the dominant communities would bring about social change.

ACKNOWLEDGEMENTS

The research for this study was funded by the American Institute of Indian Studies, University of Chicago; The Memorial Foundation for Jewish Culture, New York; The Roscoe Martin Fund; and the Syracuse University Senate Grant to which bodies I am grateful. I also gratefully acknowledge the valuable comments and suggestions given by Dr. Ephraim H. Mizruchi, Dr. Gary Spencer, Dr. Susan Wadley, Dr. Barry Glassner, Dr. T.N. Madan, Annie Mathew and Pradeep Singh. A very big debt is acknowledged to the members of the Indian Jewish communities in India and Israel, especially Sattoo and Gladis Koder, Mr. Bezalel and Mrs. Bathzion Eliahu, Bina Eliahu, Mr. Ezra Moses and family, Mr. and Mrs. Nissim Talkar, Mr. Enoch and Mrs. Erusha Eliyahu, Mr. N. Nahoum and Mr. David Nahoum.

NOTES

1. The thirty thousand estimate is based on Ezekiel Musleah, *On the Banks of the Ganga: The Sojourn of the Jews in Calcutta* (North Quincy, Massachusetts, 1975). He does not give the year for the estimate. However, based on some other readings and secondary sources, it was probably between 1947 and 1951. Also, see Benjamin Israel, *The Bene Israel of India: Some Studies* (Bombay, 1984). There are no census data available for the Jewish population. The 5,300 number is based on: 1. an estimate given by the leaders of the community and calculated by a rough growth rate, 2. the number of people immigrating to Israel, and 3. estimates given by Nathan Katz, another researcher on the Indian Jews. Since the Kerala and Calcutta communities are so small, an approximate count of the members could be obtained. Both communities together comprise about 200 members. The rest of the population is comprised of the Bene Israel.
2. T.V. Parasuram, *India's Jewish Heritage* (New Delhi, 1982); Barbara Cottle Johnson, 'Our Community in Two Worlds: The Cochin Pardesi Jews in India and Israel' (unpublished Ph.D. thesis, University of Massachusetts, 1985); Margaret Abraham, 'Ethnic Identity and Marginality Among Indian Jews in Contemporary, India', *Ethnic Groups* 9 (1991), pp. 33-60; Joan G. Roland, *Jews in British India: Identity in a Colonial Era* (Hanover and London, 1989); Benjamin Israel, *The Bene Israel of India: Some Studies;* Schifra Strizower 1. 'Jews as an Indian Caste', *The Jewish Journal of Sociology*, 1:1 (April 1959), pp. 43-57; 2. *Exotic Jewish Communities* (London, 1962); 3. 'The Bene Israel in Israel', *Middle Eastern Studies*, 2 (1966), pp. 123-43; 4. *The Children of Israel: The Bene Israel of Bombay* (Oxford, 1971); Shirley Berry Isenberg, *India's Bene Israel* (Bombay: Popular Prakashan and Judah, L. Magnes Museum, California, 1988).
3. David Mandelbaum, 'Social Stratification Among the Jews of Cochin', *The Jewish Journal of Sociology*, XVIII: 2 (December 1975); T.V. Parasuram, *India's Jewish Heritage*; Barbara Cottle Johnson, *Our Community in Two Worlds: The Cochin Pardesi Jews in India and Israel;* Margaret Abraham, 'The Cochin Jews of India: A socio-historical study in Asian Culture', *Tradition and Diaspora Selected Proceedings* of the 1993 National

Conference, edited by Daisy Cocco De Fillipis, York College, CUNY. The following articles by Walter Fischel: 1. 'David d' Beth Hillel: A Hitherto Unknown Jewish Traveller in India', *Oriens* (Leiden) 10: 2 (1957), pp. 240-7; 2. 'Cochin in Jewish History: Prologomena to a History of the Jews of India', in an off-print from *American Academy for Jewish Research Proceedings*, 30 (1962), pp. 37-59; 3. 'Exploration of the Jewish Antiquities of Cochin on the Malabar Coast', *Journal of American Oriental Society*, 87 (1967), pp. 230-48.

4. 'Shema', is the fundamental tenet of the Jewish faith. For more details, see Shirley Berry Isenberg, *India's Bene Israel*.
5. For details see, Margaret Abraham, 'Ethnic Identity and Marginality: A Study of the Jews of India' (unpublished thesis, Syracuse University, 1989); Also see Joan G. Roland, *Jews in British India: Identity in a Colonial Era*; Benjamin Israel, *The Bene Israel of India: Some Studies*; Schifra Strizower, 'Jews as an Indian Caste', '*Exotic Jewish Communities*; 'The Bene Israel in Israel'; *The Children of Israel: The Bene Israel of Bombay*; Shirley Berry Isenberg, *India's Bene Israel*.
6. For further historical details, see Ezekiel Musleah, *On the Banks of the Ganga: The Sojourn of the Jews in Calcutta;* Esmond David Ezra, *Turning Back the Pages: A Chronicle of Calcutta Jewry*, vol. 1 (London, 1986).
7. For details on the Zionist movement in India, see, Walter Fischel, 'Early Zionism in India', in a reprint from *Herzl Year Book*, vol. I (1961-2), pp. 309-28.
8. Strizower, *The Children of Israel: The Bene Israel of Bombay*; Carl Mark Gussin, 'The Bene Israel: Politics, Religion and Systemic Change' (unpublished Ph.D. thesis, Syracuse University, 1972); Benjamin Israel, *The Jews of India* (New Delhi: Centre for Jewish Inter Faith Studies, 1982).
9. Provided by an official of The Jewish Agency in Jerusalem, Israel. For details on causal factors for migration, see, Margaret Abraham, 'The Normative and the Factual: An Analysis of Emigration Factors of the Jews of India', *Jewish Journal of Sociology*, XXXIII (1991), pp. 5-19.
10. Ephraim H. Mizruchi and, Robert Perucci, 'Norm Qualities and Deviant Behavior', in Ephraim H. Mizruchi (ed.), *The Substance of Sociology* (New York, 1973).
11. Shalva Weil, 'Bene Israel Indian Jews in Lod, Israel: A Study of the Persistence of Ethnicity and Ethnic Identity', vol. 1 (unpublished Ph.D. thesis, University of Sussex, 1977).
12. Carl Mark Gussin, *The Bene Israel: Politics, Religion and Systemic Change*.
13. Walter Fischel, 'Early Zionism in India'.
14. Ben Raphael, *The Emergence of Ethnicity: Cultural Groups and Social Conflict in Israel* (Greenwood Press, Connecticut, 1982), p. 14.

15. Weil, op. cit., p. 83.
16. Judah, Matras, *Social Change in Israel* (Aldine Publication Co., 1965).
17. Weil, *Bene Israel Indian Jews*.
18. The term 'halitzah' means untying. It refers to the ceremony of taking off a brother-in-law's shoe by the widow of a brother who died childless. This ceremony allows the brother-in-law to be released from marrying the deceased brother's widow. The Bene Israel were doubted by the Arabic-speaking orthodox Jews since they had not practiced this custom, either when they obtained a divorce or when a husband died childless and was survived by his widow. For further details see, Isenberg, *India's Bene Israel*, p. 102.
19. In December 1994, Mr. Bezalel Eliahu, a Cochin Jewish immigrant, was honored by Israel's Prime Minister and Labor Minister in the Knesset with the 'Kaplan Prize' which is the highest award of labor in Agricultrure.
20. Israel, *Bene Israel of India;* Weil, *Bene Israel India Jews*.

PART III

SUMMING UP

CHAPTER 13

Indian Diaspora in West Asia

HIGH LEVEL COMMITTEE,
GOVERNMENT OF INDIA

This chapter contains short notes on the various countries of the Gulf region. In addition to the GCC countries, we have included brief sketches on several others as well. India has been the source of supply of some of the expertise and equipment, and also a considerable portion of the equally essential skilled, semi-skilled, as well as manual workers that have been instrumental in transforming this region in a relatively short time into prosperous economies. This is an area where, consequent on the discovery and exploitation of hydrocarbons during the last three decades, the Indian presence has increased manifold. Our purpose in presenting this chapter has been to provide a panoramic view, however sketchy, of this region. A statistical table has been added below in order to give a comparative idea of the size of the Indian Diaspora in this region in the year 2001, when viewed against the total population of these countries.

BAHRAIN

With a population of 643,000 and a total area of 691 sq. kms, Bahrain is the smallest of the GCC States. This island country is relatively less endowed with hydrocarbon resources than most of its neighbours. Nevertheless, its proximity to them and its central location in the Gulf have enabled it to flourish by developing a sophisticated telecommunications centre and by venturing into offshore banking. Its other distinguishing features have been an enlightened and modern education policy and a moderate policy towards non-Islamic religions. The trade and commercial activity

TABLE 13.1: THE INDIAN DIASPORA IN THE COUNTRIES OF THE GULF AND ITS NEIGHBOURING REGIONS

Countries	*Population*	*PIOs*	*NRIs*	*Stateless*	*Percentage of Population*
Bahrain	643,000	NIL	130,000	–	20.22
Iraq	23,000,000	50	60	–	Insignificant
Kuwait	2,254,000	1,000	294,000	–	12.80
Libya	5,800,000	400	12,000	–	Insignificant
Oman	2,300,000	1,000	311,000	–	13.52
Qatar	525,000	1,000	130,000	–	23.81
Saudi Arabia	21,500,000	NIL	1,500,000	–	6.90
UAE	2,900,000	50,000	900,000	–	30.00
Yemen	17,676,000	100,000	9,000	–	0.62

generated by the discovery of oil in 1932, and especially the oil boom years of the early 1970s, brought home the need to discard its earlier conservative policy towards foreigners and, instead, to permit the entry of a large expatriate community. Currently, they constitute nearly 50 per cent of the total population of Bahrain.

Indians are known to have gone to Bahrain in pursuit of trade as early as 3000 BC when their ships plied from the Harappan settlements to Oman and Bahrain, on their way to Mesopotamia. Though several Indian families have been residing in Bahrain for many decades, only a few of them have been granted local citizenship. Of the total population of 643,000 persons, Bahrainis number only 391,000. There are nearly 130,000 NRIs in the country, mostly from Kerala and other South Indian states. They are not only the island country's largest expatriate community, but they also constitute over 30 per cent of its total workforce. Our unskilled and semiskilled workers, numbering 65-70 per cent of the NRI population in Bahrain, are employed in the contracting, construction, maintenance and service sectors. They enjoy a good reputation in terms of their conduct, loyalty, higher productivity and non-involvement in local affairs. Being a large expatriate community, it is not surprising that some among them can encounter consular problems like a change in contractual terms, non-payment of wages when due, disputes relating to remuneration or working hours, etc. In the case of the relatively small number of housemaids, estimated at around eight to ten thousand, there are occasional complaints relating to maltreatment and odd cases of assault. However, the overall situation is not alarming, either in terms of numbers or frequency.

Those engaged in retail and other business activities deal in miscellaneous items like provisions, hardware, jewellery, electronics, etc. Others have taken up jobs as storekeepers, chemists, carpenters, barbers, etc. The economic boom of the early 1970s, which led to the quadrupling of oil prices, opened up increasing avenues for job opportunities, not only for manual workers, but also for a discernible number of Indian doctors, teachers, engineers, accountants, bank executives, architects and many other such high grade professionals. There is hardly any established Bahraini business organisation that does not have a senior or middle level Indian employee playing an important role in its operations.

The Indian community has established in Bahrain as many as 43 socio-cultural organizations including a *Keraleeya Samajam*, as well as five schools. Most of the associations have been brought under the umbrella of the Coordination Committee of Indian Associations (CCIA) which has been able to present a united front and organise joint functions on occasions like Republic Day. The Indian associations are actively engaged in projecting Indian culture in Bahrain. They have also been active in varied social work such as running specialised institutions for mentally retarded persons and spastic children, rendering assistance to geriatric wards, giving donations to Bahraini philanthropic organisations, etc. The Bahraini Government is very appreciative of such contribution of the community. Its liberal attitude towards non-Muslims in observing their religious practices, provided this is done indoors, has enabled the NRIs to build and maintain five churches, a Hindu temple and three gurudwaras in the country.

IRAQ

At the end of World War I, what is now Iraq was awarded to Britain as a 'mandated territory' by the League of Nations. The British administration thereupon started taking Indians to this country to build its railways and ports, establish its post and telegraph department, its inland water transport system and various other public utilities.

Some Indians began to man minor posts in Iraq as clerks, technicians and accountants, both in the government as well as in private organisations.

It was only as late as 1932 that Iraq finally became independent. The end of World War II saw the arrival in the country of the descendants of Indian pilgrims who had gone there some decades earlier and stayed on. This new wave of Indians was gradually absorbed in the country and became Iraqi citizens. They are now mainly found in Najaf and Kerbala.

There was considerable excitement in Iraq when it was discovered at the end of the 1960s that the country had enormous hydrocarbon reserves, just waiting to be exploited. With the rise in oil prices in 1973, Iraq began an ambitious programme of modernisation. This meant undertaking a number of infrastructure projects in the transport and communications sector, and in health, education, housing, etc. Indian companies were successful in winning a number of civil construction contracts. Thousands of Indian workers arrived in Iraq for the execution of those projects. Their number peaked to nearly 80,000 by the late 1980s. By and large, they earned a good name for themselves and for India by their hard work, skill and competence. They also got on well with their Iraqi colleagues, both socially and professionally Unfortunately, their number began to decline during the protracted Iran-Iraq war and finally came to an abrupt end after Desert Storm in 1990. Presently, the number of Indians in Iraq, excluding members of the Indian Embassy, is estimated to be only around 50. Almost all of them are temporary residents. They are either UN officials or businessmen in search of trading opportunities under the UN's Oil-for-Food Programme. There are five Indian students in the country on Iraqi Government scholarships and also some employees of a few Indian companies who have continued their presence in the country despite the UN sanctions. Due to Iraq's severe economic crisis resulting from those sanctions, pension and other claims filed by former Indian workers with the Iraqi authorities continue to remain pending. There is no likelihood of their clearance until the sanctions are lifted and the situation returns to normal again. One Indian citizen has landed in an Iraqi jail where he is undergoing a prison sentence.

An Indian Central School, which was run under the supervision of our Embassy in happier times, has remained closed since the beginning of the Gulf War. A gurdwara where, apart from weekly gatherings, special religious ceremonies used to be held in former years with the permission of the Iraqi authorities, still continues to function.

KUWAIT

Out of nearly 2.2 million persons currently residing in Kuwait, as many as 65 per cent are foreign nationals. The Indian Diaspora constitutes the single largest expatriate community in the country, accounting for almost 20 per cent of the total resident population. All of them are NRIs as foreigners do not normally qualify for local citizenship. Only foreign women married to Kuwaiti nationals are the exception to this rule. The exact number of Kuwaiti PIOs is not known. But it has been estimated that there are currently only about a thousand women falling in this category.

Prior to the Iraqi invasion of the country in 1990, the number of NRIs in Kuwait was approximately 170,000. With the commencement of hostilities, those who could do so left immediately on their own. Those who could not had to be repatriated through Air India's repeated sorties into the country. Interestingly, the size of the Indian Diaspora in Kuwait has increased to more that 294,000 since the expulsion of Iraqi forces from the country.

As in other Gulf countries, NRIs need the sponsorship of a Kuwaiti national or organisation for admission to the country. Being foreign nationals, they are also not permitted to own a business or purchase immovable property in their own name. The small number of Indian businessmen that reside in the country have successfully conformed to these regulations by forging the necessary partnerships with local persons or entities. Mostly engaged in foodstuffs, jewellery, garments and motor parts trading, they are very well off. As for the remaining Indians in Kuwait, while a majority are unskilled and semi-skilled workers, there are among them a sizeable number of professionals like engineers, doctors, chartered accountants, scientists, software experts, management consultants and architects, as well as skilled workers like technicians and nurses. Only about 14,000 have jobs with various government departments. As many as 120,000 have gone there as domestic servants, a large number of whom are housemaids and governesses working with Kuwaiti families.

Various segments of the Indian community have organised their own cultural associations. There are about 100 of them, each based on common interests, place of origin, home language or religion. The various groups regularly organize cultural functions featuring either artists from India or local talent. These functions are held either in the big Indian Arts Circle Auditorium that the community as a whole has set up, or in the smaller auditorium of the Indian Embassy. In addition to projecting Indian culture in Kuwait, such functions help in acquainting the community's younger generation with their land of origin. Another welcome feature is that nine Indian Schools have been established in Kuwait with affiliation to the Central Board of Secondary Education. The Indian Embassy has been authorized by the CBSE to supervise the conduct of its board examinations in Kuwait.

LIBYA

The Indian community in Libya was almost 40,000 strong in the mid-1980s. The number of PIOs in this country has now come down to only about 12,000. Most of the local Indians are skilled or semi-skilled workers and they are non-matriculates. However, in addition to many doctors, paramedics and engineers, there are also several highly educated and qualified professors and academics in the faculties of the prestigious universities in Benghazi and Tripoli. A few professionals are also to be found in the oil sector.

The Indian community has set up in Libya an Indian Community Association that has chapters in the major centres of the country The activities of the ICA include, *inter-alia,* promotion of Indian culture.

OMAN

People-to-people contacts are believed to have existed between Indians and Omanis as early as the seventh century. Indian merchants were already undertaking commercial activities in Muscat in the fifteenth century. At that time, the Indian community consisted essentially of traders and financiers from Kutch and Sindh. It was only in the nineteenth century that some Khojas also arrived here. They are presently well integrated in Oman, some of them even holding ministerial positions. Meanwhile, a few of the old Indian trading companies have developed into big business houses. The oldest Indian family in Oman has been in the country for at least eight generations.

Oman is possibly the only Arab country that is liberal in the grant of its citizenship to foreign nationals. Irrespective of his or her religion, any person who has lived in the country for at least 20 years is eligible to apply for citizenship. Almost a thousand Indians have so far been accorded such a status. Oman is also exceptional among the Gulf countries in the sense that the 'Basic Law of the State' which was promulgated in December 1996 guarantees freedom of worship to all its residents. Muscat has two Hindu temples where congregations are held regularly and *pujas* are performed every day One of these two temples was apparently established over a hundred years ago. Two gurdwaras have been constructed recently in the labour camps. There are also seven churches in Oman to serve the various Christian sects that are found here.

Currently numbering around 311,000 persons out of Oman's total population of 2.3 million, the Indian community in this country constitutes a little less than 14 per cent of its total population. It is the largest expatriate group in Oman, being 58 per cent of its foreign population. The local Indian Diaspora is composed of almost equal numbers of unskilled (25 per cent), semi-skilled (30 per cent) and skilled (35 per cent) workers. The balance (10 per cent) is constituted of professionals such as engineers, bankers, financial experts and managers. There are almost 2,000 Indian doctors in the country. Unlike in other Gulf countries, the PIOs of Oman hold most of the middle and senior management positions in the corporate sector, including a substantial number of posts of CEOs. Several Indians hold responsible positions in various ministries, government departments and public sector undertakings. Some Indians are employed in the local newspaper establishments, particularly the English language ones. Almost 80 per cent of the Diaspora are from South India, with Kerala alone contributing as many as 60 per cent. A large number of Indian companies are represented here, while several joint venture projects have already been completed or are in various stages of implementation.

The contributions of the Indian Diaspora in Oman to the

development of the Omani community as a whole, and particularly so in the fields of commerce, healthcare, the construction industry and in communications is not only considerable but also widely acknowledged. The goodwill earned by it through its hard work and its commitment have added a very positive dimension to India's bilateral relationship with this country.

At the same time, the members of the Diaspora are conscious and proud of their cultural heritage and maintain very strong links with their motherland. This is manifested in the large number of cultural events organised by them, very often with the participation of visiting artists from India. As many as fourteen Indian schools have been established in the Sultanate, all of which follow the CBSE pattern, except one that is affiliated to the Kerala State Board. Several cinema halls in Muscat screen only Hindi and Malayalam films. Until 1994, the community had established no less than 25 separate Indian associations. They were based on linguistic or other such identities. With the promulgation of a decree by the government of Oman that only one social club would be permitted per community, it is now a happy consequence that the Indian Social Club is currently the only authorised representative of the Indian Diaspora in Oman. It organises cultural activities and also hosts visiting cultural troupes, besides undertaking philanthropic work. The community has always responded generously with financial and other contributions at times of national crisis, whether for earthquake relief in Gujarat or to alleviate the suffering of families of the Kargil martyrs.

QATAR

Most of the Gulf countries have a long history of Indian nationals having migrated there, usually for business, at least a couple of centuries ago. In the case of Qatar, however, the arrival there of numerous Indians seems to have started only around the mid-1970s. Again unlike its other neighbours in the region, Qatar has been a late starter in the commercial exploitation of its oil, as also in commencing its infrastructure and other development work with the help of labour and expertise from abroad. But the situation underwent a drastic change by the 1980s. The size of the Indian community began increasing rapidly and it is presently estimated as at least 130,000. According to a recent report of the Qatar Chamber of Commerce and Industry, the number of Indian expatriates may have even reached a figure of 170,000 which is almost a third of the total number of residents in the country. This sudden and increasing influx of our nationals into Qatar is due to the high reputation they have built for themselves in this country for their sincerity, hard work and expertise, as well as their law-abiding nature. Practically every local establishment, whether governmental, business or industrial, employs Indians in various capacities. It seems more Indians would be recruited if the necessary work permits could be obtained from the Qatari government!

A major chunk of the Indian community is engaged in unskilled or semi-skilled work, which means that it may be considered as belonging to the low or middle income-earning group. A much smaller number, around fifteen to twenty thousand, consists of professionals such as doctors, engineers, chartered accountants and bankers. Some of them have even become entrepreneurs. This segment of the Diaspora must be regarded as well off, considering that the annual remittances from Qatar to India are estimated to aggregate around Rs 1,200 crores.

The local Indian community had established two schools in Qatar nearly three decades ago, to meet the educational requirements of its children. Both of them were affiliated to the CBSE as well as the Kerala streams of education. As they became insufficient to meet the growing needs of the community, two more have been added since last year – the Shanthi Niketan Indian School and the Modern Indian School. To begin with, they cater only to younger children, but higher classes for study upto the secondary level will be progressively added. Another high school, which will be managed by the UAE-based Varkey Group, is likely to come up later this year.

An Indian Cultural Centre that functions under the aegis of the Indian Embassy, serves as a cultural nerve centre for the Indian community. It has over 50 Indian socio-cultural organisations affiliated to it. The ICC is not only popular among the Indian Diaspora, but its activities win favourable notice from other expatriate groups and also from the local population.

SAUDI ARABIA

Upto around the late 1960s, the 'India connection' was the most significant political, economic and cultural link between the people of the Arabian Peninsula and the outside world. During that period, the Saudi economy was still under-developed and most of its people eked out a marginal existence. Indian goods and merchants frequently traversed the waters of the Indian Ocean, the Gulf and the Red Sea, while Indian towns like Hyderabad and Bombay provided congenial homes to Arab businessmen.

In the wake of the oil boom in the Saudi Kingdom, there was a steady increase in the employment of Indian nationals in that country. By 1983 the number of Indian workers had increased from a mere 15,000 in 1975 to 270,000. It further rose to 650,000 by 1990. After the Gulf crisis of that year, Yemeni workers, who were then a million strong lost their privileged status of not requiring a visa to enter the country or a sponsor to work in it. There was a mass exodus of Yemeni workers from the Kingdom. This resulted in Saudi employers recruiting Indians in large numbers to replace them. Consequently, the Indian Diaspora in this country, numbering about a million and half persons, is the largest Indian passport-holding community abroad.

The Indian Diaspora in Saudi Arabia may be divided into three broad categories. There are, firstly, professionals like doctors, engineers, chartered accountants and managers who are employed both with the government and the private sector on the basis of specific time-bound contracts. They constitute no more than 5 per cent of the Indian community. A somewhat larger non-professional group of 10 per cent includes white collar staff employed as clerks, secretaries, accountants, store keepers, booking clerks, etc. Finally, there is the remaining 85 per cent consisting of organised labour and technicians working on project sites and industrial establishments, as well as on operations and maintenance jobs. Outside these three main groups, there is the unorganised labour which includes a small number of illegal entrants who are either working in the country without legal sponsors or who had come to the Kingdom on *Haj* or *Umrah* visas and then stayed on to work there. Periodically, the Saudi government declares an amnesty to flush out and deport such illegal residents.

The Indian community in Saudi Arabia has been well received and accepted at all echelons of the Saudi society, as is evident from an almost three-fold growth in its numbers over the last decade or so. It is regarded as a community that is vital to the development of the country and to the proper operation and functioning of its infrastructure and its industrial and agricultural establishments. The Saudi employer is convinced that Indians give value for money, that they are loyal and disciplined, and that they are dedicated workers. They are seen as peaceful persons, not given to illegal activities and well adjusted to the constraints of Saudi social life. A major plus point in their favour is the fact that a negligible number of them get involved in criminal activities of any kind.

Most members of the Diaspora in Saudi Arabia have been able to adapt themselves to their environment and to create for themselves and their families a social and cultural life that gives them some satisfaction, though it is usually based narrowly on their Indian regional identity. They play a positive role in their community life, assuming responsibilities for organizing social and cultural events, or participating constructively in school activities. The economic and educational profile of the Indian community is directly linked to its professional composition. There is no role for the expatriates in the Saudi political system.

The community has set up a number of International Indian schools in Riyadh, Jeddah, Damman, Jubail, Taif, Buraidah and Tabuk. Approximately 32,000 students attend these schools daily. Most of them follow the CBSE pattern and have facilities for teaching upto Class XII.

The Indians in Saudi Arabia have been remitting to India annually about US $4 billion. This is the largest amount inward flow of foreign exchange from any single country. They have also been major contributors to the Resurgent India Bonds of 1998 and the India Millennium Deposits bonds of the year 2000. They responded generously to calls for assistance to the flood-affected people of Orissa last year and to the earthquake-affected people of Gujarat in January this year.

UNITED ARAB EMIRATES

After our extensive yet succinct *tour d'horizon* in the preceding pages, of many of the countries of the Gulf region, the Committee feels it may be adequate to summarise below the parallels that exist between the situation in the United Arab Emirates and its neighbouring countries. Simultaneously, an attempt will be made to show the differences that have set these Emirates apart from the rest of the region. We feel that an account on these lines would be able to indicate why the UAE has been so successful in mounting the express train of infrastructure and economic development and proceeding on its fast track in such a short time:

(i) The bilateral contacts between the UAE and India date back to the early nineteenth century when pearls and dates from the former and spices, provisions and clothing from the latter, were energetically traded to their mutual advantage.

(ii) Although some Indian trading families began settling down in places like Dubai, Sharjah and Fujairah around that time, it was only after World War I that their numbers started increasing exponentially.

(iii) The various emirates that constitute the UAE do not permit naturalization or permanent residence of foreign nationals in their territories.

(iv) Nevertheless, since the formation of the UAE in 1971, a small number of Indian emigrants have been permitted to hold UAE passports. They have been accorded some economic privileges, but they do not have any political role in the country.

(v) Only foreign wives of UAE nationals can aspire to local citizenship. But such a status would subsequently be forfeited in the event of divorce or the husband's death. Such an event would also render them into stateless persons if they happen to be PIOs, according to provisions contained in the Indian constitution and laws.

(vi) Unlike several of its regional neighbours, the UAE has not been endowed with limitless hydrocarbon resources to finance its economic development.

(vii) If it has been able to launch an ambitious programme of infrastructure and all-round economic development from the 1970s, this was the result of its imaginative schemes that began to fill its treasuries with the wherewithal for rapid development.

(viii) These schemes included total exemption of income and other taxes, the setting up of sophisticated duty-free economic zones and, as the necessary infrastructure became available, the promotion of high-grade and exotic tourism with facilities that acted as a magnet to well-heeled persons from all over the world.

(ix) Massive infrastructure and development projects meant the induction of virtually tens of thousands of experts and labour – unskilled, semiskilled and skilled.

(x) India was an obvious choice to become a preferred resource country to meet most of these requirements. The inflow of NRI professionals and workers increased steadily until it peaked at 1.2 million persons by 1996. As a rule, three fourths of our personnel in the UAE were labourers, with the unskilled workers being half the number. A majority went from the southern Indian states, especially from Kerala.

(xi) Unlike the workers, the professionals (who constituted about a quarter of the total Indian community) were well paid and eagerly sought after, for their expertise and competence.

(xii) The Indian Diaspora in the UAE has been able to establish a number of socio-cultural associations based on regional, linguistic or religious grounds. They meet frequently at various functions organised by them which, apart from enriching their own lives, are able to project Indian culture to a wider audience in their host country.

(xiii) In addition to such activities, the community has established as many as 30 Indian schools following Indian curricular systems, for the benefit of its children. The local government's relatively liberal policy towards religions other than Islam has enabled the NRIs to build a few temples and gurdwaras where devotees can gather together in private for communal prayers. They have also been allowed to set up a number of cremation grounds, one or two of which have even been built at government expense, for the benefit of persons who are not permitted by their religion to bury their dead.

(xiv) The Indian Diaspora maintains a close relationship with India. It has always responded generously with sizeable financial contributions at times of national crisis such as the earthquakes in Latur and Gujarat, the cyclone in Orissa and the Kargil crisis.

(xv) With the progressive reduction in the volume of construction activity, the UAE government has begun to worry about the fact that three fourths of all the residents in the country are foreign nationals. It has become alarmed also that NRIs currently constitute over 50 per cent of the country's expatriate workforce, followed by Pakistanis with 22 per cent. Accordingly, it has embarked on a policy of gradual '*emiratisation*' which is expected to result in local citizens forming at least 40 per cent of the country's workforce by the year 2015.

(xvi) Alarm bells have started ringing already, as employment opportunities in the UAE will progressively start becoming scarcer for our people. This is not likely to affect our professionals and highly qualified personnel in the knowledge-based sectors, at least not in the near future. Nevertheless, it is learned that many of them have already started exploring alternative opportunities for more secure employment in one or other of the western developed countries.

YEMEN

The people of India and Yemen have had deep-rooted historical, cultural and trade relations since ancient times. But in order to appreciate the current situation of the Indian Diaspora in this country, it is necessary to review briefly the recent history of Yemen. The UK had incorporated the port town of Aden into the British Empire in 1839 as a sentinel to guard the southern entrance to the Red Sea. Britain administered it from the then Bombay Presidency. During that period, many Indians migrated to Aden – mainly from Andhra Pradesh, Gujarat, Karnataka and Maharashtra. Britain finally withdrew from Aden in 1967, whereupon a leftist government took over and Aden and its adjoining areas came to be known as the People's Democratic Republic of Yemen. Pursuant to the new government's socialist policies, the private properties belonging to members of the Indian community began to be taken over by it. This resulted in the hasty departure from Aden of many PIOs, either for India or some other country. But a large number belonging to the Bohra, Khoja and Kachchi communities decided to remain behind and gradually became Yemeni citizens.

Meanwhile, the northern part of Yemen, had ended its internal civil strife and become the Yemen Arab Republic. In 1990 the two parts of Yemen decided to merge together and became the Republic of Yemen. Presently, out of a total population of over 17.6 million, the size of the Indian Diaspora in this country is estimated at a hundred thousand. Of them, only about 9,000 are NRIs. They and the PIOs are concentrated in and around the relatively bigger towns like Aden, Sana'a, Mukalla, Haraz, Seyun, Taiz, and Hodeidah. Many of the NRIs are academics and professionals. The majority consists of white-collar workers, nurses and paramedical staff, as well as skilled and semi-skilled workers and housemaids.

The Indian Embassy in Sana'a has installed a statue of Gandhiji in Aden's Mahatma Gandhi Memorial Hall with the collaboration of the locally based Indian Association. A school named 'The Mahatma Gandhi Memorial Indian Embassy School' is run in this hall for the benefit of the children of NRIs and PIOs. As many as ten Hindu and Parsi temples have survived in Aden since the time when it was still a British colony. But most of them are now objects of neglect because of the small size of their remaining congregations. As these properties are strategically located, they have become attractive targets for illegal encroachment and demolition. The Indian Ambassador in Sana'a is continuing his *démarches* with the Yemeni government to secure protection for these endangered sites. In cooperation with several western Ambassadors, he had succeeded last year in persuading the country's President to restore similarly endangered Church properties.

Various proposals have been made by our Embassy in Sana'a to provide better services to the Indian community in Yemen. These include the strengthening of its Consular Section; the opening of a branch of any nationalized Indian bank in Aden or Sana'a; and increased shipping services between Indian and Yemeni ports. These proposals are currently under Government's consideration.

IRAN

Relations between India and Iran have traditionally been very close. Historically, there have been many instances of movement of people overland between the two countries. In more recent times, around

1925, the first lot of Indians – about 180 families – went to the Iranian border town of Zahidan. They drove there from the western districts of the then Punjab province of India, in the company of truck drivers who used to transport goods to Iran. After their initial influx, these Indians gradually started settling down in the nearby towns of Zabol, Birijand and Mashhad. In 1950, some more Indians went to Iran and settled down en bloc in Teheran. They were predominantly Sikhs, but there were also some Gujaratis among them.

In the 1960s and early 1970s, the Shah of Iran permitted immigration into the country of about a million expatriate professionals to run its essential services. Among the new arrivals were about 10,000 Indian doctors, engineers and teachers. However, most of them, except a few doctors, left Iran after the Iranian revolution which ended the Shah's rule. As of now, the number of Indians who have settled down in the country consists of approximately a hundred and fifty families in Teheran, thirty-five in Zahidan and only two in Isfahan. A majority of these people are engaged in various business activities. Several of the Indian women have married Iranians and now reside in different parts of the country including Mashhad. Some Kashmiri students are studying at the Imam Khomeini University in Qazvin, while a number of other Indians are pursuing theological studies at Qom.

Almost all the Indians in Iran belonging to the third and fourth generation of emigrants have continued to retain their Indian citizenship. Only about ten families among them have become Iranian nationals. Similarly, a majority of fifth generation Indian emigrants have also adopted local citizenship because of work and tax related problems.

The Indian community in Iran, unlike its counterpart in some other countries, maintains strong links with India. Several of its members own properties in this country and even send their children to study in Indian schools. Most of them seek marriage partners for their children in India. Their loyalty to their country of origin is really touching. It manifests itself in responding to national calamities and crises in India such as the Kargil incursions and the Gujarat earthquake with the spontaneous remittance of contributions for disaster relief.

ISRAEL

Basic Facts

POPULATION OF THE COUNTRY:	6.3 million (as of October 2000)
APPROXIMATE NUMBER OF THE INDIAN COMMUNITY:	
(a) Persons of Indian Origin:	45,000
(b) Indian Citizens (NRIs):	300
(c) Stateless persons, if any:	Figures not available, but we have not come across any such cases

Profile

According to available data, between 25,000 and 30,000 Indian Jews have migrated to Israel starting from the late 1940s, with the major waves going there in the 1950s and 1960s The migrants from India belong essentially to three groups: the Bene-Israel of Maharashtra (20,000 plus); the Cochin Jews (3,500); and the so called Baghdadi Jews. Of these, the first two groups had lived in India for thousands of years and were thoroughly Indian in their language (Marathi and Malayalam, respectively), food habits and other cultural traits. The Baghdadis had a shorter sojourn in India starting from the nineteenth century onwards; they retained many elements of Iraqi Jewish culture but technically many of them could also claim Indian origin in terms of the definition in Article 5 of the Citizenship Act. In the last few years a fourth group has emerged – the Bnei Menashe of Mizoram who were accepted as a 'lost tribe' of Israel. A small number have settled in Israel. The available information about this group is scanty.

The Jews have never faced discrimination in India. Some of them went to Israel because of their religious affiliation and hopes for a better economic life. Initially, they found a country established by Ashkenazi (European) Jews. It was run by the latter on their terms, and many of the migrants from India had a difficult time adjusting and assimilating. Lacking adequate economic and social support systems, the Israelis from India had to struggle in the small 'development towns' and agricultural settlements to establish themselves in Israel. The community today has a good reputation for being law abiding and modest. They belong, by and large, to the middle class. A large proportion of the Bene-Israel lives in small towns and works as employees in firms and government agencies. A few have become business executives, while some own small businesses. Many of the Cochinis took to agriculture (in contrast to their professions while in India) and have succeeded. One migrant from Cochin ranks amongst the largest exporters of roses from Israel.

Since the younger generation born in Israel are mainly conversant with Hebrew (all immigrants have to study the language) and are being absorbed in the Israeli Jewish melting pot, the community is losing the 'Indianness' which the first generation had taken with it. Knowledge of Marathi and Malayalam, for example, is diminishing among the Jews born and raised in Israel. There is, however, considerable interest among them in maintaining cultural links with India. Israelis of Indian origin have participated in gatherings of Marathi speakers from all over the world, and a session of the World Marathi Conference was held in Israel some years ago. The most evident cultural link today, however, comes through the pop culture, particularly Hindi films and the dance forms associated with the film world. This is popular with many young people in the Indian Jewish communities, irrespective of whether or not they understand the language fully.

As they are of modest means with little political 'activism', Israelis of Indian origin have had limited economic involvement with India, or any political status in the country of their adoption. There are a number of 'Indian Jewish' and 'Bene-Israel' associations in small towns, along with a loosely structured umbrella organisation, the Central Council for Indian Jews in Israel. But the community does not have a high degree of political mobilization at the national level and consequently little bargaining power in the intensively competitive Israeli political system. There is only one person of Indian origin in the Knesset – Eli Ben Menachem – a Labour (One Israel) MK who was born in Mumbai in a Baghdadi family. A few PIOs have been successful in local politics, in town councils in cities like Lod and Ramle where there are concentrations of PIOs. A Cochini is presently the Council President of a small town (Yesod Hamala) in northern Israel. In recent years, a group of young Indian Jews started a movement (Hodaya) to mobilize the community for political action. They had marginal impact in the 1999 elections, but are seeking to continue their organisational activity.

The basic problem of the Israelis of Indian origin is socio-economic advancement. Given the fact that the Israeli economy has developed very rapidly in the last two decades, the community does have reasonable prospects for development, particularly if it emphasizes higher education more than in the past. The Indians in Israel are broadly classed as 'Sephardic' Jews and have a few Rabbis among them. In religious terms, they are quite well integrated among the 'Sephardim' of Israel.

Non-Resident Indians

The small community of Indian citizens in Israel is mostly of Gujaratis engaged in the diamond business. There are about 20 families (most of whom can trace their origin to Palanpur) and some of their employees are resident in Israel with employment permits. They play an important part in the diamond trade, which constitutes about half of overall Indo-Israeli trade. The Gujarati community is socially active and, by and large, well respected in Israel. It has set up an informal association called the Gujarati Indian Association that celebrates major cultural festivals.

There is also a small and fluctuating population of students and scholars, numbering about 50 to 60 and a few Indian workers engaged in construction, the hospitality industry and domestic work. Their numbers are hard to verify but they have been estimated to be a few hundred only.

Cultural and Other Associations

The following associations have been formed by the PIOs in Israel:

(i) *The Indo-Israel Cultural Association:* This association organizes a variety of cultural events in Israel including lectures on India and artistic performances.
(ii) *The Central Organisation of Indian Jews is* the main association of Jews of Indian origin in Israel. It conducts meetings of all Indian Jews once in a year and organizes cultural events, especially popular Hindi and Marathi song and dance

programmes. The Central Organisation of Indian Jews also publishes a quarterly journal.

(iii) *The Centre of Jewish Heritage* is broadly the main organisation of the Cochin Jews in Israel. It administers the Museum on Jewish Heritage in India. This is located at Moshav Nevatim in Israel.

(iv) *The Gujarati Indian Association* has been referred to above.

DEMANDS AND EXPECTATIONS OF THE DIASPORA

The older generation of the Israeli community of Indian origin has notions about India that are based on nostalgia for the past. Members of the second generation have high expectations from India, derived from what it has heard from the older generation. They expect things in India to conform to standards in Europe and Israel, and get a culture shock when they visit India and find that this is not so.

Contributors

MARGARET ABRAHAM is a Professor of Sociology at Hofstra University in Long Island, New York and served as Chair of the Department from 2000 to 2003. Her teaching and research interest include issues around ethnicity, gender, globalization, immigration and domestic violence. Her early research was on the Indian Jewish community in India and Israel. She is the author of *Speaking the Unspeakable: Marital Violence among South Asian Immigrants in the United States* (2000).

AKBAR S. AHMED, Ibn Khaldun Chair and Professor of Islamic Studies, American University in Washington DC and former High Commissioner of Pakistan in London is an anthropologist, writer and filmmaker. His books include *Discovering Islam: Making Sense of Muslim History and Society*; *Postmodernism and Islam: Predicament and Promise*; *Islam Today: A Short Introduction to the Muslim World*; and *Islam Under Siege: Living Dangerously in a Post-Honor World*. His latest, *After Terror: Promoting the Dialogue of Civilizations* was co-edited with Brian Forst.

CALVIN H. ALLEN, Jr. is currently Dean of the College of Arts and Sciences at Shenandoah University having previously served in faculty positions at the College of the Ozarks and The University of Memphis. He has written three books on Oman and more than 40 articles dealing with Oman and the Gulf region. Allen continues to work on the Indian Diaspora and recently served as a consultant on an exhibition 'India-Oman 5000 Years of Friendship' at Bait al-Zubair Museum in Muscat. His current project is a book on the Indian merchant role in the globalization of Muscat, Oman at the turn of the twentieth century.

RAM BUXANI is a prominent Indian businessman who has made

Dubai his home for over 40 years. He is the Group Executive Vice-Chairman of the world-wide International Traders (Middle East) Ltd. Group of Companies. A prominent spokesperson of the NRIs, Dr. Buxani has played a key role in interacting with the Indian government on behalf of Overseas Indians. He was the founder Chairman of 'Overseas Indians Economic Forum – U.A.E', now a part of 'Indian Business & Professional Council' of which he was a founder board member. His memoirs about his life in Dubai and the City's transformation over the decades were serialized in the *Gulf Today*. His autobiographical accounts are published under the title *Taking the High Road* (2003).

ABDULLAH ELMADANI is a prominent Bahraini journalist based at Manama. He is an expert on Indo-Gulf relations.

SURENDRA GOPAL, Professor and Head (Superannuated), Department of History, Patna University has been involved in research on the maritime history of India and Indian Diaspora in medieval times for around four decades. His published monographs include *Commerce and Crafts in Gujarat, 16th-17th Century* (1975), *Indians in Russia in the 17th and 18th Centuries* (1983) and *India and Central Asia: Cultural, Economic and Political Links* (2001), *Dialogue and Understanding: Central Asia and India: The Soviet and the Post-Soviet Era* (2005). He is currently preparing a monograph on Indian Diaspora in the seventeenth and eighteenth Centuries.

PRAKASH C. JAIN is on the faculty of the School of International Studies, Jawaharlal Nehru University, New Delhi. The author of *Racial Discrimination against Overseas Indians: A Class Analysis* (1990), *Indians in South Africa: Political Economy of Race Relations* (1999) and *Population and Society in West Asia: Essays in Comparative Demography* (2001), Dr. Jain has to his credit a number of articles published in Indian and foreign journals. He has also co-edited a book on *Contemporary Iran and Emerging Indo-Iranian Relations* (1996). Dr. Jain has done fieldwork on Overseas Indians in Canada, Guyana, South Africa and some of the Persian Gulf countries.

MAGANMAL J. PANCHOLIA is a leading Indian businessman of Dubai and chairman of the Arabian Trading Agency – an apex multinational company that has been into a wide variety of businesses such as textile, gold, electronics, watches, banking and currency exchange etc. Residing in Dubai for over six decades now, Mr. Pancholia has seen the Emirate grow and prosper from a tiny village to a cosmopolitan city in which his own contribution is quite significant. A Gandhian by nature he has also been deeply involved in the community affairs of the Indian expatriates in general and the Thattai Sindhi Bhatias in particular.

B.A. PRAKASH is currently Professor and Head, Department of Economics, University of Kerala, Thiruvananthapuram, Kerala. He has been the recipient of two prestigious fellowships, the Young Social Scientist Fellowship of the Indian Council of Social Science Research (1980-82) and the Career Award of the University Grant Commission (1986-89). Professor Prakash has edited a volume on *Economic Development of Kerala* (2004, 3rd edn.).

S. IRUDAYA RAJAN is an associate fellow at the Centre for Development Studies, Thiruvananthapuram. A Ph.D in demography, his research interests include historical and social demography, population economics, family planning, ageing and studies on Kerala. His publications include *Catholics in Bombay; India's Demographic Transition: A Reassessment* (ed.); Demogrphic *Transition in Kerala in the 1980s* (co-author); *Mortality and Fertility Transition in Kerala: A Historical Investigation* (co-author); *Kerala's Demographic Transition: Determinants and Consequences* (co-edited); *India's Elderly: Burden or Challenge* (co-author); and *Dynamics of Migration in Kerala: Dimensions, Differentials and Consequences* (co-author).

FATMA AL-SAYEGH is a Professor of History at the United Arab Emirates University in Al Ain, United Arab Emirates.

MYRON WEINER (1931-99) was Ford Professor of Political Science and director of the Center for International Studies at the Massachusetts Institute of Technology (MIT). He was also chair of the External Research Advisory Committee of the United Nations High Commissioner for Refugees (UNHCR). He is the author of several books on Indian politics and society, including *The Child and the State in India: Child Labor and Education Policy in Comparative Perspective (1991)*, and among others, studies on the politics of demography.

K.C. ZACHARIAH is currently honorary fellow at the Centre for Development Studies, Thiruvananthapuram, India. He was a senior demographer at the World Bank, Washington D.C. (1971-87); the UN expert in demography at the Cairo Demographic Centre (1966-70) and Deputy Director of International Institute for Population Sciences, Mumbai (1957-66). He holds a Ph.D. degree in Sociology from the University of Pennsylvania. He has published several books on migration and fertility including two books on demographic transition in Kerala.

HIGH LEVEL COMMITTEE on the Indian Diaspora constituted by the Ministry of External Affairs, Government of India consisted of Chairman: Dr. L.M. Singhvi, Member of Parliament and former High Commissioner of India to U.K.; Members: (i) Mr. R.L. Bhatia, Member of Parliament and former Minister of State for External Affairs; (ii) Mr. J.R. Hiremath, Indian Foreign Service (Retd.); (iii) Mr. Baleshwar Agrawal, Secretary-General, Antar Rashtriya Sahyog Parishad, New Delhi; Member Secretary: Mr. J.C. Sharma, Additional Secretary (NRI & PV), Ministry of External Affairs. Committee's report was subsequently published under the title *High Level Committee Report on the Indian Diaspora* in 2001 by the Indian Council of World Affairs, New Delhi.

Index